AMERICAN
VERSE
OF THE
NINETEENTH
CENTURY

Edited
with an introduction by
Richard Gray
LECTURER IN LITERATURE
UNIVERSITY OF ESSEX

DENT, LONDON
ROWMAN AND LITTLEFIELD, TOTOWA, N.J.

Contents

CONTENTS

CONTENTS

Introduction

The history of American poetry in the nineteenth century can, with some justice, be described as one of self-discovery and self-definition. The making of a new nation, in other words, and the making of a new national poetry went hand in hand. Of course, a considerable body of poetry was written during the colonial period, and there were even one or two quite impressive poets: but no distinctive poetic tradition ever emerged. There was no sign of a characteristically American 'voice'. How could there be, indeed, as long as the states of the Atlantic seaboard remained politically and culturally dependent on the mother country; to the extent that one Virginian living in the seventeenth century even complained that his state was more like a second-rate version of the Home Counties than anything which might justifiably be described as a 'New World'? Worse still, where individual settlements did differ from the English model it was in ways least calculated to encourage the growth of a vital literature. In the states to the South, for example, the educated man was more often than not a public figure, whose attention was about equally divided between his estates and political affairs. If he did find time for literature, it was as a reader rather than a writer; and even then the staple of his reading diet was provided by such works as were most likely to increase his competence as a planter and politician. Poetry was of minimal, if any, importance to him. Nor was the situation much better in the North, where the clergy remained a potent ideological force until well into the eighteenth century. There the common opinion was that God's word, as expressed in the Bible and interpreted by the theologian, was to be studied rather than man's. The devout might occasionally turn to verse for recreation but, as the New England divine Cotton Mather advised some candidates for the ministry, they were not to do so too often or for too long:

Be not so set upon poetry, as to be always poring on the passionate and measured pages. . . . Beware of a boundless and sickly appetite for the reading of . . . poems . . . and let not the Circean cup intoxicate you.

With awful warnings of this kind hanging over his head, it is little wonder that Edward Taylor, one of the few significant poets that colonial New England produced, felt obliged to keep his poeticizing secret and to leave instructions that his work should never be published after his death.

Of course, no sudden flowering of poetic talent occurred when the American colonies did finally make the political break with England, nor was there any reason why the political break should immediately and generally be followed by a cultural one as well. For quite a long period after the Revolution, in fact, observers of America were confronted with the anomalous situation of a democratic society still dependent on an aristocratic culture. One distinguished observer, Alexis de Tocqueville, made the point well in his *Democracy in America* (1835):

Although America now perhaps pays less attention to literature than any other civilized country, there is nevertheless a large number of people who take an interest in things of the mind . . . But it is England which supplies them with most of the books they need. Almost all important English books are republished in the United States . . . I remember reading the feudal drama of *Henry V* for the first time in a log cabin.

Not only do the Americans constantly draw upon the treasures of English literature, but one can truly say that English literature flourishes on their own soil. Most of the small band of American men of letters are English in origin and, notably, in ways of thought. So they transplant into democracy thoughts and ways of writing current in the aristocratic nation which they have taken as their model.

Strangely enough, this was a situation that some Americans seemed to regard with satisfaction. Benjamin Franklin, to take one example, had stated several years earlier that the making of a truly American literature would have to await the coming of a more 'refined state of society'. Until then, he contended, it would be at best an irrelevance and at worst an impediment, distracting men from the necessary business of creating a new society. Franklin's argument was based, of course, on the assumption that poetry was a product and an adornment of polite drawing-rooms only. It is an argument that still has its supporters, not least in America; and it is one also that generations of American poets have found a special need to encounter.

Benjamin Franklin might deprecate the writing of anything as flippant as poetry while there was a nation to be built, but many of his contemporaries preferred to see the matter in a rather different light. For them, the creation of poetry became an integral part of the process of creating a new nation. It was not simply that they wished to celebrate their release from the colonial yoke: to describe, in other words, the condition from which they had freed themselves. This was only a minor part of their purpose. What they really needed and wanted to do was to arrive at some understanding of their new status: to define, even if only in a provisional way, the *positive* forms which their freedom had assumed. 'The American is a new man', de Crèvecœur had proclaimed, and those poets who were interested in the development of a genuinely American poetry wanted now to find out just who this new man was. The situation was in many ways unprecedented. Here was a nation that had been devised by a few men at a particular moment in time and according to a specific conception of human nature: as Abraham Lincoln later put it, it was a nation conceived in liberty and dedicated to the propositon that all men are created free and equal. No parallel could be offered by history, and it was likely, therefore, that the poetic voice of this infant republic would be radically different from the voice of 'old Europe', whatever points of resemblance and dependence more ingenious commentators might find. And the difference would naturally enough demonstrate to the less percipient all that was 'new' about this 'strange new world' across the Atlantic. It would tell Americans something about themselves.

The problem of a distinctively American poetry, its forms and its possibilities, was not an easy one to solve. The various writers represented in this anthology suggest as much and, given their example, it would be foolish to attempt any definite kind of solution now. Always bearing this point in mind, however, it *is* possible for us to push towards some tentative conclusions about the nature of the 'new man' as he emerged in the United States; and then to examine the principal American poets of the nineteenth century within the context of these conclusions. We will then have a clearer idea of the specific difficulties with which these poets were confronted, and of the degree and nature of their success in confronting them. Like any work of literature, the poetry written in America between 1800 and 1900 deserves to be judged according to its intentions, and those intentions are so bound up with the 'new man' and the ideology of the new republic as to make some knowledge of both imperative.

The crucial thing to be said about the new American 'type', as he was pictured by writer and statesman alike, was that he was a man who had opted out of society in all but its most elementary forms. For him, repudiation of Europe and the past—a repudiation implicit in his migrating and confirmed by the Revolution—was tantamount to a rejection of all external restraint on the individual. And as a result of this rejection, several of the given conditions or circumstances of the European writer had been destroyed. So far as subject was concerned the dominating theme of European literature, the life of man *in* society, had more or less been wiped out at one blow. There *was* no society in which the hero could be seen making his way and against which the writer could test his own values. Instead, the poet was left with the isolated self, and had either to assert that self in defiance of all the rest of the world or to discover, indeed create, some kind of relationship between the two. The most important result of this was that the problems which have preoccupied writers and intellectuals of all Western nations for the last fifty years— problems relating to the nature of the Self and the relation between that Self and the external world—were precisely those which American poets were concerned with from the moment they began to regard themselves as Americans.

Predictably enough, such problems of content proved to be inseparable from the problems of poetic form and audience with which the American poet found himself confronted as well. For once the isolated self was accepted as the supreme reality, the point from which all poetic explorations were to begin, the poet found that he had to decide how far, if at all, he could trust other people, either as guides or as an audience. To put it less cryptically: could he whose principal allegiance was to himself and the uniqueness of his own experiences ever be justified in using forms, such as the sonnet or the Spenserian stanza, which were devised to express other types of experience, and which were even meant to 'communalize' that experience to some extent, to render it less individualistic and eccentric? Was not the free man denying his freedom immediately he put himself and his beliefs within the strait-jacket of iambic pentameter or rhymed couplets? And were not these difficulties multiplied by the simple fact that the American poet and his audience were not necessarily part of the same community, sharing customs and beliefs and nuances of expression? There were therefore very few assumptions with which the American poet could begin and which he could exploit. He had to create his language: a language which could at once be a true expression of himself and comprehensible to his audience. Even more important, he had in effect to create that audience, create the taste for his own particular type of poetry, in a way and to an extent that no English poet ever did. The task was a complicated one but all the complications derived ultimately from the same ideological premise, a situation implicit in the American Dream. On the one hand there was the inviolate but isolated Self, on the other the world of the Not-Self; and the American poet had somehow to establish a relationship between the two. He had to do so explicitly in *what* he said, the kinds of values he formulated, and implicitly also, in *how* and *to whom* he said it.

The first poet to be noticeably aware of the difficulties involved in becoming an American poet was one whose name is now largely forgotten: Philip Freneau (1752–1832). Born in New York City of a French Huguenot father and a Scottish mother, Freneau began his poetic career as a minor celebrant of 'lovely Fancy'; but events soon conspired to turn his interests in other directions. There was a growing tide of feeling in favour of separation from England, and it was especially strong at colleges and intellectual centres like that at which Freneau spent his young manhood. There, in fact, Freneau wrote in collaboration with a student friend some *Satires Against the Tories* (1770) and a long poem in celebration of *The Rising Glory of America*. The latter, written in 1771 and drastically revised in 1786, marked Freneau's full conversion, poetic and political, to the American cause: a cause he was later to serve both as a satirical poet and as a strongly partisan editor and journalist. Yet for all its rhetorical energy this poem about the emerging splendour of the new world is as much a tribute to the continuing importance of the old world, at least in matters cultural and intellectual, as anything else. The theme may be new but the form is essentially imitative, a pale echo of Miltonic orotundities, and so the poem tends to confirm the power of the mother country even while Freneau struggles to deny it.

Part of Freneau's problem stemmed from the fact that he was possessed of only a slight poetic talent: but only part. More important, perhaps, was the fact that he was writing at one of the most unpropitious times possible for verse and versifiers. As Freneau put it in *To An Author* (1788):

An age employed in edging steel
Can no poetic raptures feel.

Freneau in fact recognized the difficulties with which he and any poet were confronted during the Revolution and it is much to his credit that he did so. He even recognized the difficulty, the virtual impossibility, of escaping from British cultural domination when times *were* more settled. In *Literary Importation* (1788), for example, he asked indignantly,

Can we never be thought to have learning or grace
Unless it be brought from that damnable place?

and must have known that most of his own work answered him in the
negative. He was writing, as he sensed, in the wrong place at the
wrong time; yet he continued to write, not just occasional pieces
either, but poems which demonstrated a genuine attempt to arrive at
universal significance in and through a firm sense of the local. *The
Indian Burying Ground* (1788) is an instance, one of the first attempts to
understand the new country in terms of a people who had themselves
become an integral part of it. So is *The Wild Honey Suckle* (1788), in
which Freneau focuses his attention on a detail of the American scene
and discovers in that detail one truth about the American psyche;
namely, its fundamental loneliness and privacy, the apart-ness of
what Whitman was to call 'the essential Me'. There is, too, in
contrast with the florid style of Freneau's early couplets, a gesture
towards a more precise and simpler diction here, concrete and appro-
priate to the delineation of minute particulars.

Too much should not be claimed for the poem, however: it could
just as easily have been written by a minor Romantic poet living in
England as by an inhabitant of New York and New Jersey. What we
have been discovering in it is probably as much the result of hind-
sight as anything else, the outcome of our knowledge that certain
elements and interests implicit in Freneau's later poetry did assume
importance in the characteristically American verse of the rest of
the century. Freneau may have been aware of the need for a new
mode of poetic discourse but he confined himself for the most part
to the old. This is also true of William Cullen Bryant (1794–1878),
who was honoured by many of his contemporaries as the founding
father of American poetry. Certainly, the honour was justified as far
as the subjects of his poetic landscapes were concerned. Although he
was raised in Massachusetts and spent most of his adult life as a
newspaper editor in New York, *The Prairies* (1834) is adequate proof
both of his awareness of the great lands to the West and, more im-
portant, of his realization that all the new regions of America might
require the development of new tools of expression. All the same,
whatever the native loyalties involved in Bryant's choice of subject,
and whatever he might say about the irrelevance to that subject of
'the speech of England', when it came to writing rather than talking
about poetry Bryant preferred to imitate European models. The suc-
cess of *Inscription for the Entrance to a Wood* (1821), for example,
depends upon the reader accepting the somewhat factitious assump-
tion that he and the poet form part of the same polite community.

Bryant becomes almost Augustan in his dependence upon large abstractions (Truth, Guilt, Nature), poetic diction ('haunts of Nature', 'the marge'), and unparticularized description: all used in the apparent belief that the poet, although broad and even vague in his gestures, will be understood because he is talking to men with interests and values similar to his own. The poem confirms rather than demonstrates or explores. It depends for its effect upon the reader giving immediate assent to the context of moral assumptions within which Bryant is operating; and then admiring, with a certain detachment, the felicity of the operation. It need hardly be added that dependence of this kind does not help to bridge the gap between poet and audience which was one of the conditions of American poetry: on the contrary, that gap is simply ignored.

To leave the matter there, of course, would be to do Bryant a considerable disservice. At the very least, he is a superb craftsman: witness *To A Waterfowl* (1821), in which the alternating pattern of long and short lines captures the hovering movement of the bird's flight. And at his best, as in *Thanatopsis* (1821), he achieves an immense hortatory power which almost compensates for the sense that, for all he might have said in depreciation of 'the speech of England', it was upon that speech that he invariably relied. Without any doubt, he was a more fluent writer than Ralph Waldo Emerson (1803–1882), a founding member of the Transcendental Club and leading poet and essayist of the Transcendentalist movement; and yet when we read poems like Emerson's *Uriel* (1847) we begin to realize all that Bryant missed. More important, we sense too that, with Emerson, we are listening for the first time to something which sounds like a genuinely American voice.

That it should be Emerson who was one of the first to supply this voice is not surprising when his famous and influential rejection of the European past in *The American Scholar* (1837) is recalled, or his call for an American bard in *The Poet* (1844):

We have had no genius in America . . . , which knew the value of our incomparable materials, and saw, in . . . the times, another carnival of the same gods whose picture he so much admires in Homer . . . America is a poem in our eyes; its ample geography dazzles the imagination, and it will not wait long for metres.

Unlike Freneau and Bryant, Emerson managed to practise what he preached and to devise a poetry as 'free, peremptory, clear' as its subjects and its creator. At its finest, such poetry *dramatizes* the liberated self that earlier American poets are only able to talk about. As the supreme creative power, illuminating and transforming all that comes within its orbit, the self is placed at the centre of the poem. As far as style is concerned, this new egocentrism is reflected in the unusual degree of freedom that Emerson allows himself to vary lines and metres at will. In other words, while accepting the preliminary discipline of a particular rhyme and rhythm-scheme, he never lets that scheme inhibit his patterns of speech and thought. Any degree of irregularity and disruption is permissible, as long as the basic sense of 'rhythmic speech'—of speech coming directly from the primitive and oracular self—is retained:

The rhyme of the poet
Modulates the King's affairs;
Balance-loving Nature
Made all things in pairs
To every foot its antipode
Each colour with its counter glowed;
To every tone beat answering tones,
Higher or graver.
                    (*Merlin*, 1847.)

More important still is the effect of this egocentrism upon the physical and emotional landscapes which Emerson describes. In poem after poem, the self is actually shown in the process of re-creating the world, transmuting it into something freshly seen and fully discovered. Thus, in *The Snow-Storm* (1847), the poetic vision seems to be re-fashioning the scene even as the falling snow is described re-fashioning familiar objects into fresh and unfamiliar shapes; and in poems like *Uriel* and *Merlin* the poetic persona is translated into an incarnation of God, whose acts of seeing or naming are quite on a par with the Creation. This is at least one way of solving the problem of the relationship between the self and the world: by subjectifying the object or, as Emerson once put it in his famous essay on *Nature* (1836), by seeing the universe as no more and no less than 'the externalization of the soul'. The isolated man re-creates the world and makes it his own; and the isolated poet re-creates the language and the line so as to make of them a unique form of expression.

That is all very well, one might reasonably reply, but where does this leave the reader? Emerson's answer would probably be that his intention is to 're-create' the reader as well: in the sense that new powers of seeing and naming are opened to him and that the power of his own self is demonstrated by example. The reader, having been shown what can be done, might go on to transmute his own sur-roundings and thereby become a poet too—of event if not of word. It is an answer that would probably have pleased Emerson's fellow Transcendentalist and disciple, Henry David Thoreau (1817–1872), as Thoreau's poem *The Inward Morning* (1895) testifies: but it would never have satisfied Longfellow. For Henry Wadsworth Longfellow (1807–1882), believed in the value of the community, and more particularly of the American-European community. So convinced was he of this, indeed, that he even inserted a long didactic passage into one of his novels, in order to explain to his audience exactly how he thought the American literature of the future *must* depend on European forms and traditions:

As the blood of all nations is mingled with our own, so will their thoughts and feelings finally mingle in our literature. We shall draw from the Germans tenderness; from the Spaniards, passion; from the French, vivacity—to mingle more and more with our solid English sense.

(*Kavanagh: A Tale.* 1849.)

Longfellow's deliberate strategy was, in effect, to deny the existence of a problem. The European forms and legends had been good enough for the European poets, so why should the American poet reject them? Even if he did write about the American scene, could he not borrow consciously and heavily from the European tradition, so as to give a sense of authority and universality to his verse? *My Lost Youth* (1858) demonstrates the latter conviction. It is a poem about Longfellow's youth in Portland, Maine, about as personal a subject as one can get; and yet the tone is somehow impersonal, the result mostly of the quotations from and allusions to earlier poets with which the lines are packed. Even the famous refrain, it turns out, is derived from a German translation of a Lapland song. There is nothing intrinsically wrong with this kind of adaptation, of course, as the work of Pound and Eliot indicates. It is just that whereas in a poem like *The Waste Land* the echoes and allusions are employed for their associative effects, to *add to* a situation directly apprehended, Long-fellow more often than not seems to be looking at the subject in and through the associations. That is, he tends to look at life through books: at best, to identify his experiences with something he has read already and at worst, to reduce person and event to literary stereotype.

The kinds of values Longfellow derives from his books and then applies in his poetry are equally significant. For there is an extra-

ordinary sense of self-assurance in most of his verse; a feeling that all
that is relevant to experience, and has been discovered by previous
writers to be relevant to experience, occurs within the compass of the
respectable fire-side. This is most obvious in a poem like *Nature*
(1875), where the wilderness which awed Melville and terrified
Poe is reduced to 'a fond mother', whose every aspect can be attri-
buted to a pervasive concern for human welfare; but it is also at the
root of a poem such as *The Village Blacksmith* (1842), in which a figure
actually outside the sphere of Longfellow's society and sympathy is
rendered acceptable—to Longfellow, that is, and to his more genteel
readers—by being transformed into a rustic gentleman. In either
instance, the subject is reduced to comparative insignificance by the
moral framework, and that framework is founded upon the assump-
tion that the poet, the European past, and the American present
form one domestic circle.

A similar reduction of the community to fit the proportions of the
self occurs in the poetry of John Greenleaf Whittier (1807–1892), only
in this case the reduction is a conscious one. As his *Proem* (1849)
indicates, he had no vast ambitions. All he wanted to do was to excori-
ate those whose preoccupation with self—the slave-owner, for
example, and the unscrupulous industrialist—was such as to make
them oblivious to other considerations; and beyond this to offer as
an imaginative alternative to such selfishness the kind of small and
tightly knit community of interests described in *First-Day Thoughts*
(1853) and *Snow-Bound* (1866). Whittier was born in Massachusetts
of poor Quaker parents, and the Quaker experience remained
fundamental to him throughout his life. It was this, in fact, which
supplied him with his ideal: of a group of people held together by
common values and by the belief that each member of the group is
possessed of a certain 'inner light'. In *Snow-Bound* for instance, as
in the Quaker poems of Bayard Taylor (1825–1878), the reader
receives a strong sense of the particularity and individuality of the
characters presented; but he receives a strong sense of their 'apart-
ness' as a group as well, and therefore a sense of their mutuality.
Cut off from the rest of the world by a snow-storm, the various
members of the household that Whittier describes pass the time in
recalling childhood memories; and as the memories accumulate it
becomes clear that an act of communion is being realized, comparable
to the moment in a Quaker meeting when the various members
recount and thereby share their spiritual experiences with their
friends. More than this, the poem itself gradually assumes the status
of an act of communion. For Whittier is describing a particular
winter of his childhood: he also is remembering and meditating and,

in a way, offering a part of himself to the individual reader. The intention is not, of course, to settle once and for all that great war between the self and the world with which every American writer has been confronted. The range of thought and feeling in this and other poems of communion is too limited, too special, for that. But it is Whittier's purpose to make a separate peace with the individual reader, however temporary such a peace might be; to create the sense that for a moment at least a current of sympathy has passed between the poet and his audience. It is at once a humble aim and a magnificent one, and it is surely to Whittier's credit that he achieved it.

To the extent that Whittier depended on a specific community, the Quakers of New England, to present his paradigm of the good life he could perhaps be called a 'minority writer'; that is, he *could* be called this were it not that the phrase, with all it implies of limitation and alienation from the dominant culture, seems more appropriate as a description of the most famous black poet of the century, Paul Laurence Dunbar (1872–1906). And even in Dunbar's case the phrase is not a completely satisfactory one, since it tends to minimize the fact that Dunbar's problems as a *black* poet were only a more exacerbated version of his contemporaries' problems as *American* poets. He was caught between his private self and his public role just as they were, the only difference being that in his case the sense of himself was that much more indefinite and the roles attributed to him as black man were that much more fixed and inappropriate. He also was presented with a language that had little to do with his own sense of life; again the only difference being that in his case this language, as the expression of a specifically white culture, was that much more alien to him and so in need of an especially drastic transformation. The situation is one that has perhaps been best located in terms of the paradox favoured by Leroi Jones:

I am inside
Someone who hates me.

That is, as Jones sees it, the roles available to the black in American society are so very much the products of a strange culture—a culture which regards him as at best inferior and at worst an enemy—that he seems to risk schizophrenia if he accepts them. The situation, to repeat, is both a typical and—because of its extremity—an unusual one, implying enormous difficulties. And given this, it is not so surprising that Dunbar found his task impossible to fulfil. All he could do, in effect, was either adopt the language of white culture wholesale, as in the poem to *Harriet Beecher Stowe* (1899), or accept a mask created for him by the white man. The latter is what he is doing in a poem like *When De Co'n Pone's Hot* (1896): surrendering his personal feelings in favour of a fixed and essentially false public role. For not only does this kind of Negro dialect poetry subscribe to a stereotype of the black man created by the white; it belongs in general to a tradition of nigger minstrel literature devised by white writers, and is in itself a close imitation of a *white* dialect poem, *When the Frost is on the Punkin* (1883), by the Mid-Western author James Whitcomb Riley (1849–1916). Acceptance of a public mask could not go much further than this; and it leads to the inescapable conclusion that although Dunbar discovered many of the problems facing the black writer in America, he could supply few of the solutions.

The principal advantage enjoyed by Whittier, and the principal disadvantage suffered by Dunbar, sprang initially, then, from the same situation: each writer had a definite community with which he felt he could or should identify himself, and to which he possessed some degree of commitment. The crucial fact in the case of Edgar Allan Poe (1809–1849), on the other hand, was his belief that he could never thoroughly identify himself with anyone or anything. Born in Boston to a pair of strolling actors and then adopted at the age of three by a merchant in Richmond, Virginia, Poe might try to orientate himself by assuming the role of Southern gentleman—and even espousing the Southern political and literary cause—but he could never believe in the role for very long. In fact, he could not believe in any of the parts available to him in the society of early America for very long because, more than any other poet of his time, he was out of sympathy with that society. All he had, as he never tired of saying, was himself and an imaginative world which he called Eternity but which was really a larger extension of his own ego: an infinitely expansible space in which his dreams and desires could receive their full satisfaction. This was the domain of his poetry: the poet, Poe insisted, if he was to merit the name, had to translate the reader out of the 'jarring and tumultuous chaos' of mundane reality and into a 'circumscribed Eden of . . . dreams'. It was an egocentrism and an egocentric theory of poetry profoundly different from Emerson's. For whereas Emerson regarded the poetic 'I' as a transformative agency, a radiant node which illuminated the ordinary world, Poe believed that it supplied the beginning and end of the creative process. It signified and illuminated nothing but itself.

The consequences of this belief are everywhere manifest in Poe's poetry. His subject is invariably some region 'Out of SPACE—out of TIME', blanketed in mists or darkness. There is little sense of the concrete and definite, nor does he intend there to be. On the contrary, every resource of his poetic technique is used to increase the impression of impalpability, of deliquescent scene and shadowy character. The style, for example, is incantatory, full of repetitions, unexpected rhymes and hidden melodies. The syntax is sometimes so contorted that it becomes difficult to make out just what Poe is saying; and even when it is not, individual words may offer a certain resistance to the understanding because they have been chosen more for their euphony than for their denotative value. It is as if Poe were using all kinds of complicated means to communicate a sense of nothing; and that in a sense is what he *is* trying to do. He is trying to describe a transcendent world of the self which exists in and beyond the normal world of language and which has no connection with that world. His tools are words and yet his subject is a state beyond words. The most he *can* do, therefore, is invoke or point towards rather than dramatize or define. He is using the signs supplied by the material world to suggest a sense, and only a sense, of the spiritual. That the task Poe set himself was an impossible one is true: all he is able to do, in effect, is to employ a vocabulary in order to demonstrate its limitations. But that his assumption of this task was significant is equally true. For, quite apart from the enormous influence that his poetic enterprise exerted on the French Symboliste movement of the later nineteenth century and so upon all modern poetry, there is the simple fact that his work marks one extreme in the continuing dialectic between the isolated self of the American Dream on the one hand and the world of community and responsibility on the other. Further than Poe the isolated self could never venture.

Poe's initial difficulties may have sprung from an inability to identify himself with his adoptive region, but it is doubtful if this served to his ultimate disadvantage. Certainly, the evidence offered by the two other important Southern poets of the century seems to indicate that it did not. Henry Timrod (1828–1867) may have achieved a measure of fame as a result of his poetic espousal of the Southern cause—as his honorific title 'the laureate of the Confederacy' implies—but the fame carried with it some crippling limitations. For in assuming the role of public poet, Timrod became little more than the spokesman for a cause. His best works are as moving and as narrow in their emotional range as a really good national anthem. Sidney Lanier (1842–1881) is a different matter. A native of Georgia and at one time a Confederate soldier, Lanier tried to devote himself to the regional cause, as a poem like *Corn* (1877) testifies. But the effort was, happily, unsuccessful. Even in *Corn* Lanier transcends the limits of public poetry to offer an almost pagan hymn to the regenerative powers of Nature; and in later years, when all hope of establishing a comfortable niche in society for himself had vanished, he deliberately turned to new subjects and a new mode of expression. *The Marshes of Glyn* (1884), with its intricate verbal melodies and its sense of Nature as a brooding and mysterious entity, is characteristic of this later phase. Lanier's was a career cut short by premature death but even within the short time allotted to him he had nearly completed the transition from the verse speeches of Timrod to the private lyrics of Poe.

A few poets, like Lanier, might move between the opposing impulses to freedom and to community during the course of their lives, but they were the exception. Most writers tended to identify themselves with one impulse or the other and then tried to develop it into a profitable stance towards reality. Oliver Wendell Holmes (1809–1894), for example, opted like Whittier for identification with a special group; in his case, the men of sense and taste with whom he came into contact as a distinguished member of Bostonian society. It is to just such a group that his poems are addressed: either explicitly, as in *At the 'Atlantic' Dinner* (1875) or by implication. *The Last Leaf* (1836) is an instance of the latter, a poem in which Holmes, in describing a decrepit old man, manages to keep a fine balance between sympathy and amusement. The point of equilibrium is supplied by commonsense, which prevents Holmes from becoming either cruel or sentimental. It prevents him, too, from meditating upon the larger implications of this emblem of old age or even from analysing the reasons for his refusal to meditate. It would, apparently, be to consider too deeply to consider so. The most Holmes will say is that he hopes people will smile in as kindly and detached a way on him when he is old: a conclusion that is as just and sensible as it is deliberately limited and limiting.

Whereas Holmes opted for a community composed of men of sense, however small it might have to be, a contemporary and neighbour of his chose a spiritual isolation which some of his acquaintances interpreted as madness. Jones Very (1813–1880) was a lay preacher given to mystical experiences. As a youth he had been forced to withdraw from Harvard University after experiencing a religious frenzy; and throughout his life he had visions which convinced him that his will and God's will were one. This conviction might have turned him into fanatic and bigot. Instead it enabled him to write poetry which, though neglected during his life-time, some recent critics have felt justified in calling great. It is, certainly, unique. The means of expression is traditional—Very rarely used anything other than the sonnet form—but it belies a poetic stance that is as individualistic as that of Huckleberry Finn or Rimbaud. In one of his poems, for instance, ordinary people in the street are transformed into *The Dead* (1839), whose grotesque and lurid shapes are an outward and visible sign of an inward and spiritual poverty. In another, Very claims to see, with the aid of his 'spiritgaze', his 'brother's blood' on the hand of every man he meets: the blood, that is, of guilt and damnation. Very's is in effect the innocent and often savage eye of the outsider, ignoring the masks that most people use to evade self-knowledge. He has no connection with the world he observes and exposes, and in a sense no audience either. For as the poem *Yourself* (1839) makes clear, he did not expect his revelations of his inner being and his secret pact with God to be thoroughly understood by those around him.

Holmes addressing his fellow littérateurs at a fashionable dinner-party and Very watching with horror the antics of the 'strangers' surrounding him offer a characteristically American contrast which is repeated in a subtler manner by two other New Englanders: James Russell Lowell (1819–1891) and Frederick Goddard Tuckerman (1821–1873). Lowell, poet and professor, first editor of the *Atlantic Monthly* and member of one of the foremost families in Boston, did not, like Holmes, content himself with a small group of educated men for an audience. Rather, he sought a larger group whom he could educate. He assumed that people would readily assent to the justice of just opinions once they were offered them, and that therefore the task of creating an audience was an easy one. This breezy optimism was clearly one reason why he wrote *The Biglow Papers* (1848 and 1867), a series of satirical attacks on the slave-holders of the South and their political representatives. By adopting the mask of Josiah Biglow, a crude but honest Yankee farmer, Lowell evidently believed that he could use the power of the word to direct people into right ways of thinking. It was symptomatic of difficulties of which he was hardly aware, however, that like some later poets of the Mid-West, such as James Whitcomb Riley, he felt obliged to assume a rustic persona; in other words, that he felt he had to 'lower' himself so as to talk convincingly to his readers. And it was further symptomatic of those difficulties that Lowell sometimes felt uncomfortable in the clothes of Biglow: in a poem like *The Courtin'* (1867), for example, the voice of the Harvard professor, pointing the moral and adorning the tale, *will* keep breaking through the accents of the farmer. No matter how hard he tried, or how much he reassured himself, Lowell could never quite reconcile the demands of his self with what he believed to be the demands of his public.

By contrast, Tuckerman was never tempted to cater to the various tastes of his contemporaries, or even to put on the robes of the pedagogue. He was by nature a solitary and his solitude was confirmed, psychologically as well as in fact, when his wife died in childbirth. He had already published, before her death, a book of poems which went largely unnoticed; and now in response to his loss and a deepening sense of melancholy he wrote the work on which his poetic reputation rests: a series of sonnet-sequences, written in the periods 1854–1860, 1860–1872 and partly published in 1860, and a long poem entitled *The Cricket*, which was not published until 1950. These poems are not, as Tuckerman explains in sonnet I of the first sequence, addressed to anyone. They are merely and triumphantly an attempt to give objective life to a subjective complex of emotions. The result is in some respects similar to recent verse, Imagist verse for example, in which a sequence of sense-impressions is presented as the equivalent of a sequence of emotions. Similarity, however, is not identity. The poetic voice of Tuckerman is a unique one, expressive of a man who feels alienated from nature, from other men, and from God; who is aware that there might possibly exist 'signs' in his natural environment which could lead him to philosophical certainty but who is equally aware that those signs are beyond his deciphering. Thrust into a state of extreme isolation, and unable to see beyond appearances, the most that the 'I' of Tuckerman's poetry can do is to use those appearances as an alphabet to spell out his own moods. A comparison with Emerson might seem appropriate: but whereas the ego for Emerson is an assertive presence, illuminating the world and creating the real, the self in poems like Tuckerman's is essentially on the defensive and making the most it can of its own defensiveness.

A radical uncertainty about the ability of the ego to see anything beyond itself is also to be found in the poetry of Emily Dickinson (1830–1886) and Herman Melville (1819–1891). Like Tuckerman, both were what Melville once described as 'isolatoes'. Emily Dickinson spent nearly all of her life in the small village of Amherst, Massachusetts, where she was born. She never married and her acquaintances were comparatively few. Even her writing of verse did not lead to many contacts with the outside world. The one person of whom she asked literary advice, Thomas Wentworth Higginson, was out of sympathy with her poems and in any case only seven of them were published during her life-time. She had, as she said, no 'monarch' in her life to help or even encourage her in her poeticizing; and yet despite this handicap, or perhaps because of it, she managed to write a vast number of lyrics, some of which must be numbered among the greatest produced in any country during the century.

Given Emily Dickinson's situation, her subject was perhaps inevitable: the world contained within the circumference of herself and the difficulty or impossibility of ever moving outside that circumference. Nature is for her a mysterious entity, a 'stranger yet' which only gives back a picture of oneself and one's own preoccupations. The creatures in which she is interested are symptomatic of her attitude. For they are invariably the smaller, more elusive inhabitants of the fields and woods: the cricket, the robin, the fly, 'narrow fellows' all, that reflect the fickle and freckled character of man's environment, its capacity for mystery or surprise. Pushed back from these creatures and their surrounds by their irremediable 'other-ness', Emily Dickinson turns to her internal geography in the knowledge that it is all she can really know. Her self, and her feelings, encompass her world, and her recognition of this fact explains the extraordinary intensity with which she describes pleasure and melancholy and suffering. They are the only things she has and so of necessity they assume enormous and all-encompassing proportions: the eruption of pain becomes an apocalyptic event, comparable to the ending of the world, and exultation seems when it comes to irradiate all existence. By such means, Emily Dickinson tries to make up in depth of experience for what she lacks in breadth. In the face of a shattering event, pleasant or unpleasant, seconds are translated by her into eternities and the span of her body into the measure of the universe. The process of translation is illusory, of course, as she herself recognizes in her poems about the one experience, death, which marks the definite conclusion to her world. It is an experience which, in her best poems at least, is confronted with both excitement and trepidation. For it might possibly lead to a 'title divine', the final escape of the self from its limitations; or, on the other hand, it might be the prelude to annihilation and nothingness. All she can be sure of is that she cannot be sure, and so in poem after poem she approaches the gates of death only to stop short just before she enters. The scene then goes blank, and poet and reader alike are left gazing at the blankness, aware only that they have arrived at the boundaries of human consciousness. The poem is open-ended because, granted Emily Dickinson's subject and standpoint, that is the only kind of ending available to her.

This sense of the unfinished is not confined to the endings of a few specific poems. On the contrary, it characterizes every line of her best verse, being a necessary consequence of her attitude towards man and his environment. As she put it in one of her lyrics, she dwells in the 'fair house' of possibility where the most she can do is offer a series of provisional names for the furniture. The names must be provisional because of her belief that she is a prisoner, caught within the circumference of her own consciousness: she is therefore not describing the world as it is or even might be but merely constructing a language-system, and by implication a system of values, acceptable to her own individual self. Like any system based on limited evidence it is partial and open to continual alteration, qualities which are emphasized by Emily Dickinson's preference for the paratactic over the more conventional forms of syntax. For by placing phrases and clauses side by side in what *seems* to be an indiscriminate way, she avoids the kind of finished effect that is inseparable from more sophisticated types of syntactical structure: the shaping of experience and the organizing of priorities which inevitably accompany the use of main and subordinate clauses. Her disruptive use of rhythm, too, and her frequent choice of discords or half-rhymes rather than rhymes adds to the sense of the random in her verse; a sense which is appropriate here since it reinforces in the most dramatic way possible her lyric account of a self that is paradoxically both circumscribed and dynamic, engaged in a quest which it knows it can never properly complete.

Much of what has been said about Dickinson is equally applicable to Herman Melville. True, Melville's sense of isolation had different causes. Born in New York City, a sailor as soon as he was an adolescent, his early life was hardly that of a recluse. But whatever he might have been or planned to be in those early years, events soon conspired to drive him into himself. After an initial success with his stories of the South Seas, Melville found fame slipping away from him: *Moby Dick* (1851) was a financial and critical disappointment and *Pierre* (1852) a disaster. Discouraged by the reception of these books, he abandoned fiction and, much to the dismay of his relatives, took to the writing of poetry. The poems were ignored during his life-time, and perhaps for the same reasons as his later novels were. For, like the novels, they are concerned with the tragic dualities and discords of experience and express these concerns in and by means of a style which is itself often discordant, often abrupt. In *The Portent* (1886), for instance, Melville presents John Brown, the subject of the poem, as an alien and grotesque Christ-figure, whose thwarted aspirations and misdirected zeal become an emblem of the failure visited on all men when they try to realise their inner dreams in the outer world. The poem, for all its ironic use of the Christ-analogy and its deflating and anti-rhetorical half-rhymes, is not cynical. It does not deny John Brown a certain greatness of ambition and courage. As in *Moby Dick*, however, admiration for such courage, such an Ahab-like capacity for going beyond the ordinary limitations of experience, is more than tempered by the belief that the acceptance of such limitations is a condition of survival. The self, Melville insisted, may of its nature try to re-create the world in its own image: but if it does it will fail and inevitably be destroyed.

Walt Whitman (1819–1892) would not have entirely agreed. For Whitman, the son of a struggling carpenter-farmer, was all his life inclined to identify his ego with the world, and more particularly with the democratic 'en-masse' of America. This identification on which his poems depend, or rather this dialectic from which they derive their energy, is stated quite clearly in the opening lines of *Song of Myself* (1855):

I celebrate myself, and sing myself,
And what I assume you shall assume,
For every atom belonging to me as good belongs to you.

It was Whitman's intention not to reject the world, like Poe, nor to reduce the relative importance of the ego, as Lowell and Longfellow did, but to achieve a dynamic and mutually enriching equilibrium between the two. The sort of relationship that might result from this is given imaginative expression in *The Dalliance of the Eagles* (1881) in which two birds, flying and mating at the same time, and dramatically transformed into equivalents of the Self and the Not-Self, are described as being united and yet separate, 'twain yet one'. Their paths *have* been different in the past, it is clear, and *will* be different in times to come; but for a moment, in the brief space of the poem, the two forces that Whitman presents attain a kind of transcendent contact.

It is exactly this quality of contact that Whitman is aiming for in all his finest poems. In *Song of Myself* for instance, the poetic 'I' is presented as being capable of sympathetic identification with all manner of peoples, but of an identification which does not involve any loss of personal identity. The claim may sound self-contradictory but Whitman, like Emerson, is never afraid of contradicting himself. More important, he is nearly always able to suspend the reader's disbelief: to convince his audience that he can immerse himself in the being of another and yet still remain 'Walt Whitman . . . of Manhattan the son'. This is partly because he is able to create a feeling of empathy for the characters he describes—the runaway slave, the lonely woman, the Texas volunteers—even while retaining his distinctive voice, with its dynamic patterns of speech and its predisposition towards the 'fleshy, sensual' aspects of experience. And it is partly because the reader himself is drawn into the continuing process of relationships, with Whitman and the people he presents, yet still remains 'the reader', a man standing on the outside of this world of words. Right at the end of *Song of Myself* Whitman states quite explicitly and even emphasizes that the empathetic relationship he has been describing is a triangular one, between poet and world *and reader*; and, beyond this, that he expects such a relationship to continue after the poem has been read. For when he declares,

If you want me again look for me under your boot-soles,

he is in effect identifying himself and his poem with the 'spear of summer's grass' by means of which he first achieved a mystical sense of unity with the given world. Whitman and his *Song*, the implication is, will hopefully act as a source of continuing inspiration and contact; an agent of communion and a means of mystical insight quite as efficacious as the leaf of grass was for the poet.

This idea of the poem as a continuing process is, of course, crucial since Whitman is as much concerned with possibility as Emily Dickinson is. The self, as Whitman sees it, is free and continually evolving, and nothing but the most open of poetic forms is capable of expressing its energies. Consequently, Whitman uses a line the principal characteristic of which is its flexibility: it can then be varied at will to catch the inflections of individual speech or the quality of a particular occasion. The syntax is as loose as possible, too, with phrases and lines left lying alongside one another in the hope that thereby their natural force and unity will emerge. Even the grammar and diction suggest a sense of process and open-endedness. The participle is normally preferred to the active verb, because to use the latter would be to fix the event in time—the self, as it appears in Walt Whitman's verse, is 'doing' but never quite 'done'—and terms are invariably drawn from every level of experience, high or low, in an attempt to reflect, in the variety of the words being used, the variety of the life described. Under the pressure of such techniques a unique voice is created, as multiform and individualistic as the self which is the object of celebration. On several occasions during his life, when he was discussing this voice, Whitman insisted that it was the most appropriate form of utterance for the 'American bard' to use. The claim had a characteristic tinge of arrogance to it, but it also contained an element of truth. For the poetic voice of which Whitman was so proud supplied, at its very best, the most effective expression possible of the belief, implicit in the American Dream from the beginning, that the impulse towards freedom and the impulse towards community could be reconciled without doing a disservice to either.

The enormous feeling of liberation that Whitman's poetry generated was something that a number of other writers of the time attempted as well. Among several possible examples, it was a characteristic aim of those who, either by birth or inclination, could be described as the poets of the West. This was perhaps predictable, given their association with a place still very close to the frontier stage of existence; for, even in the later decades of the century, the West was still something of a New World. It could still be said to demonstrate the promise of American life—what Whitman called the sense of the 'open road'—without many of the inhibitions and complications implicit in the genteel life of the Atlantic seaboard. Illustrative of the kind of optimism it could continue to inspire are the opening lines of *Westward Ho!* (1897) by Joaquin Miller (1841?–1913):

What strength! what strife! what rude unrest!
What shocks! what half-shaped armies met!
A mighty nation moving west,
With all its steely sinews set
Against the living forests.

Unfortunately, the lines are also illustrative of the difficulties most writers of the West encountered when trying to forge a medium suited to their message. Miller's work, vivid and invigorating though it often is, is nevertheless rhetoric: the expression of a man who has denied the struggles and complexities of his own personality in favour of the public voice. The same is true of the Western verse of Bayard Taylor and Bret Harte (1876–1902). Certainly, there are aspects of their method which serve to differentiate Harte from Taylor, or both from Joaquin Miller. In a poem like *On Leaving California* (1862), for instance, Taylor employs a rhetoric much more formal and elaborate than that which Miller commonly favours; while Harte in his dialect verse employs a strategy that makes him more comparable to James Russell Lowell than to either. That is, he adopts an assumed character who may perhaps be expressive of a specific social group but who is certainly no more than tangentially related to the poet himself. Granted these differences of method, however, the beginning and end of the poetic enterprise remains in each case the same. In effect, the writer has made a radical adjustment in order to speak to his audience; and in many ways, perhaps in most, he has denied himself and the energies of his own being in doing so. The result is that there is in this verse little sense of that continuing inter-action between the individual and the society, between personal and public, which is Whitman's principal strength.

It is tempting to leave the American poetry of the nineteenth century on the triumphant note registered by Whitman, or even on the more crudely expansive note sounded in the work of the Western poets: but this is a temptation that has to be resisted. Theirs were not the last voices to be heard before the century ended, nor were they even characteristic of the final years of that century. By then, a new pessimism had entered American life, the social implications of which were perhaps best reflected in *The Man with the Hoe* (1899) by Edwin Markham (1852–1940). As Markham's poem illustrates, the accelerating growth of industry, and the corresponding decline of the traditionally agricultural economy of the nation, did much to shape the pessimistic mood of the times. But just as important a factor was the spread of Darwinism and deterministic scientific theories. This is perhaps most immediately obvious in the early work of William Vaughn Moody (1869–1910). A poem like his *Gloucester Moors* (1901), for example, communicates a sense of profound disorientation. And this disorientation seems to stem at once from a failure of idealistic purpose in American life, and from a more general loss of meaning and faith. Quite simply, the starting-point for much of Moody's philosophizing in verse is the feeling that all men, American or otherwise, have missed their way. A similar pessimism is to be found in the work of Stephen Crane (1871–1900) and the early volumes of Edwin Arlington Robinson (1865–1935). Doubt, and sometimes despair, characterize the writing of both; doubt about the quality of human relationships, about the nature of the communication between man and his environment, doubt even about the integrity of the self. In Robinson's *Richard Cory* (1897), for instance, the titular character is presented as a puzzling and opaque phenomenon. He is far too strange and alien for the narrators of the poem, a collective 'we', to understand. More telling still, these narrators themselves remain unrealized: Robinson does not offer the reader either a strong personal voice, as Emerson does, or even a thoroughly dramatized persona along the lines of Lowell's Josiah Biglow. The word 'we' is used in a vacuum, as a shape to fill a lack—of knowledge and of belief in the value of individual personality. It is a product of the same kind of uncertainty about the integrity of the self as is found, in more explicit terms, in the verse of Stephen Crane, where man is described as a creature driven by forces beyond his control and acted upon by circumstances he can rarely understand. In such a context the idea of the self, of a force within man enabling him to shape his destiny and environment as he will, can appear no more than an illusion. Instead of a self, indeed, the poet confronts the reader with a set of conditioned reflexes.

The note that Stephen Crane and Edwin Arlington Robinson struck in the declining years of the century was a discordant one, but the discord would probably have pleased the ears of Freneau or Emerson could they have heard it. For whatever else might be said about a poem like *Richard Cory*, or one of Crane's enigmatic little lyrics, it was clear that in both instances the poet was developing his personal talent in a distinctively national context. By the end of the century, in other words, an area of concern and possibility had been mapped out within which the American writer had found and was to find most of his poetic explorations taking place. True, the explorations could assume a number of different directions. The self might be celebrated as the creative principle, a light that illuminated and revitalized the rest of the world, or it might simply be accepted as marking the limits of human vision. An established community of some restricted kind might be accepted as a touchstone of value, or the writer might try to create the sense of a new community between himself and his audience. Numerous as the directions might be, though, they were all recognizably the result of a particular national dilemma, a consequence of what Americans hoped and believed themselves to be. A series of problems had been defined, germane to the American environment, together with a series of possible strategies for dealing with those problems, and these every subsequent American poet has had to accept and develop: not, of course, because he is under any tangible obligation to do so but quite simply because he is an American. In examining himself he necessarily examines the same dilemmas as others did; only the task is easier for him to the extent that possible means of articulating and dealing with these dilemmas have already been formulated. The American poet can now build on the discoveries of his predecessors; and the fact that he can do so, is, ultimately, one measure of their achievement. For quite apart from the individual and quite considerable merits of poets like Emerson and Longfellow, Poe and Dickinson, Whitman and Melville, it is to their lasting credit as a group that together they helped create a tradition of poetry which was, in the most genuine and significant sense, an American one.

ACKNOWLEDGMENTS

'Richard Cory', 'Aaron Stark', 'The House on the Hill' and 'Luke Havergal' are reprinted by permission of Charles Scribner's Sons from *The Children of Night* by Edwin Arlington Robinson (1897). Acknowledgments are also due to Rutgers University Press for permission to include 'Yourself' from *Jones Very: Selected Poems*, ed. Nathan Lyons, Rutgers University Press, New Brunswick, New Jersey, U.S.A., 1966; to Alfred A. Knopf Inc. for permission to include the poems by Stephen Crane; and to Virgil Markham for permission to include 'The Man with the Hoe' by Edwin Markham.

Select Bibliography

The reader requiring comprehensive or specialized information is
advised to consult the *Literary History of the United States*, ed. R. E.
Spiller *et al.* (New York, 1948; with a bibliographical supplement in
1959), or the *Bibliographical Guide to the Study of the Literature of the
U.S.A.*, compiled by C. Gohdes (Durham, N.C., 1963).

SOME GENERAL WORKS

Allen, G. W. *American Prosody* (New York, 1935)
Arms, G. *The Fields Were Green* (Stanford, 1953)
Conner, F. *Cosmic Optimism* (Gainesville, Fla., 1949)
Donoghue, D. *Connoisseurs of Chaos* (London, 1966). Interesting
    readings of a number of American poets, including several from
    the nineteenth century (i.e. Whitman, Tuckerman, Dickinson,
    Robinson). Recommended.
Kreymborg, A. *A History of American Poetry* (New York, 1934)
Matthiesson, F. O. *American Renaissance* (New York, 1941). A pioneer-
    ing work on American literature of the nineteenth century and
    still indispensable. Highly recommended.
Parrington, V. L. *Main Currents in American Thought* (New York, 1927–
    1930). A valuable discussion of the intellectual background.
    Recommended.
Pearce, R. H. *The Continuity of American Poetry* (New York, 1961).
    A stimulating critical account of American poetry from the
    beginning until the present day, to which I am deeply indebted.
    Highly recommended.
Wells, H. W. *The American Way of Poetry* (New York, 1964)
Winters, Y. *In Defence of Reason* (Denver, Col., 1947). A series of
    invigorating and controversial essays on American writing,
    including discussions of Poe, Dickinson, Emerson and Very.
    Recommended.

SOME WORKS ON INDIVIDUAL AUTHORS

Axelrad, J. *Philip Freneau, Champion of Democracy* (Austin, Texas, 1967)
Leary, L. *That Rascal Freneau: A Study in Literary Failure* (New Brunswick, N.J., 1949)

Godwin, P. *A Biography of William Cullen Bryant* (New York, 1883)
McLean, A. F., Jr. *William Cullen Bryant* (New York, 1964)

Carpenter, F. I. *Emerson Handbook* (New York, 1953)
Rusk, R. L. *The Life of Ralph Waldo Emerson* (New York, 1949)
Whicher, S. E. *Freedom and Fate: An Inner Life of Ralph Waldo Emerson* (Philadelphia, 1953)

Arvin, N. *Longfellow: His Life and Work* (Boston, 1963)
Wagenknecht, E. *Henry Wadsworth Longfellow: Portrait of an American Humanist* (New York, 1966)

Mordell, A. *Quaker Militant: John Greenleaf Whittier* (Boston, 1933)
Pickard, S. T. *Life and Letters of John Greenleaf Whittier* (Boston, 1894)

Davidson, E. H. *Poe: A Critical Study* (Cambridge, Mass., 1957)
Quin, A. H. *Edgar Allan Poe: A Critical Biography* (New York, 1941)
Quinn, P. F. *The French Face of Edgar Poe* (Carbondale, Ill., 1957)

Howe, M. A. de W. *Holmes of the Breakfast-Table* (Oxford, 1939)
Small, M. R. *Oliver Wendell Holmes* (New York, 1962)

Bartlett, W. J. *Jones Very: Emerson's 'Brave Saint'* (Durham, N.C., 1942)
Winters, Y. 'Jones Very and R. W. Emerson: Aspects of New England Mysticism' in *In Defence of Reason* (New York, 1947)

Canby, H. S. *Thoreau* (Boston, 1939)
Cook, R. L. *Passage to Walden* (Boston, 1949)
Krutch, J. W. *Henry David Thoreau* (New York, 1948)

Duberman, M. *James Russell Lowell* (Boston, 1966)
Scudder, H. E. *James Russell Lowell: A Biography* (Boston, 1901)

Arvin, N. *Herman Melville* (New York, 1950)

Sedgwick, W. E. *Herman Melville: The Tragedy of the Mind* (Cambridge, Mass., 1944)

Stein, W. B. *The Poetry of Melville's Later Years: Time, History, Myth, and Religion* (New York, 1970)

Allen, G. W. *The Solitary Singer: A Critical Biography of Walt Whitman* (New York, 1955)

Chase, R. *Walt Whitman Reconsidered* (New York, 1955)

Pearce, R. H. (ed.) *Whitman: A Collection of Critical Essays* (Englewood Cliffs, N.J., 1962)

Bynner, W. 'Introduction' to *The Sonnets of Frederick Goddard Tuckerman* (New York, 1931)

Winters, Y. 'A Discovery', in *Hudson Review*, III (1950), 453–458

Beatty, R. C. *Bayard Taylor: Laureate of the Gilded Age* (Norman, Oklahoma, 1936)

Thompson, H. T. *Henry Timrod: Laureate of the Confederacy* (Columbia, S.C., 1928)

Griffith, C. *The Long Shadow: Emily Dickinson's Tragic Poetry* (Princeton, 1964)

Johnson, T. H. *Emily Dickinson: An Interpretative Biography* (Cambridge Mass., 1955)

Whicher, G. F. *This Was A Poet: A Critical Biography of Emily Dickinson* (New York, 1939)

Stewart, G. R. *Bret Harte: Argonaut and Exile* (Boston, 1931)

Peterson, M. S. *Joaquin Miller, Literary Frontiersman* (Stanford, Calif., 1937)

Starke, A. H. *Sidney Lanier: A Biographical and Critical Study* (Chapel Hill, N.C., 1933)

Dickey, M. *The Youth of James Whitcomb Riley* (Indianapolis, Ill., 1919) and *The Maturity of James Whitcomb Riley* (Indianapolis, Ill., 1922)

SELECT BIBLIOGRAPHY

Stidger, W. L. *Edwin Markham* (New York, 1940)

Brawley, B. G. *Paul Laurence Dunbar: Poet of His People* (Chapel Hill, N.C., 1936)

Henry, D. D. *William Vaughn Moody: A Study* (Boston, 1934)

Winters, Y. *Edwin Arlington Robinson* (New York, 1947)

Hoffman, D. G. *The Poetry of Stephen Crane* (New York, 1957)

EDITOR'S NOTE

Poets are arranged in chronological order. In those cases where two poets were born in the same year, the date of death is used to establish precedence.

Philip Freneau (1752–1832)

Freneau was born in New York, but spent much of his life in New Jersey. While a student at the College of New Jersey (later known as Princeton), he collaborated with Hugh Brackenridge on *The Rising Glory of America*; and with Brackenridge and James Madison (who later became President) on *Satires Against the Tories*. During the Revolution he wrote more satires, against the British, and was once captured by them while making one of many voyages in the Caribbean. He later became a newspaper editor and, during the Jefferson administration, a virulent partisan of the Jeffersonians. For this he earned the enmity of Federalists like Hamilton. After a further interval of sea life, he retired to a farm in New Jersey where he died in poverty. In politics he was a Jeffersonian democrat and in religion a Deist.

From THE RISING GLORY OF AMERICA
Being part of a Dialogue pronounced on a public occasion

Acasto

Now shall the adventurous muse attempt a theme
More new, more noble and more flush of fame
Than all that went before—
Now through the veil of ancient days renew
5   The period famed when first Columbus touched
These shores so long unknown—through various toils,
Famine, and death, the hero forced his way,
Through oceans pregnant with perpetual storms,
And climates hostile to adventurous man.

*   *   *

Eugenio

10   . . . Greece and Rome no more
Detain the Muses on Citheron's brow,
Or old Olympus, crowned with waving woods,
Or Hæmus' top, where once was heard the harp,
Sweet Orpheus' harp, that gained his cause below,

15 And pierced the souls of Orcus and his bride;
That hush'd to silence by its voice divine
Thy melancholy waters, and the gales
O Hebrus! that o'er thy sad surface blow.—
No more the maids round Alpheus' waters stray,
20 Where he with Arethusa's stream doth mix,
Or where swift Tiber disembogues his waves
Into the Italian sea, so long unsung;
Hither they wing their way, the last, the best
Of countries, where the arts shall rise and grow,
25 And arms shall have their day;—even now we boast
A Franklin, prince of all philosophy,
A genius piercing as the electric fire,
Bright as the lightning's flash, explained so well,
By him, the rival of Britannia's sage.—
30 This is the land of every joyous sound,
Of liberty and life, sweet liberty!
Without whose aid the noblest genius fails,
And Science irretrievably must die.

Leander

But come, Eugenio, since we know the past—
35 What hinders to pervade with searching eye
The mystic scenes of dark futurity?
Say, shall we ask what empires yet must rise,
What kingdoms, powers and states, where now are seen
Mere dreary wastes and awful solitude,
40 Where Melancholy sits, with eye forlorn,
And time anticipates, when we shall spread
Dominion from the north, and south, and west,
Far from the Atlantic to Pacific shores,
And people half the convex of the main!—
45 A glorious theme!—but how shall mortals dare
To pierce the dark events of future years
And scenes unravel, only known to fate?

Acasto

This might we do, if warmed by that bright coal
Snatch'd from the altar of cherubic fire
50 Which touched Isaiah's lips—or if the spirit
Of Jeremy and Amos, prophets old,

Might swell the heaving breast—I see, I see
Freedom's established reign; cities, and men,
Numerous as sands upon the ocean shore,
55 And empires rising where the sun descends!—
The Ohio soon shall glide by many a town
Of note; and where the Mississippi stream,
By forests shaded, now runs weeping on,
Nations shall grow, and states not less in fame
60 Than Greece and Rome of old!—we too shall boast
Our Scipios, Solons, Catos, sages, chiefs
That in the lap of time yet dormant lie,
Waiting the joyous hour of life and light.—
O snatch me hence, ye muses, to those days
65 When, through the veil of dark antiquity,
A race shall hear of us as things remote,
That blossomed in the morn of days.—Indeed,
How could I weep that we exist so soon,
Just in the dawning of these mighty times,
70 Whose scenes are painting for eternity!
Dissentions that shall swell the trump of fame,
And ruin hovering o'er all monarchy!

*   *   *

Leander

Here independent power shall hold her sway,
And public virtue warm the patriot breast:
75 No traces shall remain of tyranny,
And laws, a pattern to the world beside,
Be here enacted first.——

Acasto

And when a train of rolling years are past . . .
A new Jerusalem, sent down from heaven,
80 Shall grace our happy earth,—perhaps this land,
Whose ample bosom shall receive, though late,
Myriads of saints, with their immortal king,
To live and reign on earth a thousand years,
Thence called Millennium. Paradise anew
85 Shall flourish, by no second Adam lost,
No dangerous tree with deadly fruit shall grow,
No tempting serpent to allure the soul

From native innocence.—A Canaan here,
Another Canaan shall excel the old,
90   And from a fairer Pisgah's top be seen.
No thistle here, nor thorn, nor briar shall spring,
Earth's curse before: the lion and the lamb
In mutual friendship linked, shall browse the shrub,
And timorous deer with softened tygers stray
95   O'er mead, or lofty hill, or grassy plain;
Another Jordan's stream shall glide along,
And Siloah's brook in circling eddies flow:
Groves shall adorn their verdant banks, on which
The happy people, free from toils and death,
100 Shall find secure repose. No fierce disease,
No fevers, slow consumption, ghastly plague,
(Fate's ancient ministers) again proclaim
Perpetual war with man: fair fruits shall bloom,
Fair to the eye, and sweeter to the taste;
105 Nature's loud storms be hushed, and seas no more
Rage hostile to mankind—and, worse than all,
The fiercer passions of the human breast
Shall kindle up to deeds of death no more,
But all subside in universal peace.——
110   Such days the world,
And such America at last shall have
When ages, yet to come, have run their round,
And future years of bliss alone remain.

LITERARY IMPORTATION

However we wrangled with Britain awhile
We think of her now in a different stile,
And many fine things we receive from her isle;
        Among all the rest,
5   Some demon possessed
Our dealers in knowledge and sellers of sense
To have a good bishop imported from thence.

The words of Sam Chandler were thought to be vain,
When he argued so often and proved it so plain
10 'That Satan must flourish till bishops should reign:'

Though he went to the wall
With his project and all,
Another bold Sammy, in bishop's array,
Has got something more than his pains for his pay.

15 It seems we had spirit to humble a throne,
Have genius for science inferior to none,
But hardly encourage a plant of our own:
If a college be planned,
'Tis all at a stand
20 'Till to Europe we send at a shameful expense,
To send us a book-worm to teach us some sense.

Can we never be thought to have learning or grace
Unless it be brought from that damnable place
Where tyranny reigns with her impudent face;
25 And popes and pretenders,
And sly faith-defenders
Have ever been hostile to reason and wit,
Enslaving a world that shall conquer them yet.

'Tis a folly to fret at the picture I draw:
30 And I say what was said by a Doctor Magraw;
'If they give us their Bishops, they'll give us their law.'
How that will agree
With such people as we,
Let us leave to the learned to reflect on awhile,
35 And say what they think in a handsomer stile.

TO AN AUTHOR

Your leaves bound up compact and fair,
In neat array at length prepare,
To pass their hour on learning's stage,
To meet the surly critic's rage;
5 The statesman's slight, the smatterer's sneer—
Were these, indeed, your only fear,
You might be tranquil and resigned:
What most should touch your fluttering mind;
Is that, few critics will be found
10 To sift your works, and deal the wound.

— 5 —

Thus, when one fleeting year is past
On some bye-shelf your book is cast—
Another comes, with something new,
And drives you fairly out of view:
With some to praise, but more to blame,
The mind returns to—whence it came;
And some alive, who scarce could read
Will publish satires on the dead.

Thrice happy Dryden, who could meet
Some rival bard in every street!
When all were bent on writing well
It was some credit to excel:—

Thrice happy Dryden, who could find
A Milbourne for his sport designed—
And Pope, who saw the harmless rage
Of Dennis bursting o'er his page
Might justly spurn the critic's aim,
Who only helped to swell his fame.

On these bleak climes by Fortune thrown,
Where rigid Reason reigns alone,
Where lovely Fancy has no sway,
Nor magic forms about us play—
Nor nature takes her summer hue
Tell me, what has the muse to do?—

An age employed in edging steel
Can no poetic raptures feel;
No solitude's attracting power,
No leisure of the noon day hour,
No shaded stream, no quiet grove
Can this fantastic century move;

The muse of love in no request—
Go—try your fortune with the rest,
One of the nine you should engage,
To meet the follies of the age:—

45 On one, we fear, your choice must fall—
The least engaging of them all—
Her visage stern—an angry style—
A clouded brow—malicious smile—
A mind on murdered victims placed—
50 She, only she, can please the taste!

THE WILD HONEY SUCKLE

Fair flower, that dost so comely grow,
Hid in this silent, dull retreat,
Untouched thy honied blossoms blow,
Unseen thy little branches greet:
5   No roving foot shall crush thee here,
       No busy hand provoke a tear.

By Nature's self in white arrayed,
She bade thee shun the vulgar eye,
And planted here the guardian shade,
10 And sent soft waters murmuring by;
       Thus quietly thy summer goes,
       Thy days declining to repose.

Smit with those charms, that must decay,
I grieve to see your future doom;
15 They died—nor were those flowers more gay,
The flowers that did in Eden bloom;
       Unpitying frosts, and Autumn's power
       Shall leave no vestige of this flower.

From morning suns and evening dews
20 At first thy little being came:
If nothing once, you nothing lose,
For when you die you are the same;
       The space between, is but an hour,
       The frail duration of a flower.

William Cullen Bryant (1794–1878)

Bryant was born in Cummington, Massachusetts. He entered Williams College in 1810; then left intending to go to Yale. Financial reasons prevented him from doing so. He was forced to give up hope of a thorough college education and study law instead. In 1815 he was admitted to the bar. In 1817 one of his most famous poems, *Thanatopsis* (the first draft of which was written when he was eighteen), was published and he was immediately hailed as an important poet. Other, equally successful poems followed and in 1825 he moved to New York, there to become editor of the *New York Evening Post*. He remained in this position for fifty years, becoming one of the finest liberal journalists of his age. His best poetry was written by the time he was forty, but in later life he continued to produce poems, criticism, tales, and travel letters.

THANATOPSIS

To him who in the love of Nature holds
Communion with her visible forms, she speaks
A various language; for his gayer hours
She has a voice of gladness, and a smile
5   And eloquence of beauty, and she glides
Into his darker musings, with a mild
And healing sympathy, that steals away
Their sharpness, ere he is aware. When thoughts
Of the last bitter hour come like a blight
10   Over thy spirit, and sad images
Of the stern agony, and shroud, and pall,
And breathless darkness, and the narrow house,
Make thee to shudder, and grow sick at heart;—
Go forth, under the open sky, and list
15   To Nature's teachings, while from all around—
Earth and her waters, and the depths of air—
Comes a still voice.—

Yet a few days, and thee
The all-beholding sun shall see no more
In all his course; nor yet in the cold ground,

– 8 –

20 Where thy pale form was laid, with many tears,
    Nor in the embrace of ocean, shall exist
    Thy image. Earth, that nourished thee, shall claim
    Thy growth, to be resolved to earth again,
    And, lost each human trace, surrendering up
25 Thine individual being, shalt thou go
    To mix for ever with the elements,
    To be a brother to the insensible rock
    And to the sluggish clod, which the rude swain
    Turns with his share, and treads upon. The oak
30 Shall send his roots abroad, and pierce thy mould.

    Yet not to thine eternal resting-place
    Shalt thou retire alone, nor couldst thou wish
    Couch more magnificent. Thou shalt lie down
    With patriarchs of the infant world—with kings,
35 The powerful of the earth—the wise, the good,
    Fair forms, and hoary seers of ages past,
    All in one mighty sepulchre. The hills
    Rock-ribbed and ancient as the sun,—the vales
    Stretching in pensive quietness between;
40 The venerable woods—rivers that move
    In majesty, and the complaining brooks
    That make the meadows green; and, poured round all,
    Old Ocean's gray and melancholy waste,—
    Are but the solemn decorations all
45 Of the great tomb of man. The golden sun,
    The planets, all the infinite host of heaven,
    Are shining on the sad abodes of death,
    Through the still lapse of ages. All that tread
    The globe are but a handful to the tribes
50 That slumber in its bosom.—Take the wings
    Of morning, pierce the Barcan wilderness,
    Or lose thyself in the continuous woods
    Where rolls the Oregon, and hears no sound,
    Save his own dashings—yet the dead are there:
55 And millions in those solitudes, since first
    The flight of years began, have laid them down
    In their last sleep—the dead reign there alone.
    So shalt thou rest, and what if thou withdraw
    In silence from the living, and no friend
60 Take note of thy departure? All that breathe
    Will share thy destiny. The gay will laugh

When thou art gone, the solemn brood of care
Plod on, and each one as before will chase
His favorite phantom; yet all these shall leave
65   Their mirth and their employments, and shall come
And make their bed with thee. As the long train
Of ages glides away, the sons of men,
The youth in life's fresh spring, and he who goes
In the full strength of years, matron and maid,
70   The speechless babe, and the gray-headed man—
Shall one by one be gathered to thy side,
By those, who in their turn shall follow them.

So live, that when thy summons comes to join
The innumerable caravan, which moves
75   To that mysterious realm, where each shall take
His chamber in the silent halls of death,
Thou go not, like the quarry-slave at night,
Scourged to his dungeon, but, sustained and soothed
By an unfaltering trust, approach thy grave,
80   Like one who wraps the drapery of his couch
About him, and lies down to pleasant dreams.

INSCRIPTION FOR THE ENTRANCE TO A WOOD

Stranger, if thou hast learned a truth which needs
No school of long experience, that the world
Is full of guilt and misery, and hast seen
Enough of all its sorrows, crimes, and cares,
5   To tire thee of it, enter this wild wood
And view the haunts of Nature. The calm shade
Shall bring a kindred calm, and the sweet breeze
That makes the green leaves dance, shall waft a balm
To thy sick heart. Thou wilt find nothing here
10   Of all that pained thee in the haunts of men,
And made thee loathe thy life. The primal curse
Fell, it is true, upon the unsinning earth,
But not in vengeance. God hath yoked to guilt
Her pale tormentor, misery. Hence, these shades
15   Are still the abodes of gladness; the thick roof
Of green and stirring branches is alive
And musical with birds, that sing and sport

In wantonness of spirit; while below
The squirrel, with raised paws and form erect,
20 Chirps merrily. Throngs of insects in the shade
Try their thin wings and dance in the warm beam
That waked them into life. Even the green trees
Partake the deep contentment; as they bend
To the soft winds, the sun from the blue sky
25 Looks in and sheds a blessing on the scene.
Scarce less the cleft-born wild-flower seems to enjoy
Existence than the wingèd plunderer
That sucks its sweets. The mossy rocks themselves,
And the old and ponderous trunks of prostrate trees
30 That lead from knoll to knoll a causey rude
Or bridge the sunken brook, and their dark roots,
With all their earth upon them, twisting high,
Breathe fixed tranquillity. The rivulet
Sends forth glad sounds, and tripping o'er its bed
35 Of pebbly sands, or leaping down the rocks,
Seems, with continuous laughter, to rejoice
In its own being. Softly tread the marge,
Lest from her midway perch thou scare the wren
That dips her bill in water. The cool wind,
40 That stirs the stream in play, shall come to thee,
Like one that loves thee nor will let thee pass
Ungreeted, and shall give its light embrace.

TO A WATERFOWL

Whither, midst falling dew,
While glow the heavens with the last steps of day,
Far, through their rosy depths, dost thou pursue
        Thy solitary way?

5   Vainly the fowler's eye
Might mark thy distant flight to do thee wrong,
As, darkly painted on the crimson sky,
        Thy figure floats along.

        Seek'st thou the plashy brink
10 Of weedy lake, or marge of river wide,
Or where the rocking billows rise and sink
        On the chafed ocean-side?

There is a Power whose care
Teaches thy way along that pathless coast—
15   The desert and illimitable air—
        Lone wandering, but not lost.

All day thy wings have fanned,
At that far height, the cold, thin atmosphere,
Yet stoop not, weary, to the welcome land,
20   Though the dark night is near.

And soon that toil shall end;
Soon shalt thou find a summer home, and rest,
And scream among thy fellows; reeds shall bend,
        Soon, o'er thy sheltered nest.

25   Thou'rt gone, the abyss of heaven
Hath swallowed up thy form; yet, on my heart
Deeply has sunk the lesson thou hast given,
        And shall not soon depart.

He who, from zone to zone,
30   Guides through the boundless sky thy certain flight,
In the long way that I must tread alone,
        Will lead my steps aright.

THE PRAIRIES

These are the gardens of the Desert, these
The unshorn fields, boundless and beautiful,
For which the speech of England has no name—
The Prairies. I behold them for the first,
5   And my heart swells, while the dilated sight
Takes in the encircling vastness. Lo! they stretch,
In airy undulations, far away,
As if the ocean, in his gentlest swell,
Stood still, with all his rounded billows fixed,
10   And motionless forever.—Motionless?—
No—they are all unchained again. The clouds
Sweep over with their shadows, and, beneath,
The surface rolls and fluctuates to the eye;
Dark hollows seem to glide along and chase
15   The sunny ridges. Breezes of the South!

Who toss the golden and the flame-like flowers,
And pass the prairie-hawk that, poised on high,
Flaps his broad wings, yet moves not—ye have played
Among the palms of Mexico and vines
20   Of Texas, and have crisped the limpid brooks,
That from the fountains of Sonora glide
Into the calm Pacific—have ye fanned
A nobler or a lovelier scene than this?
Man hath no power in all this glorious work:
25   The hand that built the firmament hath heaved
And smoothed these verdant swells, and sown their slopes
With herbage, planted them with island groves,
And hedged them round with forests. Fitting floor
For this magnificent temple of the sky—
30   With flowers whose glory and whose multitude
Rival the constellations! The great heavens
Seem to stoop down upon the scene in love,—
A nearer vault, and of a tenderer blue,
Than that which bends above our eastern hills.

35   As o'er the verdant waste I guide my steed,
Among the high rank grass that sweeps his sides
The hollow beating of his footstep seems
A sacrilegious sound. I think of those
Upon whose rest he tramples. Are they here—
40   The dead of other days?—and did the dust
Of these fair solitudes once stir with life
And burn with passion? Let the mighty mounds
That overlook the rivers, or that rise
In the dim forest crowded with old oaks,
45   Answer. A race, that long has passed away,
Built them;—a disciplined and populous race
Heaped, with long toil, the earth, while yet the Greek
Was hewing the Pentelicus to forms
Of symmetry, and rearing on its rock
50   The glittering Parthenon. These ample fields
Nourished their harvests, here their herds were fed,
When haply by their stalls the bison lowed,
And bowed his manèd shoulder to the yoke.
All day this desert murmured with their toils,
55   Till twilight blushed, and lovers walked, and wooed
In a forgotten language, and old tunes,
From instruments of unremembered form,

Gave the soft winds a voice. The red man came—
The roaming hunter tribes, warlike and fierce,
60 And the mound-builders vanished from the earth.
The solitude of centuries untold
Has settled where they dwelt. The prairie-wolf
Hunts in their meadows, and his fresh-dug den
Yawns by my path. The gopher mines the ground
65 Where stood their swarming cities. All is gone;
All—save the piles of earth that hold their bones,
The platforms where they worshipped unknown gods,
The barriers which they builded from the soil
To keep the foe at bay—till o'er the walls
70 The wild beleaguerers broke, and, one by one,
The strongholds of the plain were forced, and heaped
With corpses. The brown vultures of the wood
Flocked to those vast uncovered sepulchres,
And sat unscared and silent at their feast.
75 Haply some solitary fugitive,
Lurking in marsh and forest, till the sense
Of desolation and of fear became
Bitterer than death, yielded himself to die.
Man's better nature triumphed then. Kind words
80 Welcomed and soothed him; the rude conquerors
Seated the captive with their chiefs; he chose
A bride among their maidens, and at length
Seemed to forget—yet ne'er forgot—the wife
Of his first love, and her sweet little ones,
85 Butchered, amid their shrieks, with all his race.

Thus change the forms of being. Thus arise
Races of living things, glorious in strength,
And perish, as the quickening breath of God
Fills them, or is withdrawn. The red man, too,
90 Has left the blooming wilds he ranged so long,
And, nearer to the Rocky Mountains, sought
A wilder hunting-ground. The beaver builds
No longer by these streams, but far away,
On waters whose blue surface ne'er gave back
95 The white man's face—among Missouri's springs,
And pools whose issues swell the Oregon—
He rears his little Venice. In these plains
The bison feeds no more. Twice twenty leagues
Beyond remotest smoke of hunter's camp,

100   Roams the majestic brute, in herds that shake
       The earth with thundering steps—yet here I meet
       His ancient footsprints stamped beside the pool.

           Still this great solitude is quick with life.
       Myriads of insects, gaudy as the flowers
105   They flutter over, gentle quadrupeds,
       And birds, that scarce have learned the fear of man,
       Are here, and sliding reptiles of the ground,
       Startlingly beautiful. The graceful deer
       Bounds to the wood at my approach. The bee,
110   A more adventurous colonist than man,
       With whom he came across the eastern deep,
       Fills the savannas with his murmurings,
       And hides his sweets, as in the golden age,
       Within the hollow oak. I listen long
115   To his domestic hum, and think I hear
       The sound of that advancing multitude
       Which soon shall fill these deserts. From the ground
       Comes up the laugh of children, the soft voice
       Of maidens, and the sweet and solemn hymn
120   Of Sabbath worshippers. The low of herds
       Blends with the rustling of the heavy grain
       Over the dark brown furrows. All at once
       A fresher wind sweeps by, and breaks my dream,
       And I am in the wilderness alone.

Ralph Waldo Emerson (1803–1882)

Emerson was born in Boston. His father was a Unitarian minister
and, after studying at Harvard and Cambridge Divinity School, he
too became a minister at the 'Second Church' of Boston in 1829. In
1832, however, he resigned his clerical position on doctrinal grounds.
After various trips abroad, he settled in Concord in 1834 and in the
next year began to lecture in Boston and elsewhere. In 1836 his first
book, *Nature*, appeared which was to become a key text for the group
known as the Transcendentalists. Most of Emerson's important work
was written in the next twenty-five years, including *The American*

Scholar which O. W. Holmes described as an 'intellectual declaration of independence'. During this time Emerson also founded the Transcendental Club and edited the Transcendentalist periodical, *The Dial*. In later years his health and memory failed, and he became a kind of father-figure for the genteel society of New England : an ironic fate, considering the revolutionary nature of his earlier writings.

EACH AND ALL

Little thinks, in the field, yon red-cloaked clown,
Of thee from the hill-top looking down;
The heifer that lows in the upland farm,
Far-heard, lows not thine ear to charm;
5   The sexton, tolling his bell at noon,
Deems not that great Napoleon
Stops his horse, and lists with delight,
Whilst his files sweep round yon Alpine height;
Nor knowest thou what argument
10   Thy life to thy neighbour's creed has lent.
All are needed by each one;
Nothing is fair or good alone.
I thought the sparrow's note from heaven,
Singing at dawn on the alder bough;
15   I brought him home, in his nest, at even;
He sings the song, but it pleases not now,
For I did not bring home the river and sky;—
He sang to my ear,—they sang to my eye.
The delicate shells lay on the shore;
20   The bubbles of the latest wave
Fresh pearls to their enamel gave;
And the bellowing of the savage sea
Greeted their safe escape to me.
I wiped away the weeds and foam,
25   I fetched my sea-born treasures home;
But the poor, unsightly, noisome things
Had left their beauty on the shore,
With the sun and the sand and the wild uproar.
The lover watched his graceful maid,
30   As 'mid the virgin train she strayed,
Nor knew her beauty's best attire
Was woven still by the snow-white choir.

At last she came to his hermitage,
Like the bird from the woodlands to the cage;—
35   The gay enchantment was undone,
A gentle wife, but fairy none.
Then I said, 'I covet truth;
Beauty is unripe childhood's cheat;
I leave it behind with the games of youth.'—
40   As I spoke, beneath my feet
The ground-pine curled its pretty wreath,
Running over the club-moss burrs;
I inhaled the violet's breath;
Around me stood the oaks and firs;
45   Pine-cones and acorns lay on the ground;
Over me soared the eternal sky,
Full of light and of deity;
Again I saw, again I heard,
The rolling river, the morning bird;—
50   Beauty through my senses stole;
I yielded myself to the perfect whole.

URIEL

It fell in the ancient periods
    Which the brooding soul surveys,
Or ever the wild Time coined itself
    Into calendar months and days.

5   This was the lapse of Uriel,
Which in Paradise befell.
Once, among the Pleiads walking,
Seyd overheard the young gods talking;
And the treason, too long pent,
10   To his ears was evident.
The young deities discussed
Laws of form, and metre just,
Orb, quintessence, and sunbeams,
What subsisteth, and what seems.
15   One, with low tones that decide,
And doubt and reverend use defied,
With a look that solved the sphere,
And stirred the devils everywhere,

Gave his sentiment divine
20 Against the being of a line.
'Line in nature is not found;
Unit and universe are round;
In vain produced, all rays return;
Evil will bless, and ice will burn.'
25 As Uriel spoke with piercing eye,
A shudder ran around the sky;
The stern old war-gods shook their heads;
The seraphs frowned from myrtle-beds;
Seemed to the holy festival
30 The rash word boded ill to all;
The balance-beam of Fate was bent;
The bounds of good and ill were rent;
Strong Hades could not keep his own,
But all slid to confusion.

35 A sad self-knowledge, withering, fell
On the beauty of Uriel;
In heaven once eminent, the god
Withdrew, that hour, into his cloud;
Whether doomed to long gyration
40 In the sea of generation,
Or by knowledge grown too bright
To hit the nerve of feebler sight.
Straightway, a forgetting wind
Stole over the celestial kind,
45 And their lips the secret kept,
If in ashes the fire-seed slept.
But now and then, truth-speaking things
Shamed the angels' veiling wings;
And, shrilling from the solar course,
50 Or from fruit of chemic force,
Procession of a soul in matter,
Or the speeding change of water,
Or out of the good of evil born,
Came Uriel's voice of cherub scorn,
55 And a blush tinged the upper sky,
And the gods shook, they knew not why.

HAMATREYA

Bulkeley, Hunt, Willard, Hosmer, Meriam, Flint,
Possessed the land which rendered to their toil
Hay, corn, roots, hemp, flax, apples, wool, and wood.
Each of these landlords walked amidst his farm,
5   Saying, ''Tis mine, my children's, and my name's:
How sweet the west wind sounds in my own trees!
How graceful climb those shadows on my hill!
I fancy these pure waters and the flags
Know me, as does my dog: we sympathize;
10   And, I affirm, my actions smack of the soil.'
Where are these men? Asleep beneath their grounds;
And strangers, fond as they, their furrows plough.
Earth laughs in flowers, to see her boastful boys
Earth-proud, proud of the earth which is not theirs;
15   Who steer the plough, but cannot steer their feet
Clear of the grave.
They added ridge to valley, brook to pond,
And sighed for all that bounded their domain.
'This suits me for a pasture; that's my park;
20   We must have clay, lime, gravel, granite-ledge,
And misty lowland, where to go for peat.
The land is well,—lies fairly to the south.
'Tis good, when you have crossed the sea and back,
To find the sitfast acres where you left them.'
25   Ah! the hot owner sees not Death, who adds
Him to his land, a lump of mould the more.
Hear what the Earth says:—

EARTH-SONG

'Mine and yours;
Mine, not yours.
30   Earth endures;
Stars abide—
Shine down in the old sea;
Old are the shores;
But where are old men?
35   I who have seen much,
Such have I never seen.

'The lawyer's deed
Ran sure,

In tail,
40   To them, and to their heirs
Who shall succeed,
Without fail,
Forevermore.

'Here is the land,
45   Shaggy with wood,
With its old valley,
Mound, and flood,
But the heritors?
Fled like the flood's foam,—
50   The lawyer, and the laws,
And the kingdom,
Clean swept herefrom.

'They called me theirs,
Who so controlled me;
55   Yet every one
Wished to stay, and is gone.
How am I theirs,
If they cannot hold me,
But I hold them?'

60   When I heard the Earth-song,
I was no longer brave;
My avarice cooled
Like lust in the chill of the grave.

THE SNOW-STORM

Announced by all the trumpets of the sky,
Arrives the snow, and, driving o'er the fields,
Seems nowhere to alight: the whited air
Hides hills and woods, the river, and the heaven,
5   And veils the farm-house at the garden's end.
The sled and traveller stopped, the courier's feet
Delayed, all friends shut out, the housemates sit
Around the radiant fireplace, enclosed
In a tumultuous privacy of storm.

10   Come see the north wind's masonry.
Out of an unseen quarry evermore
Furnished with tile, the fierce artificer
Curves his white bastions with projected roof
Round every windward stake, or tree, or door.
15   Speeding, the myriad-handed, his wild work
So fanciful, so savage, naught cares he
For number or proportion. Mockingly,
On coop or kennel he hangs Parian wreaths;
A swan-like form invests the hidden thorn;
20   Fills up the farmer's lane from wall to wall,
Maugre the farmer's sighs; and, at the gate,
A tapering turret overtops the work.
And when his hours are numbered, and the world
Is all his own, retiring, as he were not,
25   Leaves, when the sun appears, astonished Art
To mimic in slow structures, stone by stone,
Built in an age, the mad wind's night-work,
The frolic architecture of the snow.

MERLIN

I

Thy trivial harp will never please
Or fill my craving ear;
Its chords should ring as blows the breeze,
Free, peremptory, clear.
5   No jingling serenader's art,
Nor tinkle of piano strings,
Can make the wild blood start
In its mystic springs.
The kingly bard
10   Must smite the chords rudely and hard,
As with hammer or with mace;
That they may render back
Artful thunder, which conveys
Secrets of the solar track,
15   Sparks of the supersolar blaze.
Merlin's blows are strokes of fate,

Chiming with the forest tone,
When boughs buffet boughs in the wood;
Chiming with the gasp and moan
20   Of the ice-imprisoned flood;
With the pulse of manly hearts;
With the voice of orators;
With the din of city arts;
With the cannonade of wars;
25   With the marches of the brave;
And prayers of might from martyrs' cave.

Great is the art,
Great be the manners, of the bard.
He shall not his brain encumber
30   With the coil of rhythm and number;
But, leaving rule and pale forethought,
He shall aye climb
For his rhyme.
'Pass in, pass in,' the angels say,
35   'In to the upper doors,
Nor count compartments of the floors,
But mount to paradise
By the stairway of surprise.'

Blameless master of the games,
40   King of sport that never shames,
He shall daily joy dispense
Hid in song's sweet influence.
Forms more cheerly live and go,
What time the subtle mind
45   Sings aloud the tune whereto
Their pulses beat,
And march their feet,
And their members are combined.

By Sybarites beguiled,
50   He shall no task decline;
Merlin's mighty line
Extremes of nature reconciled,—
Bereaved a tyrant of his will,
And made the lion mild.
55   Songs can the tempest still,
Scattered on the stormy air,

Mould the year to fair increase,
And bring in poetic peace.

He shall not seek to weave,
In weak, unhappy times,
Efficacious rhymes;
Wait his returning strength.
Bird, that from the nadir's floor
To the zenith's top can soar,
The soaring orbit of the muse exceeds that journey's length.
Nor profane affect to hit
Or compass that, by meddling wit,
Which only the propitious mind
Publishes when 't is inclined.
There are open hours
When the God's will sallies free,
And the dull idiot might see
The flowing fortunes of a thousand years;—
Sudden, at unawares,
Self-moved, fly-to the doors,
Nor sword of angels could reveal
What they conceal.

II

The rhyme of the poet
Modulates the king's affairs;
Balance-loving Nature
Made all things in pairs.
To every foot its antipode;
Each colour with its counter glowed;
To every tone beat answering tones,
Higher or graver;
Flavour gladly blends with flavour;
Leaf answers leaf upon the bough;
And match the paired cotyledons.
Hands to hands, and feet to feet,
In one body grooms and brides;
Eldest rite, two married sides
In every mortal meet.
Light's far furnace shines,
Smelting balls and bars,
Forging double stars,
Glittering twins and trines.

The animals are sick with love,
Lovesick with rhyme;
Each with all propitious time
100 Into chorus wove.

Like the dancers' ordered band,
Thoughts come also hand in hand;
In equal couples mated,
Or else alternated;
105 Adding by their mutual gage,
One to other, health and age.
Solitary fancies go
Short-lived wandering to and fro,
Most like to bachelors,
100 Or an ungiven maid,
Not ancestors,
With no posterity to make the lie afraid,
Or keep truth undecayed.
Perfect-paired as eagle's wings,
115 Justice is the rhyme of things;
Trade and counting use
The self-same tuneful muse;
And Nemesis,
Who with even matches odd,
120 Who athwart space redresses
The partial wrong,
Fills the just period,
And finishes the song.

Subtle rhymes, with ruin rife,
125 Murmur in the house of life,
Sung by the Sisters as they spin;
In perfect time and measure they
Build and unbuild our echoing clay,
As the two twilights of the day
130 Fold us music-drunken in.

THE APOLOGY

Think me not unkind and rude
  That I walk alone in grove and glen;
I go to the god of the wood
  To fetch his word to men.

5 Tax not my sloth that I
  Fold my arms beside the brook;
Each cloud that floated in the sky
  Writes a letter in my book.

Chide me not, laborious band,
10 For the idle flowers I brought;
Every aster in my hand
  Goes home loaded with a thought.

There was never mystery
  But 't is figured in the flowers;
15 Was never secret history
  But birds tell it in the bowers.

One harvest from thy field
  Homeward brought the oxen strong;
A second crop thine acres yield,
20 Which I gather in a song.

HYMN

SUNG AT THE COMPLETION OF THE CONCORD MONUMENT
April 19, 1836

By the rude bridge that arched the flood,
  Their flag to April's breeze unfurled,
Here once the embattled farmers stood,
  And fired the shot heard round the world.

5 The foe long since in silence slept;
  Alike the conqueror silent sleeps;
And Time the ruined bridge has swept
  Down the dark stream which seaward creeps.

On this green bank, by this soft stream,
10   We set to-day a votive stone;
That memory may their deed redeem,
    When, like our sires, our sons are gone.

Spirit, that made those heroes dare
    To die, or leave their children free,
15 Bid Time and Nature gently spare
    The shaft we raise to them and thee.

DAYS

Damsels of Time, the hypocritic Days,
Muffled and dumb like barefoot dervishes,
And marching single in an endless file,
Bring diadems and faggots in their hands.
5 To each they offer gifts after his will,
Bread, kingdoms, stars, and sky that holds them all.
I, in my pleached garden, watched the pomp,
Forgot my morning wishes, hastily
Took a few herbs and apples, and the Day
10 Turned and departed silent. I, too late,
Under her solemn fillet saw the scorn.

Henry Wadsworth Longfellow (1807–1882)

Born in Portland, Maine, to a comparatively old and well-established family, Longfellow graduated from Bowdoin College in 1826 and then spent three years in Europe. He returned to become professor of modern languages at Bowdoin and then, in 1836, he was appointed to a chair at Harvard. During the next few years he consolidated his position as one of America's most famous and popular poets; continued to travel in Europe extensively; and in 1843 married Frances Appleton, receiving as his wedding-gift from his father-in-law the deeds to Craigie House, which has since become a Longfellow shrine. In 1854, he resigned his chair at Harvard to devote himself to poetry and translations. A mark of his fame abroad was that in 1868 he received honorary degrees from both Oxford and Cambridge and that, immediately after his death, his bust was placed in the Poets' Corner at Westminster Abbey.

A PSALM OF LIFE

WHAT THE HEART OF THE YOUNG MAN SAID TO THE PSALMIST

Tell me not, in mournful numbers,
    Life is but an empty dream!—
For the soul is dead that slumbers,
    And things are not what they seem.

5 Life is real! Life is earnest!
    And the grave is not its goal;
Dust thou art, to dust returnest,
    Was not spoken of the soul.

Not enjoyment, and not sorrow,
10   Is our destined end or way;
But to act, that each to-morrow
    Find us farther than to-day.

Art is long, and Time is fleeting,
    And our hearts, though stout and brave,
15 Still, like muffled drums, are beating
    Funeral marches to the grave.

In the world's broad field of battle,
    In the bivouac of Life,
Be not like dumb, driven cattle!
20   Be a hero in the strife!

Trust no Future, howe'er pleasant!
    Let the dead Past bury its dead!
Act,—act in the living Present!
    Heart within, and God o'erhead!

25 Lives of great men all remind us
    We can make our lives sublime,
And, departing, leave behind us
    Footprints on the sands of time;

Footprints, that perhaps another,
  Sailing o'er life's solemn main,
A forlorn and shipwrecked brother,
  Seeing, shall take heart again.

Let us, then, be up and doing,
  With a heart for any fate;
Still achieving, still pursuing,
  Learn to labor and to wait.

HYMN TO THE NIGHT

I heard the trailing garments of the Night
  Sweep through her marble halls!
I saw her sable skirts all fringed with light
  From the celestial walls!

I felt her presence, by its spell of might,
  Stoop o'er me from above;
The calm, majestic presence of the Night,
  As of the one I love.

I heard the sounds of sorrow and delight,
  The manifold, soft chimes,
That fill the haunted chambers of the Night,
  Like some old poet's rhymes.

From the cool cisterns of the midnight air
  My spirit drank repose;
The fountain of perpetual peace flows there,—
  From those deep cisterns flows.

O holy Night! from thee I learn to bear
  What man has borne before!
Thou layest thy finger on the lips of Care,
  And they complain no more.

Peace! Peace! Orestes-like I breathe this prayer!
  Descend with broad-winged flight,
The welcome, the thrice-prayed for, the most fair,
  The best-beloved Night!

THE VILLAGE BLACKSMITH

Under a spreading chestnut-tree
    The village smithy stands;
The smith, a mighty man is he,
    With large and sinewy hands;
5   And the muscles of his brawny arms
    Are strong as iron bands.

His hair is crisp, and black, and long,
    His face is like the tan;
His brow is wet with honest sweat,
10   He earns whate'er he can,
And looks the whole world in the face,
    For he owes not any man.

Week in, week out, from morn till night,
    You can hear his bellows blow;
15   You can hear him swing his heavy sledge,
    With measured beat and slow,
Like a sexton ringing the village bell,
    When the evening sun is low.

And children coming home from school
20   Look in at the open door;
They love to see the flaming forge,
    And hear the bellows roar,
And catch the burning sparks that fly
    Like chaff from a threshing-floor.

25   He goes on Sunday to the church,
    And sits among his boys;
He hears the parson pray and preach,
    He hears his daughter's voice,
Singing in the village choir,
30   And it makes his heart rejoice.

It sounds to him like her mother's voice,
    Singing in Paradise!
He needs must think of her once more,
    How in the grave she lies;
35   And with his hard, rough hand he wipes
    A tear out of his eyes.

Toiling,—rejoicing, —sorrowing,
    Onward through life he goes;
Each morning sees some task begin,
40   Each evening sees it close;
Something attempted, something done,
    Has earned a night's repose.

Thanks, thanks to thee, my worthy friend,
    For the lesson thou hast taught!
45 Thus at the flaming forge of life
    Our fortunes must be wrought;
Thus on its sounding anvil shaped
    Each burning deed and thought.

MEZZO CAMMIN

Half of my life is gone, and I have let
    The years slip from me and have not fulfilled
    The aspiration of my youth, to build
    Some tower of song with lofty parapet.
5 Not indolence, nor pleasure, nor the fret
    Of restless passions that would not be stilled,
    But sorrow, and a care that almost killed,
    Kept me from what I may accomplish yet;
Though, half-way up the hill, I see the Past
10   Lying beneath me with its sounds and sights,—
    A city in the twilight dim and vast,
With smoking roofs, soft bells, and gleaming lights,—
    And hear above me on the autumnal blast
    The cataract of Death far thundering from the heights.

MY LOST YOUTH

Often I think of the beautiful town
    That is seated by the sea;
Often in thought go up and down
The pleasant streets of that dear old town,
5   And my youth comes back to me.

And a verse of a Lapland song
Is haunting my memory still:
"A boy's will is the wind's will,
And the thoughts of youth are long, long thoughts."

10 I can see the shadowy lines of its trees,
  And catch, in sudden gleams,
The sheen of the far-surrounding seas,
And islands that were the Hesperides
  Of all my boyish dreams.
15   And the burden of that old song,
   It murmurs and whispers still:
 "A boy's will is the wind's will,
And the thoughts of youth are long, long thoughts."

I remember the black wharves and the slips,
20 And the sea-tides tossing free;
And Spanish sailors with bearded lips,
And the beauty and mystery of the ships,
  And the magic of the sea.
   And the voice of that wayward song
25   Is singing and saying still:
 "A boy's will is the wind's will,
And the thoughts of youth are long, long thoughts."

I remember the bulwarks by the shore,
  And the fort upon the hill;
30 The sunrise gun, with its hollow roar,
The drum-beat repeated o'er and o'er,
  And the bugle wild and shrill.
   And the music of that old song
   Throbs in my memory still:
35 "A boy's will is the wind's will,
And the thoughts of youth are long, long thoughts."

I remember the sea-fight far away,
  How it thundered o'er the tide!
And the dead captains, as they lay
40 In their graves, o'erlooking the tranquil bay,
  Where they in battle died.
   And the sound of that mournful song
   Goes through me with a thrill:
 "A boy's will is the wind's will,
45 And the thoughts of youth are long, long thoughts."

I can see the breezy dome of groves,
    The shadows of Deering's Woods;
And the friendships old and the early loves
Come back with a Sabbath sound, as of doves
50   In quiet neighborhoods.
      And the verse of that sweet old song,
        It flutters and murmurs still:
    "A boy's will is the wind's will,
And the thoughts of youth are long, long thoughts."

55 I remember the gleams and glooms that dart
    Across the school-boy's brain;
The song and the silence in the heart,
That in part are prophecies, and in part
    Are longings wild and vain.
60   And the voice of that fitful song
      Sings on, and is never still:
    "A boy's will is the wind's will,
And the thoughts of youth are long, long thoughts."

There are things of which I may not speak;
65   There are dreams that cannot die;
There are thoughts that make the strong heart weak,
And bring a pallor into the cheek,
    And a mist before the eye.
      And the words of that fatal song
70   Come over me like a chill:
    "A boy's will is the wind's will,
And the thoughts of youth are long, long thoughts."

Strange to me now are the forms I meet
    When I visit the dear old town;
75 But the native air is pure and sweet,
And the trees that o'ershadow each well-known street,
    As they balance up and down,
      Are singing the beautiful song,
      Are sighing and whispering still:
80   "A boy's will is the wind's will,
And the thoughts of youth are long, long thoughts."

And Deering's Woods are fresh and fair,
    And with joy that is almost pain
My heart goes back to wander there,

85 And among the dreams of the days that were,
    I find my lost youth again.
        And the strange and beautiful song,
      The groves are repeating it still:
  "A boy's will is the wind's will,
90 And the thoughts of youth are long, long thoughts."

CHAUCER

An old man in a lodge within a park;
    The chamber walls depicted all around
    With portraitures of huntsman, hawk, and hound,
    And the hurt deer. He listeneth to the lark,
5 Whose song comes with the sunshine through the dark
    Of painted glass in leaden lattice bound;
    He listeneth and he laugheth at the sound,
    Then writeth in a book like any clerk.
He is the poet of the dawn, who wrote
10   The Canterbury Tales, and his old age
    Made beautiful with song; and as I read
I hear the crowing cock, I hear the note
    Of lark and linnet, and from every page
    Rise odors of ploughed field or flowery mead.

NATURE

As a fond mother, when the day is o'er,
    Leads by the hand her little child to bed,
    Half willing, half reluctant to be led,
    And leave his broken playthings on the floor,
5 Still gazing at them through the open door,
    Nor wholly reassured and comforted
    By promises of others in their stead,
    Which, though more splendid, may not please him more;
So Nature deals with us, and takes away
10   Our playthings one by one, and by the hand
    Leads us to rest so gently, that we go
Scarce knowing if we wish to go or stay,
    Being too full of sleep to understand
    How far the unknown transcends the what we know.

THE TIDE RISES, THE TIDE FALLS

The tide rises, the tide falls,
The twilight darkens, the curlew calls;
Along the sea-sands damp and brown
The traveller hastens toward the town,
5   And the tide rises, the tide falls.

Darkness settles on roofs and walls,
But the sea, the sea in the darkness calls;
The little waves, with their soft, white hands,
Efface the footprints in the sands,
10   And the tide rises, the tide falls.

The morning breaks; the steeds in their stalls
Stamp and neigh, as the hostler calls;
The day returns, but nevermore
Returns the traveller to the shore,
15   And the tide rises, the tide falls.

ULTIMA THULE

TO G. W. G.

With favoring winds, o'er sunlit seas,
We sailed for the Hesperides,
The land where golden apples grow;
But that, ah! that was long ago.

5 How far, since then, the ocean streams
Have swept us from that land of dreams,
That land of fiction and of truth,
The lost Atlantis of our youth!

Whither, ah, whither? Are not these
10 The tempest-haunted Orcades,
Where sea-gulls scream, and breakers roar,
And wreck and sea-weed line the shore?

Ultima Thule! Utmost Isle!
Here in thy harbors for a while
15 We lower our sails; a while we rest
From the unending, endless quest.

THE CROSS OF SNOW

In the long, sleepless watches of the night,
    A gentle face—the face of one long dead—
    Looks at me from the wall, where round its head
    The night-lamp casts a halo of pale light.
5 Here in this room she died; and soul more white
    Never through martyrdom of fire was led
    To its repose; nor can in books be read
    The legend of a life more benedight.
There is a mountain in the distant West
10   That, sun-defying, in its deep ravines
    Displays a cross of snow upon its side.
Such is the cross I wear upon my breast
    These eighteen years, through all the changing scenes
    And seasons, changeless since the day she died.

John Greenleaf Whittier (1807–1892)

Whittier was born in East Haverhill, Massachusetts, and raised in
the Quaker faith by a family that had lived on the same plot of land
since the seventeenth century. His parents were poor and he had
little schooling, apart from that provided by his reading of the Bible
and favourite poets such as Burns. He was encouraged to write poetry
and one of his pieces was sent by his sister to the Abolitionist editor,
William Lloyd Garrison. Garrison accepted the poem, encouraged
Whittier to write more, and even helped the young poet to return
to school for a while. Under this influence Whittier soon became a
major propagandist for the Abolitionist movement, but as the Civil
War approached he turned to writing the more reflective poems,
coloured by the Quaker faith, for which he is now best known. In
later years he lived in seclusion with his mother and sister.

PROEM

    I love the old melodious lays
Which softly melt the ages through,
    The songs of Spenser's golden days,
    Arcadian Sidney's silvery phrase,
5 Sprinkling our noon of time with freshest morning dew.

Yet, vainly in my quiet hours
To breathe their marvellous notes I try;
I feel them, as the leaves and flowers
In silence feel the dewy showers,
10   And drink with glad, still lips the blessing of the sky.

The rigor of a frozen clime,
The harshness of an untaught ear,
The jarring words of one whose rhyme
Beat often Labor's hurried time,
15   Or Duty's rugged march through storm and strife, are here.

Of mystic beauty, dreamy grace,
No rounded art the lack supplies;
Unskilled the subtle lines to trace,
Or softer shades of Nature's face,
20   I view her common forms with unanointed eyes.

Nor mine the seer-like power to show
The secrets of the heart and mind;
To drop the plummet-line below
Our common world of joy and woe.
25   A more intense despair or brighter hope to find.

Yet here at least an earnest sense
Of human right and weal is shown;
A hate of tyranny intense,
And hearty in its vehemence,
30   As if my brother's pain and sorrow were my own.

O Freedom! if to me belong
Nor mighty Milton's gift divine,
Nor Marvell's wit and graceful song,
Still with a love as deep and strong
35   As theirs, I lay, like them, my best gifts on thy shrine!

FIRST-DAY THOUGHTS

In calm and cool and silence, once again
I find my old accustomed place among
My brethren, where, perchance, no human tongue

Shall utter words; where never hymn is sung,
5   Nor deep-toned organ blown, nor censer swung,
Nor dim light falling through the pictured pane!
There, syllabled by silence, let me hear
The still small voice which reached the prophet's ear;
Read in my heart a still diviner law
10   Than Israel's leader on his table saw!
There let me strive with each besetting sin
         Recall my wandering fancies, and restrain
         The sore disquiet of a restless brain;
         And, as the path of duty is made plain,
15   May grace be given that I may walk therein,
         Not like the hireling, for his selfish gain,
With backward glances and reluctant tread,
Making a merit of his coward dread,
         But, cheerful, in the light around me thrown,
20   Walking as one to pleasant service led;
         Doing God's will as if it were my own,
Yet trusting not in mine, but in His strength alone!

From SNOW-BOUND

A Winter Idyl

To the Memory of the Household It Describes
This Poem Is Dedicated by the Author

The sun that brief December day
Rose cheerless over hills of gray,
And, darkly circled, gave at noon
A sadder light than waning moon.
5   Slow tracing down the thickening sky
Its mute and ominous prophecy,
A portent seeming less than threat,
It sank from sight before it set.
A chill no coat, however stout,
10   Of homespun stuff could quite shut out,
A hard, dull bitterness of cold,
That checked, mid-vein, the circling race
Of life-blood in the sharpened face,
The coming of the snow-storm told.

15   The wind blew east; we heard the roar
    Of Ocean on his wintry shore,
    And felt the strong pulse throbbing there
    Beat with low rhythm our inland air.

    Meanwhile we did our nightly chores,—
20   Brought in the wood from out of doors,
    Littered the stalls, and from the mows
    Raked down the herd's-grass for the cows:
    Heard the horse whinnying for his corn;
    And, sharply clashing horn on horn,
25   Impatient down the stanchion rows
    The cattle shake their walnut bows;
    While, peering from his early perch
    Upon the scaffold's pole of birch,
    The cock his crested helmet bent
30   And down his querulous challenge sent.

    Unwarmed by any sunset light
    The gray day darkened into night,
    A night made hoary with the swarm
    And whirl-dance of the blinding storm,
35   As zigzag, wavering to and fro,
    Crossed and recrossed the wingëd snow:
    And ere the early bedtime came
    The white drift piled the window-frame,
    And through the glass the clothes-line posts
40   Looked in like tall and sheeted ghosts.

    So all night long the storm roared on:
    The morning broke without a sun;
    In tiny spherule traced with lines
    Of Nature's geometric signs,
45   In starry flake, and pellicle,
    All day the hoary meteor fell;
    And, when the second morning shone,
    We looked upon a world unknown,
    On nothing we could call our own.
50   Around the glistening wonder bent
    The blue walls of the firmament,
    No cloud above, no earth below,—
    A universe of sky and snow!

The old familiar sights of ours
55   Took marvellous shapes; strange domes and towers
Rose up where sty or corn-crib stood,
Or garden-wall, or belt of wood;
A smooth white mound the brush-pile showed,
A fenceless drift what once was road;
60   The bridle-post an old man sat
With loose-flung coat and high cocked hat;
The well-curb had a Chinese roof;
And even the long sweep, high aloof,
In its slant splendor, seemed to tell
65   Of Pisa's leaning miracle.

A prompt, decisive man, no breath
Our father wasted: "Boys, a path!"
Well pleased, (for when did farmer boy
Count such a summons less than joy?)
70   Our buskins on our feet we drew;
With mittened hands, and caps drawn low,
To guard our necks and ears from snow,
We cut the solid whiteness through.
And, where the drift was deepest, made
75   A tunnel walled and overlaid
With dazzling crystal: we had read
Of rare Aladdin's wondrous cave,
And to our own his name we gave,
With many a wish the luck were ours
80   To test his lamp's supernal powers.
We reached the barn with merry din,
And roused the prisoned brutes within.
The old horse thrust his long head out,
And grave with wonder gazed about;
85   The cock his lusty greeting said,
And forth his speckled harem led;
The oxen lashed their tails, and hooked,
And mild reproach of hunger looked;
The hornëd patriarch of the sheep.
90   Like Egypt's Ammon roused from sleep.
Shook his sage head with gesture mute,
And emphasised with stamp of foot.

All day the gusty north-wind bore
The loosening drift its breath before;

95   Low circling round its southern zone,
The sun through dazzling snow-mist shone.
No church-bell lent its Christian tone
To the savage air, no social smoke
Curled over woods of snow-hung oak.
100   A solitude made more intense
By dreary-voicèd elements,
The shrieking of the mindless wind,
The moaning tree-boughs swaying blind,
And on the glass the unmeaning beat
105   Of ghostly finger-tips of sleet.
Beyond the circle of our hearth
No welcome sound of toil or mirth
Unbound the spell, and testified
Of human life and thought outside.
110   We minded that the sharpest ear
The buried brooklet could not hear,
The music of whose liquid lip
Had been to us companionship,
And, in our lonely life, had grown
115   To have an almost human tone.

As night drew on, and, from the crest
Of wooded knolls that ridged the west,
The sun, a snow-blown traveller, sank
From sight beneath the smothering bank,
120   We piled, with care, our nightly stack
Of wood against the chimney-back,—
The oaken log, green, huge, and thick,
And on its top the stout back-stick;
The knotty-forestick laid apart,
125   And filled between with curious art
The ragged brush; then hovering near,
We watched the first red blaze appear,
Heard the sharp crackle, caught the gleam
On whitewashed wall and sagging beam,
130   Until the old, rude-furnished room
Burst, flower-like, into rosy bloom;
While radiant with a mimic flame
Outside the sparkling drift became,
And through the bare-boughed lilac-tree
135   Our own warm hearth seemed blazing free.

The crane and pendent trammels showed,
The Turks' heads on the andirons glowed;
While childish fancy, prompt to tell
The meaning of the miracle,
40   Whispered the old rhyme: "*Under the tree,*
When fire outdoors burns merrily,
There the witches are making tea."

The moon above the eastern wood
Shone at its full; the hill-range stood
45   Transfigured in the silver flood,
Its blown snows flashing cold and keen,
Dead white, save where some sharp ravine
Took shadow, or the sombre green
Of hemlocks turned to pitchy black
150   Against the whiteness at their back
For such a world and such a night
Most fitting that unwarming light,
Which only seemed where'er it fell
To make the coldness visible.

155   Shut in from all the world without,
We sat the clean-winged hearth about,
Content to let the north-wind roar
In baffled rage at pane and door,
While the red logs before us beat
160   The frost-line back with tropic heat;
And ever, when a louder blast
Shook beam and rafter as it passed,
The merrier up its roaring draught
The great throat of the chimney laughed;
165   The house-dog on his paws outspread
Laid to the fire his drowsy head,
The cat's dark silhouette on the wall
A couchant tiger's seemed to fall;
And, for the winter fireside meet,
170   Between the andirons' straddling feet,
The mug of cider simmered slow,
The apples sputtered in a row,
And, close at hand, the basket stood
With nuts from brown October's wood.

175 What matter how the night behaved?
    What matter how the north-wind raved?
    Blow high, blow low, not all its snow
    Could quench our hearth-fire's ruddy glow.
    O Time and Change!—with hair as gray
180 As was my sire's that winter day,
    How strange it seems, with so much gone
    Of life and love, to still live on!
    Ah, brother! only I and thou
    Are left of all that circle now,—
185 The dear home faces whereupon
    That fitfull firelight paled and shone.
    Henceforward, listen as we will,
    The voices of that hearth are still;
    Look where we may, the wide earth o'er,
190 Those lighted faces smile no more.
    We tread the paths their feet have worn,
        We sit beneath their orchard trees,
        We hear, like them, the hum of bees
    And rustle of the bladed corn;
195 We turn the pages that they read,
        Their written words we linger o'er,
    But in the sun they cast no shade,
    No voice is heard, no sign is made,
        No step is on the conscious floor!
200 Yet Love will dream, and Faith will trust,
    (Since He who knows our need is just,)
    That somehow, somewhere, meet we must.
    Alas for him who never sees
    The stars shine through his cypress-trees!
205 Who, hopeless, lays his dead away,
    Nor looks to see the breaking day
    Across the mournful marbles play!
    Who hath not learned, in hours of faith,
        The truth to flesh and sense unknown,
210 That Life is ever lord of Death,
        And Love can never lose its own!

    We sped the time with stories old,
    Wrought puzzles out, and riddles told,
    Or stammered from our school-book lore
215 "The Chief of Gambia's golden shore."

How often since, when all the land
Was clay in Slavery's shaping hand,
As if a far-blown trumpet stirred
The languorous sin-sick air, I heard:
220 "*Does not the voice of reason cry,*
Claim the first right which Nature gave,
From the red scourge of bondage fly,
Nor deign to live a burdened slave!"
Our father rode again his ride
225 On Memphremagog's wooded side;
Sat down again to moose and samp
In trapper's hut and Indian camp;
Lived o'er the old idyllic ease
Beneath St François' hemlock-trees;
230 Again for him the moonlight shone
On Norman cap and bodiced zone;
Again he heard the violin play
Which led the village dance away,
And mingled in its merry whirl
235 The grandam and the laughing girl.
Or, nearer home, our steps he led
Where Salisbury's level marshes spread
Mile-wide as flies the laden bee;
Where merry mowers, hale and strong,
240 Swept, scythe on scythe, their swaths along
The low green prairies of the sea.
We shared the fishing off Boar's Head,
And round the rocky Isles of Shoals
The hake-broil on the drift-wood coals;
245 The chowder on the sand-beach made,
Dipped by the hungry, steaming hot,
With spoons of clam-shell from the pot.
We heard the tales of witchcraft old,
And dream and sign and marvel told
250 To sleepy listeners as they lay
Stretched idly on the salted hay,
Adrift along the winding shores,
When favoring breezes deigned to blow
The square sail of the gundelow
255 And idle lay the useless oars.

Our mother, while she turned her wheel
Or run the new-knit stocking-heel,

Told how the Indian hordes came down
At midnight on Cocheco town,
260 And how her own great-uncle bore
His cruel scalp-mark to fourscore.
Recalling, in her fitting phrase,
So rich and picturesque and free,
(The common unrhymed poetry
265 Of simple life and country ways,)
The story of her early days,—
She made us welcome to her home;
Old hearths grew wide to give us room;
We stole with her a frightened look
270 At the gray wizard's conjuring-book,
The fame whereof went far and wide
Through all the simple country side;
We heard the hawks at twilight play,
The boat-horn on Piscataqua,
275 The loon's weird laughter far away;
We fished her little trout-brook, knew
What flowers in wood and meadow grew,
What sunny hillsides autumn-brown
She climbed to shake the ripe nuts down,
280 Saw where in sheltered cove and bay
The duck's black squadron anchored lay,
And heard the wild-geese calling loud
Beneath the gray November cloud.

Then, haply, with a look more grave,
285 And soberer tone, some tale she gave
From painful Sewel's ancient tome,
Beloved in every Quaker home,
Of faith fire-winged by martyrdom . . .

*   *   *

Brisk wielder of the birch and rule,
290 The master of the district school
Held at the fire his favored place,
Its warm glow lit a laughing face
Fresh-hued and fair, where scarce appeared
The uncertain prophecy of beard.
295 He teased the mitten-blinded cat,
Played cross-pins on my uncle's hat,

Sang songs, and told us what befalls
In classic Dartmouth's college halls.
Born the wild Northern hills among,
300   From whence his yeoman father wrung
By patient toil subsistence scant,
Not competence and yet not want,
He early gained the power to pay
His cheerful, self-reliant way;
305   Could doff at ease his scholar's gown
To peddle wares from town to town . . .

*   *   *

Happy the snow-locked homes wherein
He tuned his merry violin,
Or played the athlete in the barn,
310   Or held the good dame's winding-yarn,
Or mirth-provoking versions told
Of classic legends rare and old,
Wherein the scenes of Greece and Rome
Had all the commonplace of home,
315   And little seemed at best the odds
'Twixt Yankee pedlers and old gods . . .

*   *   *

At last the great logs, crumbling low,
Sent out a dull and duller glow,
The bull's-eye watch that hung in view,
320   Ticking its weary circuit through,
Pointed with mutely warning sign
Its black hand to the hour of nine.
That sign the pleasant circle broke:
My uncle ceased his pipe to smoke,
325   Knocked from its bowl the refuse gray,
And laid it tenderly away;
Then roused himself to safely cover
The dull red brands with ashes over.
And while, with care, our mother laid
330   The work aside, her steps she stayed
One moment, seeking to express
Her grateful sense of happiness

For food and shelter, warmth and health,
And love's contentment more than wealth,
335 With simple wishes (not the weak,
Vain prayers which no fulfilment seek,
But such as warm the generous heart,
O'er-prompt to do with Heaven its part)
That none might lack, that bitter night,
340 For bread and clothing, warmth and light.

Within our beds awhile we heard
The wind that round the gables roared,
With now and then a ruder shock,
Which made our very bedsteads rock.
345 We heard the loosened clapboards tost,
The board-nails snapping in the frost;
And on us, through the unplastered wall,
Felt the light sifted snow-flakes fall.
But sleep stole on, as sleep will do
350 When hearts are light and life is new;
Faint and more faint the murmurs grew,
Till in the summer-land of dreams
They softened to the sound of streams,
Low stir of leaves, and dip of oars,
355 And lapsing waves on quiet shores.

Next morn we wakened with the shout
Of merry voices high and clear;
And saw the teamsters drawing near
To break the drifted highways out.
360 Down the long hillside treading slow
We saw the half-buried oxen go,
Shaking the snow from heads uptost,
Their straining nostrils white with frost.
Before our door the straggling train
365 Drew up, an added team to gain.
The elders threshed their hands a-cold,
Passed, with the cider-mug, their jokes
From lip to lip; the younger folks
Down the loose snow-banks, wrestling, rolled,
370 Then toiled again the cavalcade
O'er windy hill, through clogged ravine,
And woodland paths that wound between
Low drooping pine-boughs winter-weighed.

From every barn a team afoot,
375 At every house a new recruit,
Where, drawn by Nature's subtlest law,
Haply the watchful young men saw
Sweet doorway pictures of the curls
And curious eyes of merry girls,
380 Lifting their hands in mock defence
Against the snow-ball's compliments,
And reading in each missive tost
The charm with Eden never lost.

We heard once more the sleigh-bell's sound;
385   And, following where the teamsters led,
The wise old Doctor went his round,
Just pausing at our door to say,
In the brief autocratic way
Of one who, prompt at Duty's call,
390 Was free to urge her claim on all,
    That some poor neighbor sick abed
At night our mother's aid would need.
For, one in generous thought and deed,
    What mattered in the sufferer's sight
395   The Quaker matron's inward light,
The Doctor's mail of Calvin's creed?
All hearts confess the saints elect
    Who, twain in faith, in love agree,
And melt not in an acid sect
400   The Christian pearl of charity!

So days went on: a week had passed
Since the great world was heard from last.
The Almanac we studied o'er,
Read and reread our little store
405 Of books and pamphlets, scarce a score;
One harmless novel, mostly hid
From younger eyes, a book forbid,
And poetry, (or good or bad,
A single book was all we had,)
410 Where Ellwood's meek, drab-skirted Muse,
    A stranger to the heathen Nine,
    Sang, with a somewhat nasal whine,
The wars of David and the Jews.

At last the floundering carrier bore
415 The village paper to our door.
Lo! broadening outward as we read,
To warmer zones the horizon spread;
In panoramic length unrolled
We saw the marvels that it told.
420 Before us passed the painted Creeks,
  And daft McGregor on his raids
  In Costa Rica's everglades.
And up Taygetos winding slow
Rode Ypsilanti's Mainote Greeks,
425 A Turk's head at each saddle-bow!
Welcome to us its week-old news,
Its corner for the rustic Muse,
  Its monthly gauge of snow and rain,
Its record, mingling in a breath
430 The wedding bell and dirge of death;
Jest, anecdote, and love-lorn tale,
The latest culprit sent to jail;
Its hue and cry of stolen and lost,
Its vendue sales and goods at cost,
435   And traffic calling loud for gain.
We felt the stir of hall and street,
The pulse of life that round us beat;
The chill embargo of the snow
Was melted in the genial glow;
440 Wide swung again our ice-locked door,
And all the world was ours once more!

Clasp, Angel of the backward look
  And folded wings of ashen gray
  And voice of echoes far away,
445 The brazen covers of thy book;
The weird palimpsest old and vast,
Wherein thou hid'st the spectral past;
Where, closely mingling, pale and glow
The characters of joy and woe;
450 The monographs of outlived years,
Or smile-illumed or dim with tears,
  Green hills of life that slope to death,
And haunts of home, whose vistaed trees
Shade off to mournful cypresses
455   With the white amaranths underneath.

Even while I look, I can but heed
    The restless sands' incessant fall,
Importunate hours that hours succeed,
Each clamorous with its own sharp need,
460   And duty keeping pace with all.
Shut down and clasp the heavy lids;
I hear again the voice that bids
The dreamer leave his dream midway
For larger hopes and graver fears:
465 Life greatens in those later years,
The century's aloe flowers to-day!

Yet, haply, in some lull of life,
Some Truce of God which breaks its strife,
The worldling's eyes shall gather dew,
470   Dreaming in throngful city ways
Of winter joys his boyhood knew;
And dear and early friends—the few
Who yet remain—shall pause to view
    These Flemish pictures of old days;
475 Sit with me by the homestead hearth,
And stretch the hands of memory forth
    To warm them at the wood-fire's blaze!
And thanks untraced to lips unknown
Shall greet me like the odors blown
480 From unseen meadows newly mown,
Or lilies floating in some pond,
Wood-fringed, the wayside gaze beyond;
The traveller owns the grateful sense
Of sweetness near, he knows not whence,
485 And, pausing, takes with forehead bare
The benediction of the air.

Edgar Allan Poe (1809–1849)

Born in Boston, Massachusetts, to strolling actors, Poe lost both his parents when he was two. He was received into the family of John Allan, a merchant in Richmond, Virginia; and went to England with them in 1815 to be put to school near London. On returning home he was sent to the University of Virginia, only to be expelled within the year. Mr. Allan then wanted Poe to start a commercial career. Poe was unwilling, however. He ran away from home and enlisted in the army under a pseudonym. In 1830, he was enrolled at West Point briefly, but, in a short while, was again expelled. Relations with Mr. Allan soon broke down completely and Poe subsequently had to make his own way as an editor, critic, and creative writer. His responsibilities were increased by the fact that in 1836 he married his cousin Virginia Clemm, a girl of only thirteen. He was always on the move from one position to another and his financial circumstances were never good. He died in Baltimore in mysterious circumstances.

A DREAM WITHIN A DREAM

Take this kiss upon the brow!
And, in parting from you now,
Thus much let me avow—
You are not wrong, who deem
5 That my days have been a dream;
Yet if hope has flown away
In a night, or in a day,
In a vision, or in none,
Is it therefore the less *gone?*
10 *All* that we see or seem
Is but a dream within a dream.

I stand amid the roar
Of a surf-tormented shore,
And I hold within my hand
15 Grains of the golden sand—
How few! yet how they creep
Through my fingers to the deep,

While I weep—while I weep!
O God! can I not grasp
20   Them with a tighter clasp?
O God! can I not save
One from the pitiless wave?
Is *all* that we see or seem
But a dream within a dream?

SONNET—TO SCIENCE

Science! true daughter of Old Time thou art!
    Who alterest all things with thy peering eyes.
Why preyest thou thus upon the poet's heart,
    Vulture, whose wings are dull realities?
5 How should he love thee? or how deem thee wise,
    Who wouldst not leave him in his wandering
To seek for treasure in the jewelled skies,
    Albeit he soared with an undaunted wing?
Hast thou not dragged Diana from her car?
10   And driven the Hamadryad from the wood
To seek a shelter in some happier star?
    Hast thou not torn the Naiad from her flood,
The Elfin from the green grass, and from me
The summer dream beneath the tamarind tree?

TO HELEN

Helen, thy beauty is to me
    Like those Nicéan barks of yore,
That gently, o'er a perfumed sea,
    The weary, way-worn wanderer bore
5   To his own native shore.

On desperate seas long wont to roam,
    Thy hyacinth hair, thy classic face,
Thy Naiad airs have brought me home
    To the glory that was Greece,
10   And the grandeur that was Rome.

Lo! in yon brilliant window-niche
    How statue-like I see thee stand,
The agate lamp within thy hand!
    Ah, Psyche, from the regions which
15   Are Holy-Land!

ISRAFEL

And the angel Israfel, whose heart-strings are a lute, and who has the sweetest voice of all God's creatures.—KORAN.

In Heaven a spirit doth dwell
    "Whose heart-strings are a lute;"
None sing so wildly well
As the angel Israfel,
5   And the giddy stars (so legends tell)
Ceasing their hymns, attend the spell
        Of his voice, all mute.

Tottering above
    In her highest noon,
10   The enamoured moon
Blushes with love,
    While, to listen, the red levin
    (With the rapid Pleiads, even,
    Which were seven,)
15   Pauses in Heaven.

And they say (the starry choir
    And the other listening things)
That Israfeli's fire
Is owing to that lyre
20   By which he sits and sings—
The trembling living wire
Of those unusual strings.

But the skies that angel trod,
    Where deep thoughts are a duty—
25 Where Love's a grown-up God—
    Where the Houri glances are
Imbued with all the beauty
    Which we worship in a star.

Therefore, thou art not wrong,
30   Israfeli, who despisest
An unimpassioned song;
To thee the laurels belong,
        Best bard, because the wisest!
Merrily live and long!

35 The ecstasies above
        With thy burning measures suit—
Thy grief, thy joy, thy hate, thy love,
        With the fervour of thy lute—
        Well may the stars be mute!

40 Yes, Heaven is thine; but this
        Is a world of sweets and sours;
Our flowers are merely—flowers,
And the shadow of thy perfect bliss
        Is the sunshine of ours.

45 If I could dwell
Where Israfel
        Hath dwelt, and he where I,
He might not sing so wildly well
        A mortal melody,
While a bolder note than this might swell
        From my lyre within the sky.

THE CITY IN THE SEA

Lo! Death has reared himself a throne
In a strange city lying alone
Far down within the dim West,
Where the good and the bad and the worst and the best
5 Have gone to their eternal rest.
There shrines and palaces and towers
(Time-eaten towers that tremble not!)
Resemble nothing that is ours.
Around, by lifting winds forgot,
10 Resignedly beneath the sky
The melancholy waters lie.

No rays from the holy heaven come down
On the long night-time of that town;

But light from out the lurid sea
15   Streams up the turrets silently—
Gleams up the pinnacles far and free—
Up domes—up spires—up kingly halls—
Up fanes—up Babylon-like walls—
Up shadowy long-forgotten bowers
20   Of sculptured ivy and stone flowers—
Up many and many a marvellous shrine
Whose wreathéd friezes intertwine
The viol, the violet, and the vine.

Resignedly beneath the sky
25   The melancholy waters lie.
So blend the turrets and shadows there
That all seem pendulous in air,
While from a proud tower in the town
Death looks gigantically down.

30   There open fanes and gaping graves
Yawn level with the luminous waves;
But not the riches there that lie
In each idol's diamond eye—
Not the gaily-jewelled dead
35   Tempt the waters from their bed;
For no ripples curl, alas!
Along that wilderness of glass—
No swellings tell that winds may be
Upon some far-off happier sea—
40   No heavings hint that winds have been
On seas less hideously serene.

But lo, a stir is in the air!
The wave—there is a movement there!
As if the towers had thrust aside,
45   In slightly sinking, the dull tide—
As if their tops had feebly given
A void within the filmy Heaven.
The waves have now a redder glow—
The hours are breathing faint and low—
50   And when, amid no earthly moans,
Down, down that town shall settle hence,
Hell, rising from a thousand thrones,
Shall do it reverence.

– 54 –

ELDORADO

Gaily bedight,
A gallant knight,
In sunshine and in shadow,
Had journeyed long,
5   Singing a song,
In search of Eldorado.

But he grew old—
This knight so bold—
And o'er his heart a shadow
10   Fell as he found
No spot of ground
That looked like Eldorado.

And as his strength
Failed him at length,
He met a pilgrim shadow—
15   "Shadow," said he,
"Where can it be—
This land of Eldorado?"

"Over the Mountains
Of the Moon,
20   Down the Valley of the Shadow,
Ride, boldly ride,"
The shade replied,—
"If you seek for Eldorado."

ANNABEL LEE

It was many and many a year ago,
In a kingdom by the sea,
That a maiden there lived whom you may know
By the name of ANNABEL LEE;
5   And this maiden she lived with no other thought
Than to love and be loved by me.

I was a child, and *she* was a child,
In this kingdom by the sea;

But we loved with a love that was more than love—
    I and my Annabel Lee;
With a love that the winged seraphs of heaven
    Coveted her and me.

And this was the reason that, long ago,
    In this kingdom by the sea,
A wind blew out of a cloud, chilling
    My beautiful Annabel Lee;
So that her highborn kinsmen came
    And bore her away from me,
To shut her up in a sepulchre
    In this kingdom by the sea.

The angels, not half so happy in heaven,
    Went envying her and me—
Yes!—that was the reason (as all men know,
    In this kingdom by the sea)
That the wind came out of the cloud by night,
    Chilling and killing my Annabel Lee.

But our love it was stronger by far than the love
    Of those who were older than we—
    Of many far wiser than we—
And neither the angels in heaven above,
    Nor the demons down under the sea,
Can ever dissever my soul from the soul
    Of the beautiful Annabel Lee!

For the moon never beams, without bringing me dreams
    Of the beautiful Annabel Lee;
And the stars never rise, but I feel the bright eyes
    Of the beautiful Annabel Lee;
And so, all the night-tide, I lie down by the side
Of my darling—my darling—my life and my bride,
    In the sepulchre there by the sea,
    In her tomb by the sounding sea.

Oliver Wendell Holmes (1809–1894)

Born in Cambridge, Massachusetts, Holmes was the son of a minister. He received an excellent education at Andover and Harvard and, after studying law briefly, devoted most of his adult life to medicine. In 1839, after several years of study in America and in the hospitals of Edinburgh and Paris, he became professor of anatomy and physiology at Dartmouth. Subsequently he was appointed to a chair at Harvard, which he occupied for more than thirty years. In his spare time he wrote poetry, fiction, and criticism, and a series of famous essays (*The Autocrat of the Breakfast-Table; The Professor at the Breakfast-Table* etc.) for the *Atlantic Monthly*. He died in Boston.

THE LAST LEAF

I saw him once before,
As he passed by the door,
   And again
The pavement stones resound,
5   As he totters o'er the ground
   With his cane.

They say that in his prime,
Ere the pruning-knife of Time
   Cut him down,
10   Not a better man was found
By the Crier on his round
   Through the town.

But now he walks the streets,
And he looks at all he meets
15   Sad and wan,
And he shakes his feeble head,
That it seems as if he said,
   "They are gone."

The mossy marbles rest
20   On the lips that he has prest
   In their bloom,

And the names he loved to hear
Have been carved for many a year
  On the tomb.

25 My grandmamma has said—
Poor old lady, she is dead
  Long ago—
That he had a Roman nose,
And his cheek was like a rose
30   In the snow.

But now his nose is thin,
And it rests upon his chin
  Like a staff,
And a crook is in his back,
35 And a melancholy crack
  In his laugh.

I know it is a sin
For me to sit and grin
  At him here;
40 But the old three-cornered hat,
And the breeches, and all that,
  Are so queer!

And if I should live to be
The last leaf upon the tree
45 In the spring,
Let them smile, as I do now,
At the old forsaken bough
  Where I cling.

THE CHAMBERED NAUTILUS

This is the ship of pearl, which, poets feign,
  Sails the unshadowed main,—
  The venturous bark that flings
On the sweet summer wind its purpled wings
5 In gulfs enchanted, where the Siren sings,
  And coral reefs lie bare,
Where the cold sea-maids rise to sun their streaming hair.

Its webs of living gauze no more unfurl;
    Wrecked is the ship of pearl!
    And every chambered cell,
Where its dim dreaming life was wont to dwell,
As the frail tenant shaped his growing shell,
    Before thee lies revealed,—
Its irised ceiling rent, its sunless crypt unsealed!

Year after year beheld the silent toil
    That spread his lustrous coil;
    Still, as the spiral grew,
He left the past year's dwelling for the new,
Stole with soft step its shining archway through,
    Built up its idle door,
Stretched in his last-found home, and knew the old no more.

Thanks for the heavenly message brought by thee,
    Child of the wandering sea,
    Cast from her lap, forlorn!
From thy dead lips a clearer note is born
Than ever Triton blew from wreathèd horn!
    While on mine ear it rings,
Through the deep caves of thought I hear a voice that sings:—

Build thee more stately mansions, O my soul,
    As the swift seasons roll!
    Leave thy low-vaulted past!
Let each new temple, nobler than the last,
Shut thee from heaven with a dome more vast,
    Till thou at length art free,
Leaving thine outgrown shell by life's unresting sea!

AT THE 'ATLANTIC' DINNER
December 15, 1874

I suppose it's myself that you're making allusion to
And bringing the sense of dismay and confusion to.
Of course *some* must speak,—they are always selected to,
But pray what's the reason that I am expected to?
I'm not fond of wasting my breath as those fellows do
That want to be blowing forever as bellows do;
Their legs are uneasy, but why will you jog any
That long to stay quiet beneath the mahogany?

Why, why call *me* up with your battery of flatteries?
10 You say "He writes poetry,"—that's what the matter is!
"It costs him no trouble—a pen full of ink or two
And the poem is done in the time of a wink or two;
As for thoughts—never mind—take the ones that lie uppermost,
And the rhymes used by Milton and Byron and Tupper most;
15 The lines come so easy! at one end he jingles 'em,
At the other with capital letters he shingles 'em,—
Why, the things writes itself, and before he's half done with it
He hates to stop writing, he has such good fun with it!"

Ah, that is the way in which simple ones go about
20 And draw a fine picture of things they don't know about!
We all know a kitten, but come to a catamount
The beast is a stranger when grown up to that amount,
(A stranger we rather prefer should n't visit us,
A *felis* whose advent is far from felicitous.)
25 The boy who can boast that his trap has just got a mouse
Mustn't draw it and write underneath "hippopotamus";
Or say unveraciously, "This is an elephant,"—
Don't think, let me beg, these examples irrelevant,—
What they mean is just this—that a thing to be painted well
30 Should always be something with which we're acquainted well.

You call on your victim for "things he has plenty of,—
Those copies of verses no doubt at least twenty of;
His desk is crammed full, for he always keeps writing 'em
And reading to friends as his way of delighting 'em!"
35 I tell you this writing of verses means business,—
It makes the brain whirl in a vortex of dizziness:
You think they are scrawled in the languor of laziness—
I tell you they're squeezed by a spasm of craziness,
A fit half as bad as the staggering vertigos
40 That seize a poor fellow and down in the dirt he goes!

And therefore it chimes with the word's etymology
That the sons of Apollo are great on apology,
For the writing of verse is a struggle mysterious
And the gayest of rhymes is a matter that's serious.
45 For myself, I'm relied on by friends in extremities,
And I don't mind so much if a comfort to them it is;
'Tis a pleasure to please, and the straw that can tickle us
Is a source of enjoyment though slightly ridiculous.

I am up for a—something—and since I've begun with it,
50 I must give you a toast now before I have done with it.

Let me pump at my wits as they pumped the Cochituate
That moistened—it may be—the very last bit you ate:
Success to our publishers, authors and editors
To our debtors good luck,—pleasant dreams to our creditors;
55 May the monthly grow yearly, till all we are groping for
Has reached the fulfilment we're all of us hoping for;
Till the bore through the tunnel—it makes me let off a sigh
To think it may possibly ruin my prophecy—
Has been punned on so often 't will never provoke again
60 One mild adolescent to make the old joke again;
Till abstinent, all-go-to-meeting society
Has forgotten the sense of the word inebriety;
Till the work that poor Hannah and Bridget and Phillis do
The humanized, civilized female gorillas do;
65 Till the roughs, as we call them, grown loving and dutiful,
Shall worship the true and the pure and the beautiful,
And, preying no longer as tiger and vulture do,
All read the 'Atlantic' as persons of culture do!

Jones Very (1813–1880)

Born in Salem, Massachusetts, Very spent much of his early life
making voyages with his father, a sea-captain. He graduated from
Harvard in 1836, and entered Cambridge Divinity School. He
taught Greek at Harvard at the same time, but in 1838 he was
obliged to withdraw from teaching after having what he described
as a mystical experience. He was confined in an asylum for a few
weeks, then declared sane and released. His first volume of poems
and essays appeared in 1838 and writing, together with some lay
preaching for the Unitarian Church, occupied most of his subsequent
life. He lived and died quietly at his family home in Salem.

THE NEW BIRTH

'Tis a new life;—thoughts move not as they did
With slow uncertain steps across my mind,
In thronging haste fast pressing on they bid
The portals open to the viewless wind

5   That comes not save when in the dust is laid
    The crown of pride that gilds each mortal brow,
    And from before man's vision melting fade
    The heavens and earth;—their walls are falling now.—
    Fast crowding on, each thought asks utterance strong;
10 Storm-lifted waves swift rushing to the shore,
    On from the sea they send their shouts along,
    Back through the cave-worn rocks their thunders roar;
    And I a child of God by Christ made free
    Start from death's slumbers to Eternity.

THY BROTHER'S BLOOD

    I have no brother,—they who meet me now
    Offer a hand with their own wills defiled,
    And, while they wear a smooth unwrinkled brow,
    Know not that Truth can never be beguiled;
5   Go wash the hand that still betrays thy guilt;—
    Before the spirit's gaze what stain can hide?
    Abel's red blood upon the earth is spilt,
    And by thy tongue it cannot be denied;
    I hear not with the ear,—the heart doth tell
10 Its secret deeds to me untold before;
    Go, all its hidden plunder quickly sell,
    Then shalt thou cleanse thee from thy brother's gore,
    Then will I take thy gift;—that bloody stain
    Shall not be seen upon thy hand again.

THE GARDEN

    I saw the spot where our first parents dwelt;
    And yet it wore to me no face of change.
    And while amid its fields and groves, I felt
    As if I had not sinned, nor thought it strange;
5   My eye seemed but a part of every sight,
    My ear heard music in each sound that rose;
    Each sense forever found a new delight,
    Such as the spirit's visions only knows;

Each act some new and ever-varying joy
10   Did by my Father's love for me prepare;
To dress the spot my ever fresh employ,
And in the glorious whole with Him to share;
No more without the flaming gate to stray,
No more for sin's dark stain the debt of death to pay.

THE DEAD

I see them, crowd on crowd they walk the earth
Dry, leafless trees no autumn wind laid bare;
And in their nakedness find cause for mirth,
And all unclad would winter's rudeness dare;
5   No sap doth through their clattering branches flow,
Whence springing leaves and blossoms bright appear;
Their hearts the living God have ceased to know,
Who gives the springtime to th'expectant year;
They mimic life, as if from him to steal
10   His glow of health to paint the livid cheek;
They borrow words for thoughts they cannot feel,
That with a seeming heart their tongue may speak;
And in their show of life more dead they live
Than those that to the earth with many tears they give.

THE PRAYER

    Wilt Thou not visit me?
The plant beside me feels Thy gentle dew;
    And every blade of grass I see,
From Thy deep earth its moisture drew.

5   Wilt Thou not visit me?
Thy morning calls on me with cheering tone;
    And every hill and tree
Lend but one voice, the voice of Thee alone.

    Come, for I need Thy love,
10   More than the flower the dew or grass the rain;
    Come, gently as Thy holy dove;
And let me in Thy sight rejoice to live again.

I will not hide from them,
When Thy storms come, though fierce may be their wrath,
15   But bow with leafy stem,
And strengthened follow on Thy chosen path.

   Yes, Thou wilt visit me;
Nor plant nor tree Thy eye delights so well,
   As when from sin set free,
20 My spirit loves with Thine in peace to dwell.

Not in some future world alone 'twill be,
   Beyond the grave, beyond the bounds of time;
But on the earth Thy glory we shall see,
   And share Thy triumph, peaceful, pure, sublime.

25 Lord! help me that I faint not, weary grow,
   Nor at Thy Coming slumber too, and sleep;
For Thou hast promised, and full well I know
   Thou wilt to us Thy word of promise keep.

YOURSELF

'Tis to yourself I speak; you cannot know
Him whom I call in speaking such a one,
For you beneath the earth lie buried low,
Which he alone as living walks upon:
5 You may at times have heard him speak to you,
And often wished perchance that you were he;
And I must ever wish that it were true,
For then you could hold fellowship with me:
But now you hear us talk as strangers, met
10 Above the room wherein you lie abed;
A word perhaps loud spoken you may get,
Or hear our feet when heavily they tread;
But he who speaks, or him who's spoken to,
Must both remain as strangers still to you.

THE CREATED

There is naught for thee by thy haste to gain;
'Tis not the swift with me that win the race;
Through long endurance of delaying pain.
Thine opened eye shall see thy Father's face;
Nor here nor there, where now thy feet would turn,
Thou wilt find Him who ever waits for thee;
But let obedience quench desires that burn,
And where thou art thy Father too will be.
Behold! as day by day the spirit grows,
Thou see'st by inward light things hid before;
Till what God is, thyself, His image shows;
And thou wilt wear the robe that first thou wore,
When bright with radiance from his forming hand,
He saw the lord of all His creatures stand.

THE HAND AND FOOT

The hand and foot that stir not, they shall find
Sooner than all the rightful place to go:
Now in their motion free as roving wind,
Though first no snail so limited and slow;
I mark them full of labor all the day,
Each active motion made in perfect rest;
They cannot from their path mistaken stray,
Though 'tis not theirs, yet in it they are blest;
The bird has not their hidden track found out,
The cunning fox though full of art he be;
It is the way unseen, the certain route,
Where ever bound, yet thou art ever free;
The path of Him, whose perfect law of love
Bids spheres and atoms in just order move.

THE NEW WORLD

The night that has no star lit up by God,
The day that round men shines who still are blind,
The earth their grave-turned feet for ages trod,
And sea swept over by His mighty wind,—

5   All these have passed away; the melting dream
       That flitted o'er the sleepers' half-shut eye,
       When touched by morning's golden-darting beam;
       And he beholds around the earth and sky
       What ever real stands; the rolling spheres,
10   And heaving billows of the boundless main,
       That show, though time is past, no trace of years,
       And earth restored he sees as his again,
       The earth that fades not, and the heavens that stand,
       Their strong foundations laid by God's right hand!

Henry David Thoreau (1817–1862)

Born in Concord, Massachusetts, Thoreau graduated from Harvard
in 1837. After a brief period of teaching he went to live at the home
of Emerson, where he was introduced into the Transcendentalist
circle. He contributed frequently to Emerson's magazine, *The Dial*,
and at the same time did a little lecturing, land-surveying and odd-
jobbing: just enough to secure the necessities of life. The bulk of his
poetry was written before 1840, by which time he had come to regard
himself as chiefly a writer of prose. In 1839, he made a trip with his
brother on the Concord and Merrimack Rivers; and from 1845 until
1847 he lived in seclusion at Walden Pond. From these experiences
came his two most famous books (and the only ones published during
his life-time) which enact Thoreau's version of the Transcendentalist
creed. In later years he became an ardent opponent of slavery and
of the conditions he found in New England factories. He travelled
widely in North America, but he died where he was born, in Concord.

SIC VITA

       I am a parcel of vain strivings tied
           By a chance bond together,
       Dangling this way and that, their links
           Were made so loose and wide,
5   Methinks,
               For milder weather.

A bunch of violets without their roots,
  And sorrel intermixed,
Encircled by a wisp of straw
    Once coiled about their shoots,
      The law
      By which I'm fixed.

A nosegay which Time clutched from out
  Those fair Elysian fields,
With weeds and broken stems, in haste,
  Doth make the rabble rout
    That waste
    The day he yields.

And here I bloom for a short hour unseen,
  Drinking my juices up,
With no root in the land
  To keep my branches green,
        But stand
    In a bare cup.

Some tender buds were left upon my stem
  In mimicry of life,
But ah! the children will not know,
  Till time has withered them,
        The woe
    With which they're rife.

But now I see I was not plucked for nought,
  And after in life's vase
Of glass set while I might survive,
  But by a kind hand brought
        Alive
    To a strange place.

That stock thus thinned will soon redeem its hours,
  And by another year,
Such as God knows, with freer air,
  More fruits and fairer flowers
      Will bear,
    While I droop here.

THE INWARD MORNING

Packed in my mind lie all the clothes
    Which outward nature wears,
And in its fashion's hourly change
    It all things else repairs.

5   In vain I look for change abroad,
    And can no difference find,
Till some new ray of peace uncalled
    Illumes my inmost mind.

What is it gilds the trees and clouds,
10   And paints the heavens so gay,
But yonder fast-abiding light
    With its unchanging ray?

Lo, when the sun streams through the wood,
    Upon a winter's morn,
15   Where'er his silent beams intrude
    The murky night is gone.

How could the patient pine have known
    The morning breeze would come,
Or humble flowers anticipate
20   The insect's noonday hum,—

Till the new light with morning cheer
    From far streamed through the aisles,
And nimbly told the forest trees
    For many stretching miles?

25   I've heard within my inmost soul
    Such cheerful morning news,
In the horizon of my mind
    Have seen such orient hues,

As in the twilight of the dawn,
30   When the first birds awake,
Are heard within some silent wood,
    Where they the small twigs break,

Or in the eastern skies are seen,
    Before the sun appears,
35   The harbingers of summer heats
      Which from afar he bears.

SMOKE

Light-winged Smoke, Icarian bird,
Melting thy pinions in thy upward flight;
Lark without song, and messenger of dawn,
Circling above the hamlets as thy nest;
5 Or else, departing dream, and shadowy form
Of midnight vision, gathering up thy skirts;
By night star-veiling, and by day
Darkening the light and blotting out the sun;
Go thou, my incense, upward from this hearth,
10 And ask the gods to pardon this clear flame.

WINTER MEMORIES

Within the circuit of this plodding life
There enter moments of an azure hue,
Untarnished fair as is the violet
Or anemone, when the spring strews them
5 By some meandering rivulet, which make
The best philosophy untrue that aims
But to console man for his grievances.
I have remembered when the winter came,
High in my chamber in the frosty nights,
10 When in the still light of the cheerful moon
On every twig and rail and jutting spout,
The icy spears were adding to their length
Against the arrows of the coming sun,—
How in the shimmering noon of summer past
15 Some unrecorded beam slanted across
The upland pastures where the johnswort grew;
Or heard, amid the verdure of my mind,
The bee's long smothered hum, on the blue flag
Loitering amidst the mead; or busy rill,
20 Which now through all its course stands still and dumb,
Its own memorial,—purling at its play

Along the slopes, and through the meadows next,
Until its youthful sound was hushed at last
In the staid current of the lowland stream;
25   Or seen the furrows shine but late upturned,
And where the fieldfare followed in the rear,
When all the fields around lay bound and hoar
Beneath a thick integument of snow:—
So by God's cheap economy made rich,
30   To go upon my winter's task again.

THE RESPECTABLE FOLKS

The respectable folks,—
Where dwell they?
They whisper in the oaks,
And they sigh in the hay;
5   Summer and winter, night and day,
Out on the meadow, there dwell they.
They never die,
Nor snivel, nor cry,
Nor ask our pity
10   With a wet eye.
A sound estate they ever mend,
To every asker readily lend;
To the ocean wealth,
To the meadow health,
15   To Time his length,
To the rocks strength,
To the stars light,
To the weary night,
To the busy day,
20   To the idle play;
And so their good cheer never ends,
For all are their debtors, and all their friends.

MY PRAYER

Great God, I ask thee for no meaner pelf
Than that I may not disappoint myself;
That in my action I may soar as high
As I can now discern with this clear eye.

– 70 –

5   And next in value, which thy kindness lends,
That I may greatly disappoint my friends,
Howe'er they think or hope that it may be,
They may not dream how thou'st distinguished me.

That my weak hand may equal my firm faith,
10   And my life practise more than my tongue saith;
That my low conduct may not show,
Nor my relenting lines,
That I thy purpose did not know,
Or overrated thy designs.

James Russell Lowell (1819–1891)

Born in Cambridge, Massachusetts, Lowell was the son of a Unitarian
clergyman and the member of a distinguished New England family
(subsequent members of the family include the poets Amy and Robert
Lowell). He was educated at Harvard College, where he devoted
himself more to private reading than to prescribed studies, and at
Harvard Law School: but he only practised law briefly before turning
to literature as a full-time occupation. *The Biglow Papers* (First Series)
appeared in 1846 and were an immediate success. In 1855 he was
appointed professor of modern languages at Harvard and in later
years he was editor, successively, of the *Atlantic Monthly* and the *North
American Review*. He received honorary degrees from Oxford and
Cambridge, and in 1880 became Ambassador to Great Britain. He
returned to the United States in 1885, and later died at his family
home.

From A FABLE FOR CRITICS

[EMERSON]

'There comes Emerson first, whose rich words, every one,
Are like gold nails in temples to hang trophies on,
Whose prose is grand verse, while his verse, the Lord knows,
Is some of it pr— No, 't is not even prose;

5 I'm speaking of metres; some poems have welled
  From those rare depths of soul that have ne'er been excelled;
  They're not epics, but that doesn't matter a pin,
  In creating, the only hard thing's to begin;
  A grass-blade's no easier to make than an oak;
10 If you've once found the way, you've achieved the grand stroke;
  In the worst of his poems are mines of rich matter,
  But thrown in a heap with a crush and a clatter;
  Now it is not one thing nor another alone
  Makes a poem, but rather the general tone,
15 The something pervading, uniting the whole,
  The before unconceived, unconceivable soul,
  So that just in removing this trifle or that, you
  Take away, as it were, a chief limb of the statue;
  Roots, wood, bark, and leaves singly perfect may be,
20 But, clapt hodge-podge together, they don't make a tree.

    'But, to come back to Emerson (whom, by the way,
  I believe we left waiting),—his is, we may say,
  A Greek head on right Yankee shoulders, whose range
  Has Olympus for one pole, for t' other the Exchange;
25 He seems, to my thinking (although I'm afraid
  The comparison must, long ere this, have been made),
  A Plotinus-Montaigne, where the Egyptian's gold mist
  And the Gascon's shrewd wit cheek-by-jowl coexist . . .

        *   *   *

  "'T is refreshing to old-fashioned people like me
30 To meet such a primitive Pagan as he,
  In whose mind all creation is duly respected
  As parts of himself—just a little projected;
  And who's willing to worship the stars and the sun,
  A convert to—nothing but Emerson.
35 So perfect a balance there is in his head,
  That he talks of things sometimes as if they were dead;
  Life, nature, love, God, and affairs of that sort,
  He looks at as merely ideas; in short,
  As if they were fossils stuck round in a cabinet,
40 Of such vast extent that our earth's a mere dab in it;
  Composed just as he is inclined to conjecture her,
  Namely, one part pure earth, ninety-nine parts pure lecturer;
  You are filled with delight at his clear demonstration,

Each figure, word, gesture, just fits the occasion,
45 With the quiet precision of science he'll sort 'em
But you can't help suspecting the whole a *post mortem.*

[BRYANT]

'There is Bryant, as quiet, as cool, and as dignified,
As a smooth, silent iceberg, that never is ignified,
Save when by reflection 't is kindled o' nights
50 With a semblance of flame by the chill Northern Lights.
He may rank (Griswold says so) first bard of your nation
(There's no doubt that he stands in supreme ice-olation),
Your topmost Parnassus he may set his heel on,
But no warm applauses come, peal following peal on,—
55 He's too smooth and too polished to hang any zeal on:
Unqualified merits, I'll grant, if you choose, he has 'em,
But he lacks the one merit of kindling enthusiasm;
If he stir you at all, it is just, on my soul,
Like being stirred up with the very North Pole.

[WHITTIER]

60   'There is Whittier, whose swelling and vehement heart
Strains the strait-breasted drab of the Quaker apart,
And reveals the live Man, still supreme and erect,
Underneath the bemummying wrappers of sect;
There was ne'er a man born who had more of the swing
65 Of the true lyric bard and all that kind of thing;
And his failures arise (though perhaps he don't know it)
From the very same cause that has made him a poet,—
A fervour of mind which knows no separation
'Twixt simple excitement and pure inspiration . . .

        *   *   *

70 'Like old what's-his-name there at the battle of Hastings
(Who, however, gave more than mere rhythmical bastings),
Our Quaker leads off metaphorical fights
For reform and whatever they call human rights,
Both singing and striking in front of the war,
75 And hitting his foes with the mallet of Thor;
Anne haec, one exclaims, on beholding his knocks,
Vestis filii tui, O leather-clad Fox?

Can that be thy son, in the battle's mid din,
Preaching brotherly love and then driving it in
80 To the brain of the tough old Goliah of sin,
With the smoothest of pebbles from Castaly's spring
Impressed on his hard moral sense with a sling?

[AMERICAN LITERATURE]

'There are truths you Americans need to be told,
And it never 'll refute them to swagger and scold . . .

*   *   *

85 'The most of you (this is what strikes all beholders)
Have a mental and physical stoop in the shoulders;
Though you ought to be free as the winds and the waves,
You've the gait and the manners of runaway slaves . . .

*   *   *

'You steal Englishmen's books and think Englishmen's thought.
90 With their salt on her tail your wild eagle is caught:
Your literature suits its each whisper and motion
To what will be thought of it over the ocean;
The cast clothes of Europe your statesmanship tries
And mumbles again the old blarneys and lies:—
95 Forget Europe wholly, your veins throb with blood,
To which the dull current in hers is but mud . . .

*   *   *

'O my friends, thank your God, if you have one, that he
'Twixt the Old World and you set the gulf of a sea;
Be strong-backed, brown-handed, upright as your pines,
100 By the scale of a hemisphere shape your designs,
Be true to yourselves and this new nineteenth age,
As a statue by Powers, or a picture by Page,
Plough, sail, forge, build, carve, paint, all things make new,
To your own New-World instincts contrive to be true,
105 Keep your ears open wide to the Future's first call,
Be whatever you will, but yourselves first of all,
Stand fronting the dawn on Toil's heaven-scaling peaks,
And become my new race of more practical Greeks.

LOWELL

[POE AND LONGFELLOW]

'There comes Poe, with his raven, like Barnaby Rudge,
110 Three fifths of him genius and two fifths sheer fudge,
Who talks like a book of iambs and pentameters,
In a way to make people of common sense damn metres,
Who has written some things quite the best of their kind,
But the heart somehow seems all squeezed out by the mind,
115 Who— But hey-day! What's this? Messieurs Mathews and Poe,
You mustn't fling mud-balls at Longfellow so,
Does it make a man worse that his character's such
As to make his friends love him (as you think) too much?
Why, there is not a bard at this moment alive
120 More willing than he that his fellows should thrive;
While you are abusing him thus, even now
He would help either one of you out of a slough:
You may say that he's smooth and all that till you're hoarse,
But remember that elegance also is force;
125 After polishing granite as much as you will,
The heart keeps its tough old persistency still;
Deduct all you can, *that* still keeps you at bay;
Why, he'll live till men weary of Collins and Gray.

[LOWELL]

'There is Lowell, who's striving Parnassus to climb
130 With a whole bale of *isms* tied together with rhyme,
He might get on alone, spite of brambles and boulders,
But he can't with that bundle he has on his shoulders,
The top of the hill he will ne'er come nigh reaching
Till he learns the distinction 'twixt singing and preaching;
135 His lyre has some chords that would ring pretty well,
But he'd rather by half make a drum of the shell,
And rattle away till he's old as Methusalem,
At the head of a march to the last new Jerusalem.'

From THE BIGLOW PAPERS (SECOND SERIES)

THE COURTIN'

God makes sech nights, all white an' still
    Fur 'z you can look or listen,
Moonshine an' snow on field an' hill,
    All silence an' all glisten.

5   Zekle crep' up quite unbeknown
       An' peeked in thru' the winder,
An' there sot Huldy all alone,
       'ith no one nigh to hender.

A fireplace filled the room's one side
10   With half a cord o' wood in—
There warn't no stoves (tell comfort died)
    To bake ye to a puddin'.

The wa'nut logs shot sparkles out
    Towards the pootiest, bless her,
15   An' leetle flames danced all about
    The chiny on the dresser.

Agin the chimbley crook-necks hung,
    An' in amongst 'em rusted
The ole queen's-arm thet gran'ther Young
20   Fetched back from Concord busted.

The very room, coz she was in,
    Seemed warm from floor to ceilin',
An' she looked full ez rosy agin
    Ez the apples she was peelin'.

25   'T was kin' o' kingdom-come to look
    On sech a blessed cretur,
A dogrose blushin' to a brook
    Ain't modester nor sweeter.

He was six foot o' man, A 1,
30   Clear grit an' human natur';
None could n't quicker pitch a ton
    Nor dror a furrer straighter.

He'd sparked it with full twenty gals,
    Hed squired 'em, danced 'em, druv 'em,
Fust this one, an' then thet, by speils—
    All is, he could n't love 'em.

But long o' her his veins 'ould run
    All crinkly like curled maple,
The side she breshed felt full o' sun
    Ez a south slope in Ap'il.

She thought no v'ice hed sech a swing
    Ez hisn in the choir;
My! when he made Ole Hunderd ring,
    She *knowed* the Lord was nigher.

An' she'd blush scarlit, right in prayer,
    When her new meetin'-bunnet
Felt somehow thru' its crown a pair
    O' blue eyes sot upon it.

Thet night, I tell ye, she looked *some!*
    She seemed to 've gut a new soul,
For she felt sartin-sure he'd come,
    Down to her very shoe-sole.

She heered a foot, an' knowed it tu,
    A-raspin' on the scraper,—
All ways to once her feelins flew
    Like sparks in burnt-up paper.

He kin' o' l'itered on the mat,
    Some doubtfle o' the sekle,
His heart kep' goin' pity-pat,
    But hern went pity Zekle.

An' yit she gin her cheer a jerk
    Ez though she wished him furder,
An' on her apples kep' to work,
    Parin' away like murder.

'You want to see my Pa, I s'pose?'
    'Wal . . . no . . . I come dasignin''—
'To see my Ma? She's sprinklin' clo'es
    Agin to-morrer's i'nin'.'

To say why gals acts so or so,
    Or don't, 'ould be presumin';
Mebby to mean *yes* an' say *no*
    Comes nateral to women.

He stood a spell on one foot fust,
    Then stood a spell on t' other,
An' on which one he felt the wust
    He could n't ha' told ye nuther.

Says he, 'I'd better call agin';
    Says she, 'Think likely, Mister':
Thet last word pricked him like a pin.
    An' ... Wal, he up an' kist her.

When Ma bimeby upon 'em slips,
    Huldy sot pale ez ashes,
All kin' o' smily roun' the lips
    An' teary roun' the lashes.

For she was jes' the quiet kind
    Whose naturs never vary,
Like streams that keep a summer mind
    Snowhid in Jenooary.

The blood clost roun' her heart felt glued
    Too tight for all expressin',
Tell mother see how metters stood,
    An' gin 'em both her blessin'.

Then her red come back like the tide
    Down to the Bay o' Fundy,
An' all I know is they was cried
    In meetin' come nex' Sunday.

Herman Melville (1819–1891)

Born in New York City, Melville was descended from Major Thomas Melville, one of the participants in the Boston 'tea-party' and reputedly the model for Holmes's portrait of the 'Last Leaf'. His father died bankrupt when he was twelve and, after working briefly as a clerk, Melville became a sailor on merchant and whaling ships. In 1842 he deserted in the Marquesas Islands and then returned to Boston via Tahiti. This adventure and others from his sea-faring days became the basis of his early romances, which were immensely popular. In 1850 he moved to Pittsfield, Massachusetts, where he wrote *Moby Dick*. It was not as popular as his early work, nor was his subsequent fiction; and Melville then turned to the writing of poetry, which he published privately. He returned to New York in 1863 to become a customs inspector and later died in that city largely forgotten by the public.

THE PORTENT

(1859)

Hanging from the beam,
    Slowly swaying (such the law),
Gaunt the shadow on your green,
    Shenandoah!
5   The cut is on the crown
    (Lo, John Brown),
And the stabs shall heal no more.

Hidden in the cap
    Is the anguish none can draw;
10   So your future veils its face,
    Shenandoah!
But the streaming beard is shown
    (Weird John Brown),
The meteor of the war.

SHILOH

A REQUIEM

(April, 1862)

Skimming lightly, wheeling still,
  The swallows fly low
Over the field in clouded days,
  The forest-field of Shiloh—
5   Over the field where April rain
Solaced the parched ones stretched in pain
Through the pause of night
That followed the Sunday fight
  Around the church of Shiloh—
10   The church so lone, the log-built one,
That echoed to many a parting groan
    And natural prayer
  Of dying foemen mingled there—
Foemen at morn, but friends at eve—
15   Fame or country least their care:
(What like a bullet can undeceive!)
  But now they lie low,
While over them the swallows skim,
  And all is hushed at Shiloh.

MALVERN HILL

(July, 1862)

Ye elms that wave on Malvern Hill
  In prime of morn and May,
Recall ye how McClellan's men
    Here stood at bay?
5   While deep within yon forest dim
  Our rigid comrades lay—
Some with the cartridge in their mouth,
Others with fixed arms lifted South—
    Invoking so
10   The cypress glades? Ah wilds of woe!

The spires of Richmond, late beheld
  Through rifts in musket-haze,

Were closed from view in clouds of dust
    On leaf-walled ways,
15   Where streamed our wagons in caravan;
    And the Seven Nights and Days
Of march and fast, retreat and fight,
Pinched our grimed faces to ghastly plight—
    Does the elm wood
20   Recall the haggard beards of blood?

The battle-smoked flag, with stars eclipsed,
    We followed (it never fell!)—
In silence husbanded our strength—
    Received their yell;
25   Till on this slope we patient turned
    With cannon ordered well;
Reverse we proved was not defeat;
But ah, the sod what thousands meet!—
    Does Malvern Wood
30   Bethink itself, and muse and brood?

    We elms of Malvern Hill
      Remember every thing;
    But sap the twig will fill:
    Wag the world how it will,
35   *Leaves must be green in Spring.*

THE HOUSE-TOP

A NIGHT PIECE

(July, 1863)

No sleep. The sultriness pervades the air
And binds the brain—a dense oppression, such
As tawny tigers feel in matted shades,
Vexing their blood and making apt for ravage.
5   Beneath the stars the roofy desert spreads
Vacant as Libya. All is hushed near by.
Yet fitfully from far breaks a mixed surf
Of muffled sound, the Atheist roar of riot.
Yonder, where parching Sirius set in drought,
10   Balefully glares red Arson—there—and there.

The Town is taken by its rats—ship-rats
And rats of the wharves. All civil charms
And priestly spells which late held hearts in awe—
Fear-bound, subjected to a better sway
15   Than sway of self; these like a dream dissolve,
And man rebounds whole æons back in nature.
Hail to the low dull rumble, dull and dead,
And ponderous drag that jars the wall.
Wise Draco comes, deep in the midnight roll
20   Of black artillery; he comes, though late;
In code corroborating Calvin's creed
And cynic tyrannies of honest kings;
He comes, nor parlies; and the Town, redeemed,
Gives thanks devout; nor, being thankful, heeds
25   The grimy slur on the Republic's faith implied,
Which holds that Man is naturally good,
And—more—is Nature's Roman, never to be scourged.

THE BERG

(A DREAM)

I saw a ship of martial build
(Her standards set, her brave apparel on)
Directed as by madness mere
Against a stolid iceberg steer,
5   Nor budge it, though the infatuate ship went down.
The impact made huge ice-cubes fall
Sullen, in tons that crashed the deck;
But that one avalanche was all—
No other movement save the foundering wreck.

10   Along the spurs of ridges pale,
Not any slenderest shaft and frail,
A prism over glass-green gorges lone,
Toppled; nor lace of traceries fine,
Nor pendant drops in grot or mine
15   Were jarred, when the stunned ship went down.
Nor sole the gulls in cloud that wheeled
Circling one snow-flanked peak afar,

But nearer fowl the floes that skimmed
And crystal beaches, felt no jar.
20   No thrill transmitted stirred the lock
Of jack-straw needle-ice at base;
Towers undermined by waves—the block
Atilt impending—kept their place.
Seals, dozing sleek on sliddery ledges
25   Slipt never, when by loftier edges
Through very inertia overthrown,
The impetuous ship in bafflement went down.

Hard Berg (methought), so cold, so vast,
With mortal damps self-overcast;
30   Exhaling still thy dankish breath—
Adrift dissolving, bound for death;
Though lumpish thou, a lumbering one—
A lumbering lubbard loitering slow,
Impingers rue thee and go down,
35   Sounding thy precipice below,
Nor stir the slimy slug that sprawls
Along thy dead indifference of walls.

PEBBLES

I

Though the Clerk of the Weather insist,
    And lay down the weather-law,
Pintado and gannet they wist
That the winds blow whither they list
5   In tempest or flaw.

II

Old are the creeds, but stale the schools,
    Revamped as the mode may veer,
But Orm from the schools to the beaches strays,
And, finding a Conch hoar with time, he delays
10   And reverent lifts it to ear.
That Voice, pitched in far monotone,
    Shall it swerve? shall it deviate ever?
The Seas have inspired it, and Truth—
    Truth, varying from sameness never.

III

15 In hollows of the liquid hills
    Where the long Blue Ridges run,
The flattery of no echo thrills,
    For echo the seas have none;
Nor aught that gives man back man's strain—
20 The hope of his heart, the dream in his brain.

IV

On ocean where the embattled fleets repair,
Man, suffering inflictor, sails on sufferance there.

V

Implacable I, the old implacable Sea:
    Implacable most when most I smile serene—
25 Pleased, not appeased, by myriad wrecks in me.

VI

Curled in the comb of yon billow Andean,
    Is it the Dragon's heaven-challenging crest?
Elemental mad ramping of ravening waters—
    Yet Christ on the Mount, and the dove in her nest!

VII

30 Healed of my hurt, I laud the inhuman Sea—
Yea, bless the Angels Four that there convene;
For healed I am even by their pitiless breath
Distilled in wholesome dew named rosmarine.

AFTER THE PLEASURE PARTY

LINES TRACED UNDER AN IMAGE OF AMOR THREATENING

Fear me, virgin whosoever
Taking pride from love exempt,
    Fear me, slighted. Never, never
Brave me, nor my fury tempt:
5   *Downy wings, but wroth they beat*
Tempest even in reason's seat.

Behind the house the upland falls
With many an odorous tree—
White marbles gleaming through green halls,
10 Terrace by terrace, down and down,
And meets the starlit Mediterranean Sea.

'Tis Paradise. In such an hour
Some pangs that rend might take release.
Nor less perturbed who keeps this bower
15 Of balm, nor finds balsamic peace?
From whom the passionate words in vent
After long revery's discontent?

Tired of the homeless deep,
Look how their flight yon hurrying billows urge,
20 Hitherward but to reap
Passive repulse from the iron-bound verge!
Insensate, can they never know
'Tis mad to wreck the impulsion so?

An art of memory is, they tell:
25 But to forget! forget the glade
Wherein Fate sprung Love's ambuscade,
To float pale years of cloistral life
And flush me in this sensuous strife.
'Tis Vesta struck with Sappho's smart.
30 No fable her delirious leap:
With more of cause in desperate heart,
Myself could take it—but to sleep!

Now first I feel, what all may ween,
That soon or late, if faded e'en,
35 One's sex asserts itself. Desire,
The dear desire through love to sway,
Is like the Geysers that aspire—
Through cold obstruction win their fervid way.
But baffled here—to take disdain,
40 To feel rule's instinct, yet not reign;
To dote, to come to this drear shame—
Hence the winged blaze that sweeps my soul
Like prairie fires that spurn control,
Where withering weeds incense the flame.

45   And kept I long heaven's watch for this,
        Contemning love, for this, even this?
        O terrace chill in Northern air,
        O reaching ranging tube I placed
        Against yon skies, and fable chased
50   Till, fool, I hailed for sister there
        Starred Cassiopea in Golden Chair.
        In dream I throned me, nor I saw
        In cell the idiot crowned with straw.

        And yet, ah yet scarce ill I reigned,
55   Through self-illusion self-sustained,
        When now—enlightened, undeceived—
        What gain I barrenly bereaved!
        Than this can be yet lower decline—
        Envy and spleen, can these be mine?

60   The pleasant girl demure that trod
        Beside our wheels that climbed the way,
        And bore along a blossoming rod
        That looked the sceptre of May-day—
        On her—to fire this petty hell,
65   His softened glance how moistly fell!
        The cheat! on briars her buds were strung;
        And wiles peeped forth from mien how meek.
        The innocent bare-foot! young, so young!
        To girls, strong man's a novice weak.
70   To tell such beads! And more remain,
        Sad rosary of belittling pain.

        When after lunch and sallies gay,
        Like the Decameron folk we lay
        In sylvan groups; and I—let be!
75   O, dreams he, can he dream that one
        Because not roseate feels no sun?
        The plain lone bramble thrills with Spring
        As much as vines that grapes shall bring.

        Me now fair studies charm no more.
80   Shall great thoughts writ, or high themes sung
        Damask wan cheeks—unlock his arm
        About some radiant ninny flung?
        How glad with all my starry lore,

I'd buy the veriest wanton's rose
85 Would but my bee therein repose.

Could I remake me! or set free
This sexless bound in sex, then plunge
Deeper than Sappho, in a lunge
Piercing Pan's paramount mystery!
90 For, Nature, in no shallow surge
Against thee either sex may urge,
Why hast thou made us but in halves—
Co-relatives? This makes us slaves.
If these co-relatives never meet
95 Self-hood itself seems incomplete.
And such the dicing of blind fate
Few matching halves here meet and mate.
What Cosmic jest or Anarch blunder
The human integral clove asunder
100 And shied the fractions through life's gate?

Ye stars that long your votary knew
Rapt in her vigil, see me here!
Whither is gone the spell ye threw
When rose before me Cassiopea?
105 Usurped on by love's stronger reign—
But lo, your very selves do wane:
Light breaks—truth breaks! Silvered no more,
But chilled by dawn that brings the gale
Shivers yon bramble above the vale,
110 And disillusion opens all the shore.

One knows not if Urania yet
The pleasure-party may forget;
Or whether she lived down the strain
Of turbulent heart and rebel brain;
115 For Amor so resents a slight,
And her's had been such haught disdain,
He long may wreak his boyish spite,
And boy-like, little reck the pain.

One knows not, no. But late in Rome
120 (For queens discrowned a congruous home)
Entering Albani's porch she stood
Fixed by an antique pagan stone

Colossal carved. No anchorite seer,
Not Thomas à Kempis, monk austere,
125 Religious more are in their tone;
Yet far, how far from Christian heart
That form august of heathen Art.
Swayed by its influence, long she stood,
Till surged emotion seething down,
130 She rallied and this mood she won:

Languid in frame for me,
To-day by Mary's convent shrine,
Touched by her picture's moving plea
In that poor nerveless hour of mine,
135 I mused—A wanderer still must grieve.
Half I resolved to kneel and believe,
Believe and submit, the veil take on.
But thee, armed Virgin! less benign,
Thee now I invoke, thou mightier one.
140 Helmeted woman—if such term
Befit thee, far from strife
Of that which makes the sexual feud
And clogs the aspirant life—
O self-reliant, strong and free,
145 Thou in whom power and peace unite,
Transcender! raise me up to thee,
Raise me and arm me!

Fond appeal.
For never passion peace shall bring,
Nor Art inanimate for long
150 Inspire. Nothing may help or heal
While Amor incensed remembers wrong.
Vindictive, not himself he'll spare;
For scope to give his vengeance play
Himself he'll blaspheme and betray.

155 Then for Urania, virgins everywhere,
O pray! Example take too, and have care.

THE BENCH OF BOORS

In bed I muse on Tenier's boors,
Embrowned and beery losels all:
    A wakeful brain
    Elaborates pain:
5   Within low doors the slugs of boors
Laze and yawn and doze again.

In dreams they doze, the drowsy boors,
Their hazy hovel warm and small:
    Thought's ampler bound
10   But chill is found:
Within low doors the basking boors
Snugly hug the ember-mound.

Sleepless, I see the slumberous boors
Their blurred eyes blink, their eyelids fall:
15   Thought's eager sight
    Aches—overbright!
Within low doors the boozy boors
Cat-naps take in pipe-bowl light.

IN A BYE-CANAL

A swoon of noon, a trance of tide,
The hushed siesta brooding wide
    Like calms far off Peru;
No floating wayfarer in sight,
5 Dumb noon, and haunted like the night
    When Jael the wiled one slew.
A languid impulse from the oar
Plied by my indolent gondolier
Tinkles against a palace hoar,
10   And, hark, response I hear!
A lattice clicks; and lo, I see
Between the slats, mute summoning me,
What loveliest eyes of scintillation,
What basilisk glance of conjuration!

15   Fronted I have, part taken the span
        Of portents in nature and peril in man.
        I have swum—I have been
        Twixt the whale's black flukes
            and the white shark's fin;
20   The enemy's desert have wandered in,
        And there have turned, have turned and scanned,
        Following me how noiselessly,
        Envy and Slander, lepers hand in hand.
        All this. But at the latticed eye—
25   "Hey! Gondolier, you sleep, my man;
        Wake up!" And, shooting by, we ran;
        The while I mused, This, surely now,
        Confutes the Naturalists, allow!
        Sirens, true sirens verily be,
30   Sirens, waylayers in the sea.
        Well, wooed by these same deadly misses,
        Is it shame to run?
        No! flee them did divine Ulysses,
            Brave, wise, and Venus' son.

Walt Whitman (1819–1892)

Born near Huntington, Long Island, of mixed English and Dutch parentage, Whitman left the ancestral farm with his family in 1823. He settled in Brooklyn, where he attended the local school and was then taught the printer's trade. For about twenty years after this, until 1861, he was occupied as a printer, editor, and miscellaneous writer; he was also, for a while, a teacher and a house-builder. Meanwhile, in 1855, the first edition of *Leaves of Grass* appeared and for the rest of his life Whitman devoted as much attention as he could to writing poems for the nine subsequent editions, most of which he published himself. In 1862 he began three years' service as a volunteer army nurse in the Washington hospitals. Then in 1865, with his health failing, he obtained a minor clerical post in the civil service and retained one or other position of this kind until he was stricken by paralysis in 1873. He retired to Camden, New Jersey, where he died already something of a legend.

SONG OF MYSELF

1

I celebrate myself, and sing myself,
And what I assume you shall assume,
For every atom belonging to me as good belongs to you.
I loafe and invite my soul,
5 I lean and loafe at my ease observing a spear of summer grass.

My tongue, every atom of my blood, form'd from this soil, this air,
Born here of parents born here from parents the same, and their
　　parents the same,
I, now thirty-seven years old in perfect health begin,
Hoping to cease not till death.

10 Creeds and schools in abeyance,
Retiring back a while sufficed at what they are, but never forgotten,
I harbor for good or bad, I permit to speak at every hazard,
Nature without check with original energy.

2

Houses and rooms are full of perfumes, the shelves are crowded with
　　perfumes,
15 I breathe the fragrance myself and know it and like it,
The distillation would intoxicate me also, but I shall not let it.

The atmosphere is not a perfume, it has no taste of the distillation,
　　it is odorless,
It is for my mouth forever, I am in love with it,
I will go to the bank by the wood and become undisguised and naked,
20 I am mad for it to be in contact with me.

The smoke of my own breath,
Echoes, ripples, buzz'd whispers, love-root, silk-thread, crotch and
　　vine,

My respiration and inspiration, the beating of my heart, the passing
    of blood and air through my lungs,
The sniff of green leaves and dry leaves, and of the shore and dark-
    color'd sea-rocks, and of hay in the barn,
25 The sound of the belch'd words of my voice loos'd to the eddies of the
    wind,
A few light kisses, a few embraces, a reaching around of arms,
The play of shine and shade on the trees as the supple boughs wag,
The delight alone or in the rush of the streets, or along the fields and
    hill-sides,
The feeling of health, the full-noon trill, the song of me rising from
    bed and meeting the sun.

30 Have you reckon'd a thousand acres much? have you reckon'd the
    earth much?
Have you practis'd so long to learn to read?
Have you felt so proud to get at the meaning of poems?

Stop this day and night with me and you shall possess the origin of
    all poems,
You shall possess the good of the earth and sun, (there are millions of
    suns left,)
35 You shall no longer take things at second or third hand, nor look
    through the eyes of the dead, nor feed on the spectres in books,
You shall not look through my eyes either, nor take things from me,
You shall listen to all sides and filter them from your self.

3

I have heard what the talkers were talking, the talk of the beginning
    and the end,
But I do not talk of the beginning or the end.

40 There was never any more inception than there is now,
Nor any more youth or age than there is now,
And will never be any more perfection than there is now,
Nor any more heaven or hell than there is now.

Urge and urge and urge,
45 Always the procreant urge of the world.

Out of the dimness opposite equals advance, always substance and
    increase, always sex,
Always a knit of identity, always distinction, always a breed of life.

To elaborate is no avail, learn'd and unlearn'd feel that it is so.

Sure as the most certain sure, plumb in the uprights, well entretied,
    braced in the beams,
50 Stout as a horse, affectionate, haughty, electrical,
I and this mystery here we stand.

Clear and sweet is my soul, and clear and sweet is all that is not my
    soul.
Lack one lacks both, and the unseen is proved by the seen,
Till that becomes unseen and receives proof in its turn.

55 Showing the best and dividing it from the worst age vexes age,
Knowing the perfect fitness and equanimity of things, while they
    discuss I am silent, and go bathe and admire myself.

Welcome is every organ and attribute of me, and of any man hearty
    and clean,
Not an inch nor a particle of an inch is vile, and none shall be less
    familiar than the rest.

I am satisfied—I see, dance, laugh, sing:
60 As the hugging and loving bed-fellow sleeps at my side through the
    night, and withdraws at the peep of the day with stealthy tread,
Leaving me baskets cover'd with white towels swelling the house with
    their plenty,
Shall I postpone my acceptation and realization and scream at my
    eyes,
That they turn from gazing after and down the road,
And forthwith cipher and show to me a cent,
65 Exactly the value of one and exactly the value of two, and which is
    ahead?

4

Trippers and askers surround me,
People I meet, the effect upon me of my early life or the ward and
    city I live in, or the nation,
The latest dates, discoveries, inventions, societies, authors old and
    new,
My dinner, dress, associates, looks, compliments, dues,
70 The real or fancied indifference of some man or woman I love,

The sickness of one of my folks or of myself, or ill-doing or loss or
    lack of money, or depressions or exaltations,
Battles, the horrors of fratricidal war, the fever of doubtful news, the
    fitful events;
These come to me days and nights and go from me again,
But they are not the Me myself.

75 Apart from the pulling and hauling stands what I am,
Stands amused, complacent, compassionating, idle, unitary,
Looks down, is erect, or bends an arm on an impalpable certain rest.
Looking with side-curved head curious what will come next,
Both in and out of the game and watching and wondering at it.

80 Backward I see in my own days where I sweated through fog with
    linguists and contenders,
I have no mockings or arguments, I witness and wait.

5

I believe in you my soul, the other I am must not abase itself to you,
And you must not be abased to the other.

Loafe with me on the grass, loose the stop from your throat,
85 Not words, not music or rhyme I want, not custom or lecture, not
    even the best,
Only the lull I like, the hum of your valvèd voice.

I mind how once we lay such a transparent summer morning,
How you settled your head athwart my hips and gently turn'd over
    upon me,
And parted the shirt from my bosom-bone, and plunged your tongue
    to my bare stript heart,
90 And reach'd till you felt my beard, and reach'd till you held my feet.

Swiftly arose and spread around me the peace and knowledge that
    pass all the argument of the earth,
And I know that the hand of God is the promise of my own,
And I know that the spirit of God is the brother of my own,
And that all the men ever born are also my brothers, and the women
    my sisters and lovers,
95 And that a kelson of the creation is love,
And limitless are leaves stiff or drooping in the fields,

And brown ants in the little wells beneath them,
And mossy scabs of the worm fence, heap'd stones, elder, mullein
and poke-weed.

6

A child said *What is the grass?* fetching it to me with full hands;
100 How could I answer the child? I do not know what it is any more
than he.

I guess it must be the flag of my disposition, out of hopeful green
stuff woven.

Or I guess it is the handkerchief of the Lord,
A scented gift and remembrancer designedly dropt,
Bearing the owner's name someway in the corners, that we may see
and remark, and say *Whose?*

105 Or I guess the grass is itself a child, the produced babe of the vegeta-
tion.

Or I guess it is a uniform hieroglyphic,
And it means, Sprouting alike in broad zones and narrow zones,
Growing among black folks as among white,
Kanuck, Tuckahoe, Congressman, Cuff, I give them the same, I
receive them the same.

110 And now it seems to me the beautiful uncut hair of graves.

Tenderly will I use you curling grass,
It may be you transpire from the breasts of young men,
It may be if I had known them I would have loved them,
It may be you are from old people, or from offspring taken soon out
of their mothers' laps,
115 And here you are the mothers' laps.

This grass is very dark to be from the white heads of old mothers,
Darker than the colorless beards of old men,
Dark to come from under the faint red roofs of mouths.

O I perceive after all so many uttering tongues,
120 And I perceive they do not come from the roofs of mouths for nothing.

I wish I could translate the hints about the dead young men and
    women,
And the hints about old men and mothers, and the offspring taken
    soon out of their laps.

What do you think has become of the young and old men?
And what do you think has become of the women and children?

125 They are alive and well somewhere,
    The smallest sprout shows there is really no death,
    And if ever there was it led forward life, and does not wait at the end
        to arrest it,
    And ceas'd the moment life appear'd.

    All goes onward and outward, nothing collapses,
130 And to die is different from what any one supposed, and luckier.

7

Has any one supposed it lucky to be born?
I hasten to inform him or her it is just as lucky to die, and I
    know it.

I pass death with the dying and birth with the new-wash'd babe,
    and am not contain'd between my hat and boots,
And peruse manifold objects, no two alike and every one good,
135 The earth good and the stars good, and their adjuncts all good.

I am not an earth nor an adjunct of an earth,
I am the mate and companion of people, all just as immortal and
    fathomless as myself,
(They do not know how immortal, but I know.)

Every kind for itself and its own, for me mine male and female,
140 For me those that have been boys and that love women,
    For me the man that is proud and feels how it stings to be slighted,
    For me the sweet-heart and the old maid, for me mothers and the
        mothers of mothers,
    For me lips that have smiled, eyes that have shed tears,
    For me children and the begetters of children.

145 Undrape! you are not guilty to me, nor stale nor discarded,
  I see through the broadcloth and gingham whether or no,
  And am around, tenacious, acquisitive, tireless, and cannot be
    shaken away.

8

The little one sleeps in its cradle,
I lift the gauze and look a long time, and silently brush away flies
  with my hand.

150 The youngster and the red-faced girl turn aside up the bushy hill,
  I peeringly view them from the top.

The suicide sprawls on the bloody floor of the bedroom,
I witness the corpse with its dabbled hair, I note where the pistol
  has fallen.

The blab of the pave, tires of carts, sluff of boot-soles, talk of the
    promenaders,
155 The heavy omnibus, the driver with his interrogating thumb, the
    clank of the shod horses on the granite floor,
  The snow-sleighs, clinking, shouted jokes, pelts of snow-balls,
  The hurrahs for popular favorites, the fury of rous'd mobs,
  The flap of the curtain'd litter, a sick man inside borne to the hospital,
  The meeting of enemies, the sudden oath, the blows and fall,
160 The excited crowd, the policeman with his star quickly working his
    passage to the centre of the crowd,
  The impassive stones that receive and return so many echoes,
  What groans of over-fed or half-starv'd who fall sunstruck or in fits,
  What exclamations of women taken suddenly who hurry home and
    gave birth to babes,
  What living and buried speech is always vibrating here, what howls
    restrain'd by decorum,
165 Arrests of criminals, slights, adulterous offers made, acceptances,
    rejections with convex lips,
  I mind them or the show or resonance of them—I come and I depart.

9

The big doors of the country barn stand open and ready,
The dried grass of the harvest-time loads the slow-drawn wagon,
The clear light plays on the brown gray and green intertinged,
70 The armfuls are pack'd to the sagging mow.

I am there, I help, I came stretch'd atop of the load,
I felt its soft jolts, one leg reclined on the other,
I jump from the cross-beams and seize the clover and timothy,
And roll head over heels and tangle my hair full of wisps.

10

175 Alone far in the wilds and mountains I hunt,
Wandering amazed at my own lightness and glee,
In the late afternoon choosing a safe spot to pass the night,
Kindling a fire and broiling the fresh-kill'd game,
Falling asleep on the gather'd leaves with my dog and gun by my
side.

180 The Yankee clipper is under her sky-sails, she cuts the sparkle and
scud,
My eyes settle the land, I bend at her prow or shout joyously from
the deck.

The boatmen and clam-diggers arose early and stopt for me,
I tuck'd my trowser-ends in my boots and went and had a good time;
You should have been with us that day round the chowder-kettle.

185 I saw the marriage of the trapper in the open air in the far west, the
bride was a red girl,
Her father and his friends sat near cross-legged and dumbly smoking,
they had moccasins to their feet and large thick blankets hanging
from their shoulders,
On a bank lounged the trapper, he was drest mostly in skins, his
luxuriant beard and curls protected his neck, he held his bride
by the hand,
She had long eyelashes, her head was bare, her coarse straight locks
descended upon her voluptuous limbs and reach'd to her feet.

The runaway slave came to my house and stopt outside,
190 I heard his motions crackling the twigs of the woodpile,
Through the swung half-door of the kitchen I saw him limpsy and
weak,
And went where he sat on a log and led him in and assured him,
And brought water and fill'd a tub for his sweated body and bruis'd
feet,
And gave him a room that enter'd from my own, and gave him some
coarse clean clothes,

195 And remember perfectly well his revolving eyes and his awkwardness,
And remember putting plasters on the galls of his neck and ankles;
He staid with me a week before he was recuperated and pass'd north,
I had him sit next me at table, my fire-lock lean'd in the corner.

11

Twenty-eight young men bathe by the shore,
200 Twenty-eight young men and all so friendly;
Twenty-eight years of womanly life and all so lonesome.

She owns the fine house by the rise of the bank,
She hides handsome and richly drest aft the blinds of the window.

Which of the young men does she like the best?
205 Ah the homeliest of them is beautiful to her.

Where are you off to, lady? for I see you,
You splash in the water there, yet stay stock still in your room.

Dancing and laughing along the beach came the twenty-ninth bather,
The rest did not see her, but she saw them and loved them.

210 The beards of the young men glisten'd with wet, it ran from their
     long hair,
Little streams pass'd all over their bodies.

An unseen hand also pass'd over their bodies,
It descended tremblingly from their temples and ribs.

The young men float on their backs, their white bellies bulge to the
     sun, they do not ask who seizes fast to them,
215 They do not know who puffs and declines with pendant and bending
     arch,
They do not think whom they souse with spray.

12

The butcher-boy puts off his killing-clothes, or sharpens his knife at
     the stall in the market,
I loiter enjoying his repartee and his shuffle and break-down.

Blacksmiths with grimed and hairy chests environ the anvil,
220 Each has his main-sledge, they are all out, there is a great heat in the
fire.

From the cinder-strew'd threshold I follow their movements,
The lithe sheer of their waists plays even with their massive arms,
Overhand the hammers swing, overhand so slow, overhand so sure.
They do not hasten, each man hits in his place.

13

225 The negro holds firmly the reins of his four horses, the block swags
underneath on its tied-over chain,
The negro that drives the long dray of the stone-yard, steady and
tall he stands pois'd on one leg on the string-piece,
His blue shirt exposes his ample neck and breast and loosens over
his hip-band,
His glance is calm and commanding, he tosses the slouch of his hat
away from his forehead,
The sun falls on his crispy hair and mustache, falls on the black of
his polish'd and perfect limbs.

230 I behold the picturesque giant and love him, and I do not stop there,
I go with the team also.

In me the caresser of life wherever moving, backward as well as
forward sluing,
To niches aside and junior bending, not a person or object missing,
Absorbing all to myself and for this song.

235 Oxen that rattle the yoke and chain or halt in the leafy shade, what is
that you express in your eyes?
It seems to me more than all the print I have read in my life.

My tread scares the wood-drake and wood-duck on my distant and
day-long ramble,
They rise together, they slowly circle around.

I believe in those wing'd purposes,
240 And acknowledge red, yellow, white, playing within me,
And consider green and violet and the tufted crown intentional,
And do not call the tortoise unworthy because she is not something
else,

And the jay in the woods never studied the gamut, yet trills pretty
    well to me,
And the look of the bay mare shames silliness out of me.

14

245 The wild gander leads his flock through the cool night,
    Ya-honk he says, and sounds it down to me like an invitation,
    The pert may suppose it meaningless, but I listening close,
    Find its purpose and place up there toward the wintry sky.

    The sharp-hoof'd moose of the north, the cat on the house-sill, the
        chickadee, the prairie-dog,
250 The litter of the grunting sow as they tug at her teats,
    The brood of the turkey-hen and she with her half-spread wings,
    I see in them and myself the same old law.

    The press of my foot to the earth springs a hundred affections,
    They scorn the best I can do to relate them.

255 I am enamour'd of growing out-doors,
    Of men that live among cattle or taste of the ocean or woods,
    Of the builders and steerers of ships and the wielders of axes and
        mauls, and the drivers of horses,
    I can eat and sleep with them week in and week out.

    What is commonest, cheapest, nearest, easiest, is Me,
260 Me going in for my chances, spending for vast returns,
    Adorning myself to bestow myself on the first that will take me,
    Not asking the sky to come down to my good will,
    Scattering it freely forever.

15

    The pure contralto sings in the organ loft,
265 The carpenter dresses his plank, the tongue of his foreplane whistles
        its wild ascending lisp,
    The married and unmarried children ride home to their Thanksgiving
        dinner,
    The pilot seizes the king-pin, he heaves down with a strong arm,
    The mate stands braced in the whale-boat, lance and harpoon are
        ready,

The duck-shooter walks by silent and cautious stretches,

270 The deacons are ordain'd with cross'd hands at the altar,

The spinning-girl retreats and advances to the hum of the big wheel,

The farmer stops by the bars as he walks on a First-day loafe and looks at the oats and rye,

The lunatic is carried at last to the asylum a confirm'd case,

(He will never sleep any more as he did in the cot in his mother's bed-room;)

275 The jour printer with gray head and gaunt jaws works at his case,

He turns his quid of tobacco while his eyes blurr with the manuscript;

The malform'd limbs are tied to the surgeon's table,

What is removed drops horribly in a pail;

The quadroon girl is sold at the auction-stand, the drunkard nods by the bar-room stove,

280 The machinist rolls up his sleeves, the policeman travels his beat, the gate-keeper marks who pass,

The young fellow drives the express-wagon, (I love him, though I do not know him;)

The half-breed straps on his light boots to compete in the race,

The western turkey-shooting draws old and young, some lean on their rifles, some sit on logs,

Out from the crowd steps the marksman, takes his position, levels his piece;

285 The groups of newly-come immigrants cover the wharf or levee,

As the woolly-pates hoe in the sugar-field, the overseer views them from his saddle,

The bugle calls in the ball-room, the gentlemen run for their partners, the dancers bow to each other,

The youth lies awake in the cedar-roof'd garret and harks to the musical rain,

The Wolverine sets traps on the creek that helps fill the Huron,

290 The squaw wrapt in her yellow-hemm'd cloth is offering moccasins and bead-bags for sale,

The connoisseur peers along the exhibition-gallery with half-shut eyes bent sideways,

As the deck-hands make fast the steamboat the plank is thrown for the shore-going passengers.

The young sister holds out the skein while the elder sister winds it off in a ball, and stops now and then for the knots,

The one-year wife is recovering and happy having a week ago borne her first child,

295 The clean-hair'd Yankee girl works with her sewing-machine or in the factory or mill,

The paving-man leans on his two-handed rammer, the reporter's lead flies swiftly over the note-book, the sign-painter is lettering with blue and gold,

The canal boy trots on the tow-path, the book-keeper counts at his desk, the shoemaker waxes his thread,

The conductor beats time for the band and all the performers follow him,

The child is baptized, the convert is making his first professions,

300 The regatta is spread on the bay, the race is begun, (how the white sails sparkle!)

The drover watching his drove sings out to them that would stray,

The pedler sweats with his pack on his back, (the purchaser higgling about the odd cent;)

The bride unrumples her white dress, the minute-hand of the clock moves slowly,

The opium-eater reclines with rigid head and just-open'd lips,

305 The prostitute draggles her shawl, her bonnet bobs on her tipsy and pimpled neck,

The crowd laugh at her blackguard oaths, the men jeer and wink to each other,

(Miserable! I do not laugh at your oaths nor jeer you;)

The President holding a cabinet council is surrounded by the great Secretaries,

On the piazza walk three matrons stately and friendly with twined arms,

310 The crew of the fish-smack pack repeated layers of halibut in the hold,

The Missourian crosses the plains toting his wares and his cattle,

As the fare-collector goes through the train he gives notice by the jingling of loose change,

The floor-men are laying the floor, the tinners are tinning the roof, the masons are calling for mortar,

In single file each shouldering his hod pass onward the laborers;

315 Seasons pursuing each other the indescribable crowd is gather'd, it is the fourth of Seventh-month, (what salutes of cannon and small arms!)

Seasons pursuing each other the plougher ploughs, the mower mows, and the winter-grain falls in the ground;

Off on the lakes the pike-fisher watches and waits by the hole in the frozen surface,

The stumps stand thick round the clearing, the squatter strikes deep with his axe,

Flatboatmen make fast towards dusk near the cotton-wood or pecan-trees,

320 Coon-seekers go through the regions of the Red river or through
those drain'd by the Tennessee, or through those of the Arkansas,
Torches shine in the dark that hangs on the Chattahooche or Alta-
mahaw,
Patriarchs sit at supper with sons and grandsons and great-grandsons
around them,
In walls of adobie, in canvas tents, rest hunters and trappers after
their day's sport,
The city sleeps and the country sleeps,
325 The living sleep for their time, the dead sleep for their time,
The old husband sleeps by his wife and the young husband sleeps
by his wife;
And these tend inward to me, and I tend outward to them,
And such as it is to be of these more or less I am,
And of these one and all I weave the song of myself.

16

330 I am of old and young, of the foolish as much as the wise,
Regardless of others, ever regardful of others,
Maternal as well as paternal, a child as well as a man,
Stuff'd with the stuff that is coarse and stuff'd with the stuff that is
fine,
One of the Nation of many nations, the smallest the same and the
largest the same,
335 A Southerner soon as a Northerner, a planter nonchalant and
hospitable down by the Oconee I live,
A Yankee bound my own way ready for trade, my joints the limberest
joints on earth and the sternest joints on earth,
A Kentuckian walking the vale of the Elkhorn in my deer-skin
leggings, a Louisianian or Georgian,
A boatman over lakes or bays or along coasts, a Hoosier, Badger,
Buckeye;
At home on Kanadian snow-shoes or up in the bush, or with fisher-
men off Newfoundland,
340 At home in the fleet of ice-boats, sailing with the rest and tacking,
At home on the hills of Vermont or in the woods of Maine, or the
Texan ranch,
Comrade of Californians, comrade of free North-Westerners, (loving
their big proportions,)
Comrade of raftsmen and coalmen, comrade of all who shake hands
and welcome to drink and meat,
A learner with the simplest, a teacher of the thoughtfullest,

345 A novice beginning yet experient of myriads of seasons,
Of every hue and caste am I, of every rank and religion,
A farmer, mechanic, artist, gentleman, sailor, quaker,
Prisoner, fancy-man, rowdy, lawyer, physician, priest.

I resist any thing better than my own diversity,
350 Breathe the air but leave plenty after me,
And am not stuck up, and am in my place.

(The moth and the fish-eggs are in their place,
The bright suns I see and the dark suns I cannot see are in their
place,
The palpable is in its place and the impalpable is in its place.)

17

355 These are really the thoughts of all men in all ages and lands, they
are not original with me,
If they are not yours as much as mine they are nothing, or next to
nothing,
If they are not the riddle and the untying of the riddle they are
nothing,
If they are not just as close as they are distant they are nothing.

This is the grass that grows wherever the land is and the water is,
360 This the common air that bathes the globe.

18

With music strong I come, with my cornets and my drums,
I play not marches for accepted victors only, I play marches for
conquer'd and slain persons.

Have you heard that it was good to gain the day?
I also say it is good to fall, battles are lost in the same spirit in which
they are won.

365 I beat and pound for the dead,
I blow through my embouchures my loudest and gayest for them.

Vivas to those who have fail'd!
And to those whose war-vessels sank in the sea!
And to those themselves who sank in the sea!

370 And to all generals that lost engagements, and all overcome heroes!
And the numberless unknown heroes equal to the greatest heroes
known!

19

This is the meal equally set, this the meat for natural hunger,
It is for the wicked just the same as the righteous, I make appoint-
ments with all,
I will not have a single person slighted or left away,
375 The kept-woman, sponger, thief, are hereby invited,
The heavy-lipp'd slave is invited, the venerealee is invited;
There shall be no difference between them and the rest.

This is the press of a bashful hand, this the float and odor of hair,
This the touch of my lips to yours, this the murmur of yearning,
380 This the far-off depth and height reflecting my own face,
This the thoughtful merge of myself, and the outlet again.

Do you guess I have some intricate purpose?
Well I have, for the Fourth-month showers have, and the mica on
the side of a rock has.

Do you take it I would astonish?
385 Does the daylight astonish? does the early redstart twittering through
the woods?
Do I astonish more than they?

This hour I tell things in confidence,
I might not tell everybody, but I will tell you.

20

Who goes there? hankering, gross, mystical, nude;
390 How is it I extract strength from the beef I eat?

What is a man anyhow? what am I? what are you?

All I mark as my own you shall offset it with your own,
Else it were time lost listening to me.

I do not snivel that snivel the world over,
395 That months are vacuums and the ground but wallow and filth.

Whimpering and truckling fold with powders for invalids, con-
        formity goes to the fourth-remov'd,
I wear my hat as I please indoors or out.

Why should I pray? why should I venerate and be ceremonious?

Having pried through the strata, analyzed to a hair, counsel'd with
        doctors and calculated close,
400 I find no sweeter fat than sticks to my own bones.

In all people I see myself, none more and not one a barley-corn less,
And the good or bad I say of myself I say of them.

I know I am solid and sound,
To me the converging objects of the universe perpetually flow,
405 All are written to me, and I must get what the writing means.

I know I am deathless,
I know this orbit of mine cannot be swept by a carpenter's compass,
I know I shall not pass like a child's carlacue cut with a burnt stick
        at night.

I know I am august,
410 I do not trouble my spirit to vindicate itself or be understood,
I see that the elementary laws never apologize,
(I reckon I behave no prouder than the level I plant my house by,
        after all.)

I exist as I am, that is enough,
If no other in the world be aware I sit content,
415 And if each and all be aware I sit content.

One world is aware and by far the largest to me, and that is myself,
And whether I come to my own to-day or in ten thousand or ten
        million years,
I can cheerfully take it now, or with equal cheerfulness I can wait.

My foothold is tenon'd and mortis'd in granite,
420 I laugh at what you call dissolution,
And I know the amplitude of time.

21

I am the poet of the Body and I am the poet of the Soul,
The pleasures of heaven are with me and the pains of hell are with
    me,
The first I graft and increase upon myself, the latter I translate into
    a new tongue.

425 I am the poet of the woman the same as the man,
And I say it is as great to be a woman as to be a man,
And I say there is nothing greater than the mother of men.

I chant the chant of dilation or pride,
We have had ducking and deprecating about enough,
430 I show that size is only development.

Have you outstript the rest? are you the President?
It is a trifle, they will more than arrive there every one, and still pass
    on.

I am he that walks with the tender and growing night,
I call to the earth and sea half-held by the night.

435 Press close bare-bosom'd night—press close magnetic nourishing
    night!
Night of south winds—night of the large few stars!
Still nodding night—mad naked summer night.

Smile O voluptuous cool-breath'd earth!
Earth of the slumbering and liquid trees!
440 Earth of departed sunset—earth of the mountains misty-topt!
Earth of the vitreous pour of the full moon just tinged with blue!
Earth of shine and dark mottling the tide of the river!
Earth of the limpid gray of clouds brighter and clearer for my sake!
Far-swooping elbow'd earth—rich apple-blossom'd earth!
445 Smile, for your lover comes.

Prodigal, you have given me love—therefore I to you give love!
O unspeakable passionate love.

22

You sea! I resign myself to you also—I guess what you mean,
I behold from the beach your crooked inviting fingers,

450 I believe you refuse to go back without feeling of me,
    We must have a turn together, I undress, hurry me out of sight of
        the land,
    Cushion me soft, rock me in billowy drowse,
    Dash me with amorous wet, I can repay you.

    Sea of stretch'd ground-swells,
455 Sea breathing broad and convulsive breaths,
    Sea of the brine of life and of unshovell'd yet always-ready graves,
    Howler and scooper of storms, capricious and dainty sea,
    I am integral with you, I too am of one phase and of all phases.

    Partaker of influx and efflux I, extoller of hate and conciliation,
460 Extoller of amies and those that sleep in each others' arms.

    I am he attesting sympathy,
    (Shall I make my list of things in the house and skip the house that
        supports them?)

    I am not the poet of goodness only, I do not decline to be the poet of
        wickedness also.

    What blurt is this about virtue and about vice?
465 Evil propels me and reform of evil propels me, I stand indifferent,
    My gait is no fault-finder's or rejecter's gait,
    I moisten the roots of all that has grown.

    Did you fear some scrofula out of the unflagging pregnancy?
    Did you guess the celestial laws are yet to be work'd over and
        rectified?

470 I find one side a balance and the antipodal side a balance,
    Soft doctrine as steady help as stable doctrine,
    Thoughts and deeds of the present our rouse and early start.

    This minute that comes to me over the past decillions,
    There is no better than it and now.

475 What behaved well in the past or behaves well to-day is not such a
        wonder,
    The wonder is always and always how there can be a mean man or
        an infidel.

Endless unfolding of words of ages!
And mine a word of the modern, the word En-Masse.

A word of the faith that never balks,
480 Here or henceforward it is all the same to me, I accept Time abso-
    lutely.

It alone is without flaw, it alone rounds and completes all,
That mystic baffling wonder alone completes all.

I accept Reality and dare not question it,
Materialism first and last imbuing.

485 Hurrah for positive science! long live exact demonstration!
Fetch stonecrop mixt with cedar and branches of lilac,
This is the lexicographer, this the chemist, this made a grammar of
    the old cartouches,
These mariners put the ship through dangerous unknown seas,
This is the geologist, this works with the scalpel, and this is a mathe-
    matician.

490 Gentlemen, to you the first honors always!
Your facts are useful, and yet they are not my dwelling,
I but enter by them to an area of my dwelling.

Less the reminders of properties told my words,
And more the reminders they of life untold, and of freedom and
    extrication,
495 And make short account of neuters and geldings, and favor men and
    women fully equipt,
And beat the gong of revolt, and stop with fugitives and them that
    plot and conspire.

24

Walt Whitman, a kosmos, of Manhattan the son,
Turbulent, fleshy, sensual, eating, drinking and breeding,
No sentimentalist, no stander above men and women or apart from
    them,
500 No more modest than immodest.

Unscrew the locks from the doors!
Unscrew the doors themselves from their jambs!

Whoever degrades another degrades me,
And whatever is done or said returns at last to me.

505 Through me the afflatus surging and surging, through me the current
and index.

I speak the pass-word primeval, I give the sign of democracy.
By God! I will accept nothing which all cannot have their counter-
part of on the same terms.

Through me many long dumb voices,
Voices of the interminable generations of prisoners and slaves,
510 Voices of the diseas'd and despairing and of thieves and dwarfs,
Voices of cycles of preparation and accretion,
And of the threads that connect the stars, and of wombs and of the
father-stuff,
And of the rights of them the others are down upon,
Of the deform'd, trivial, flat, foolish, despised,
515 Fog in the air, beetles rolling balls of dung.

Through me forbidden voices,
Voices of sexes and lusts, voices veil'd and I remove the veil,
Voices indecent by me clarified and transfigur'd.

I do not press my fingers across my mouth,
520 I keep as delicate around the bowels as around the head and heart,
Copulation is no more rank to me than death is.
I believe in the flesh and the appetites,
Seeing, hearing, feeling, are miracles, and each part and tag of me
is a miracle.

Divine am I inside and out, and I make holy whatever I touch or
am touch'd from,
515 The scent of these arm-pits aroma finer than prayer,
This head more than churches, bibles, and all the creeds.

If I worship one thing more than another it shall be the spread of
my own body, or any part of it,
Translucent mould of me it shall be you!
Shaded ledges and rests it shall be you!

530 Firm masculine colter it shall be you!
Whatever goes to the tilth of me it shall be you!
You my rich blood! your milky stream pale strippings of my life!
Breast that presses against other breasts it shall be you!
My brain it shall be your occult convolutions!
535 Root of wash'd sweet-flag! timorous pond-snipe! nest of guarded
duplicate eggs! it shall be you!
Mix'd tussled hay of head, beard, brawn, it shall be you!
Trickling sap of maple, fibre of manly wheat, it shall be you!
Sun so generous it shall be you!
Vapors lighting and shading my face it shall be you!
540 You sweaty brooks and dews it shall be you!
Winds whose soft-tickling genitals rub against me it shall be you!
Broad muscular fields, branches of live oak, loving lounger in my
winding paths, it shall be you!
Hands I have taken, face I have kiss'd, mortal I have ever touch'd, it
shall be you.

I dote on myself, there is that lot of me and all so luscious,
545 Each moment and whatever happens thrills me with joy,
I cannot tell how my ankles bend, nor whence the cause of my faintest
wish,
Nor the cause of the friendship I emit, nor the cause of the friendship
I take again.

That I walk up my stoop, I pause to consider if it really be,
A morning-glory at my window satisfies me more than the meta-
physics of books.

550 To behold the day-break!
The little light fades the immense and diaphanous shadows,
The air tastes good to my palate.

Hefts of the moving world at innocent gambols silently rising, freshly
exuding,
Scooting obliquely high and low.

555 Something I cannot see puts upward libidinous prongs,
Seas of bright juice suffuse heaven.

The earth by the sky staid with, the daily close of their junction,
The heav'd challenge from the east that moment over my head,
The mocking taunt, See then whether you shall be master!

560 Dazzling and tremendous how quick the sun-rise would kill me,
　　If I could not now and always send sun-rise out of me.

We also ascend dazzling and tremendous as the sun,
We found our own O my soul in the calm and cool of the daybreak.

My voice goes after what my eyes cannot reach,
565 With the twirl of my tongue I encompass worlds and volumes of
　　worlds.

Speech is the twin of my vision, it is unequal to measure itself,
It provokes me forever, it says sarcastically,
Walt you contain enough, why don't you let it out then?

Come now I will not be tantalized, you conceive too much of articula-
　　tion,
570 Do you not know O speech how the buds beneath you are folded?
Waiting in gloom, protected by frost,
The dirt receding before my prophetical screams,
I underlying causes to balance them at last,
My knowledge my live parts, it keeping tally with the meaning of
　　all things,
575 Happiness, (which whoever hears me let him or her set out in search
　　of this day.)

My final merit I refuse you, I refuse putting from me what I really
　　am,
Encompass worlds, but never try to encompass me,
I crowd your sleekest and best by simply looking toward you.

Writing and talk do not prove me,
580 I carry the plenum of proof and every thing else in my face,
With the hush of my lips I wholly confound the skeptic.

26

Now I will do nothing but listen,
To accrue what I hear into this song, to let sounds contribute toward
　　it.

I hear bravuras of birds, bustle of growing wheat, gossip of flames,
clack of sticks cooking my meals,
585 I hear the sound I love, the sound of the human voice,
I hear all sounds running together, combined, fused or following,
Sounds of the city and sounds out of the city, sounds of the day and
night,
Talkative young ones to those that like them, the loud laugh of work-
people at their meals,
The angry base of disjointed friendship, the faint tones of the sick,
590 The judge with hands tight to the desk, his pallid lips pronouncing
a death-sentence,
The heave'e'yo of stevedores unlading ships by the wharves, the
refrain of the anchor-lifters,
The ring of alarm-bells, the cry of fire, the whirr of swift-streaking
engines and hose-carts with premonitory tinkles and color'd
lights,
The steam-whistle, the solid roll of the train of approaching cars,
The slow march play'd at the head of the association marching two
and two,
595 (They go to guard some corpse, the flag-tops are draped with black
muslin.)

I hear the violoncello, ('tis the young man's heart's complaint,)
I hear the key'd cornet, it glides quickly in through my ears,
It shakes mad-sweet pangs through my belly and breast.

I hear the chorus, it is a grand opera,
600 Ah this indeed is music—this suits me.

A tenor large and fresh as the creation fills me,
The orbic flex of his mouth is pouring and filling me full.

I hear the train'd soprano (what work with hers is this?)
The orchestra whirls me wider than Uranus flies,
605 It wrenches such ardors from me I did not know I possess'd them,
It sails me, I dab with bare feet, they are lick'd by the indolent waves,
I am cut by bitter and angry hail, I lose my breath,
Steep'd amid honey'd morphine, my windpipe throttled in fakes of
death,
At length let up again to feel the puzzle of puzzles,
610 And that we call Being.

27

To be in any form, what is that?
(Round and round we go, all of us, and ever come back thither,)
If nothing lay more develop'd the quahaug in its callous shell were
      enough.

Mine is no callous shell,
615 I have instant conductors all over me whether I pass or stop,
They seize every object and lead it harmlessly through me.

I merely stir, press, feel with my fingers, and am happy,
To touch my person to some one else's is about as much as I can
      stand.

28

Is this then a touch? quivering me to a new identity,
620 Flames and ether making a rush for my veins,
Treacherous tip of me reaching and crowding to help them,
My flesh and blood playing out lightning to strike what is hardly
      different from myself,
On all sides prurient provokers stiffening my limbs,
Straining the udder of my heart for its withheld drip,
625 Behaving licentious toward me, taking no denial,
Depriving me of my best as for a purpose,
Unbuttoning my clothes, holding me by the bare waist,
Deluding my confusion with the calm of the sunlight and pasture-fields,
Immodestly sliding the fellow-senses away,
630 They bribed to swap off with touch and go and graze at the edges
      of me,
No consideration, no regard for my draining strength or my anger,
Fetching the rest of the herd around to enjoy them a while,
Then all uniting to stand on a headland and worry me.

The sentries desert every other part of me,
635 They have left me helpless to a red marauder,
They all come to the headland to witness and assist against me.

I am given up by traitors,
I talk wildly, I have lost my wits, I and nobody else am the greatest
      traitor,
I went myself first to the headland, my own hands carried me there.

640 You villain touch! what are you doing? my breath is tight in its
    throat,
    Unclench your floodgates, you are too much for me.

29

Blind loving wrestling touch, sheath'd hooded sharp-tooth'd touch!
Did it make you ache so, leaving me?

Parting track'd by arriving, perpetual payment of perpetual loan,
645 Rich showering rain, and recompense richer afterward.

Sprouts take and accumulate, stand by the curb prolific and vital,
Landscapes projected masculine, full-sized and golden.

30

All truths wait in all things,
They neither hasten their own delivery nor resist it,
650 They do not need the obstetric forceps of the surgeon,
The insignificant is as big to me as any,
(What is less or more than a touch?)

Logic and sermons never convince,
The damp of the night drives deeper into my soul.

655 (Only what proves itself to every man and woman is so,
Only what nobody denies is so.)

A minute and a drop of me settle my brain,
I believe the soggy clods shall become lovers and lamps,
And a compend of compends is the meat of a man or woman,
660 And a summit and flower there is the feeling they have for each other,
And they are to branch boundlessly out of that lesson until it becomes
    omnific,
And until one and all shall delight us, and we them.

31

I believe a leaf of grass is no less than the journey-work of the stars,
And the pismire is equally perfect, and a grain of sand, and the egg
    of the wren,
665 And the tree-toad is a chef-d'œuvre for the highest,
And the running blackberry would adorn the parlors of heaven,

And the narrowest hinge in my hand puts to scorn all machinery,
And the cow crunching with depress'd head surpasses any statue,
And a mouse is miracle enough to stagger sextillions of infidels.

670 I find I incorporate gneiss, coal, long-threaded moss, fruits, grains,
    esculent roots,
And am stucco'd with quadrupeds and birds all over,
And have distanced what is behind me for good reasons,
But call any thing back again when I desire it.

In vain the speeding or shyness,
675 In vain the plutonic rocks send their old heat against my approach,
In vain the mastodon retreats beneath its own powder'd bones,
In vain objects stand leagues off and assume manifold shapes,
In vain the ocean settling in hollows and the great monsters lying
    low,
In vain the buzzard houses herself with the sky,
680 In vain the snake slides through the creepers and logs,
In vain the elk takes to the inner passes of the woods,
In vain the razor-bill'd auk sails far north to Labrador,
I follow quickly, I ascend to the nest in the fissure of the cliff.

32

I think I could turn, and live with animals, they are so placid and
    self-contain'd,
685 I stand and look at them long and long.

They do not sweat and whine about their condition,
They do not lie awake in the dark and weep for their sins,
They do not make me sick discussing their duty to God,
Not one is dissatisfied, not one is demented with the mania of owning
    things,
690 Not one kneels to another, nor to his kind that lived thousands of
    years ago,
Not one is respectable or unhappy over the whole earth.

So they show their relations to me and I accept them,
They bring me tokens of myself, they evince them plainly in their
    possession.

I wonder where they get those tokens,
695 Did I pass that way huge times ago and negligently drop them?

Myself moving forward then and now and forever,
Gathering and showing more always and with velocity,
Infinite and omnigenous, and the like of these among them,
Not too exclusive toward the reachers of my remembrancers,
700 Picking out here one that I love, and now go with him on brotherly
terms.

A gigantic beauty of a stallion, fresh and responsive to my caresses,
Head high in the forehead, wide between the ears,
Limbs glossy and supple, tail dusting the ground,
Eyes full of sparkling wickedness, ears finely cut, flexibly moving.

705 His nostrils dilate as my heels embrace him,
His well-built limbs tremble with pleasure as we race around and
return.

I but use you a minute, then I resign you, stallion,
Why do I need your paces when I myself out-gallop them?
Even as I stand or sit passing faster than you.

33

710 Space and Time! now I see it is true, what I guessed at,
What I guess'd when I loaf'd on the grass,
What I guess'd while I lay alone in my bed,
And again as I walk'd the beach under the paling stars of the morning.

My ties and ballasts leave me, my elbows rest in sea-gaps,
715 I skirt sierras, my palms cover continents,
I am afoot with my vision.

By the city's quadrangular houses—in log huts, camping with lumber-
men,
Along the ruts of the turnpike, along the dry gulch and rivulet bed,
Weeding my onion-patch or hoeing rows of carrots and parsnips,
crossing savannas, trailing in forests,
720 Prospecting, gold-digging, girdling the trees of a new purchase,
Scorch'd ankle-deep by the hot sand, hauling my boat down the
shallow river,
Where the panther walks to and fro on a limb overhead, where the
buck turns furiously at the hunter,
Where the rattlesnake suns his flabby length on a rock, where the
otter is feeding on fish,

Where the alligator in his tough pimples sleeps by the bayou,
725 Where the black bear is searching for roots or honey, where the
   beaver pats the mud with his paddle-shaped tail;
Over the growing sugar, over the yellow-flower'd cotton plant, over
   the rice in its low moist field,
Over the sharp-peak'd farm house, with its scallop'd scum and
   slender shoots from the gutters,
Over the western persimmon, over the long-leav'd corn, over the
   delicate blue-flower flax,
Over the white and brown buckwheat, a hummer and buzzer there
   with the rest,
730 Over the dusky green of the rye as it ripples and shades in the breeze;
Scaling mountains, pulling myself cautiously up, holding on by low
   scragged limbs,
Walking the path worn in the grass and beat through the leaves of
   the brush,
Where the quail is whistling betwixt the woods and the wheat-lot,
Where the bat flies in the Seventh-month eve, where the great gold-
   bug drops through the dark,
735 Where the brook puts out of the roots of the old tree and flows to the
   meadow,
Where cattle stand and shake away flies with the tremulous shudder-
   ing of their hides,
Where the cheese-cloth hangs in the kitchen, where andirons straddle
   the hearth-slab, where cobwebs fall in festoons from the rafters;
Where trip-hammers crash, where the press is whirling its cylinders,
Wherever the human heart beats with terrible throes under its ribs,
740 Where the pear-shaped balloon is floating aloft, (floating in it myself
   and looking composedly down,)
Where the life-car is drawn on the slip-noose, where the heat hatches
   pale-green eggs in the dented sand,
Where the she-whale swims with her calf and never forsakes it,
Where the steam-ship trails hind-ways its long pennant of smoke,
Where the fin of the shark cuts like a black chip out of the water,
745 Where the half-burn'd brig is riding on unknown currents,
Where shells grow to her slimy deck, where the dead are corrupting
   below;
Where the dense-starr'd flag is borne at the head of the regiments,
Approaching Manhattan up by the long-stretching island,
Under Niagara, the cataract falling like a veil over my countenance,
750 Upon a door-step, upon the horse-block of hard wood outside,
Upon the race-course, or enjoying picnics or jigs or a good game of
   base-ball,

At he-festivals, with blackguard gibes, ironical license, bull-dances, drinking, laughter,

At the cider-mill tasting the sweets of the brown mash, sucking the juice through a straw,

At apple-peelings wanting kisses for all the red fruit I find,

755 At musters, beach-parties, friendly bees, huskings, house-raisings;

Where the mocking-bird sounds his delicious gurgles, cackles, screams, weeps,

Where the hay-rick stands in the barn-yard, where the dry-stalks are scatter'd, where the brood-cow waits in the hovel,

Where the bull advances to do his masculine work, where the stud to the mare, where the cock is treading the hen,

Where the heifers browse, where geese nip their food with short jerks,

760 Where sun-down shadows lengthen over the limitless and lonesome prairie,

Where herds of buffalo make a crawling spread of the square miles far and near,

Where the humming-bird shimmers, where the neck of the long-lived swan is curving and winding,

Where the laughing-gull scoots by the shore, where she laughs her near-human laugh,

Where bee-hives range on a gray bench in the garden half hid by the high weeds,

765 Where band-neck'd partridges roost in a ring on the ground with their heads out,

Where burial coaches enter the arch'd gates of a cemetery,

Where winter wolves bark amid wastes of snow and icicled trees,

Where the yellow-crown'd heron comes to the edge of the marsh at night and feeds upon small crabs,

Where the splash of swimmers and divers cools the warm noon,

770 Where the katy-did works her chromatic reed on the walnut-tree over the well,

Through patches of citrons and cucumbers with silver-wired leaves,

Through the salt-lick or orange glade, or under conical firs,

Through the gymnasium, through the curtain'd saloon, through the office or public hall;

Pleas'd with the native and pleas'd with the foreign, pleas'd with the new and old,

775 Pleas'd with the homely woman as well as the handsome,

Pleas'd with the quakeress as she puts off her bonnet and talks melodiously,

Pleas'd with the tune of the choir of the whitewash'd church,

Pleas'd with the earnest words of the sweating Methodist preacher,
impress'd seriously at the camp-meeting;
Looking in at the shop-windows of Broadway the whole forenoon,
flatting the flesh of my nose on the thick plate-glass,
780 Wandering the same afternoon with my face turn'd up to the clouds,
or down a lane or along the beach,
My right and left arms round the sides of two friends, and I in the
middle;
Coming home with the silent and dark-cheek'd bush-boy, (behind
me he rides at the drape of the day,)
Far from the settlements studying the print of animals' feet, or the
moccasin print,
By the cot in the hospital reaching lemonade to a feverish patient,
785 Nigh the coffin'd corpse when all is still, examining with a candle;
Voyaging to every port to dicker and adventure,
Hurrying with the modern crowd as eager and fickle as any,
Hot toward one I hate, ready in my madness to knife him,
Solitary at midnight in my back yard, my thoughts gone from me a
long while,
790 Walking the old hills of Judæa with the beautiful gentle God by my
side,
Speeding through space, speeding through heaven and the stars,
Speeding amid the seven satellites and the broad ring, and the
diameter of eighty thousand miles,
Speeding with tail'd meteors, throwing fire-balls like the rest,
Carrying the crescent child that carries its own full mother in its belly,
795 Storming, enjoying, planning, loving, cautioning,
Backing and filling, appearing and disappearing,
I tread day and night such roads.

I visit the orchards of spheres and look at the product,
And look at quintillions ripen'd and look at quintillions green.

800 I fly those flights of a fluid and swallowing soul,
My course runs below the soundings of plummets.

I help myself to material and immaterial,
No guard can shut me off, no law prevent me.

I anchor my ship for a little while only,
805 My messengers continually cruise away or bring their returns to me.

I go hunting polar furs and the seal, leaping chasms with a pike-
pointed staff, clinging to topples of brittle and blue.

I ascend to the foretruck,
I take my place late at night in the crow's-nest,
We sail the arctic sea, it is plenty light enough,
810 Through the clear atmosphere I stretch around on the wonderful
beauty,
The enormous masses of ice pass me and I pass them, the scenery is
plain in all directions,
The white-topt mountains show in the distance, I fling out my fancies
toward them,
We are approaching some great battle-field in which we are soon to
be engaged,
We pass the colossal outposts of the encampment, we pass with still
feet and caution,
815 Or we are entering by the suburbs some vast and ruin'd city,
The blocks and fallen architecture more than all the living cities of
the globe.

I am a free companion, I bivouac by invading watchfires,
I turn the bridegroom out of bed and stay with the bride myself, I
tighten her all night to my thighs and lips.

My voice is the wife's voice, the screech by the rail of the stairs,
820 They fetch my man's body up dripping and drown'd.

I understand the large hearts of heroes,
The courage of present times and all times,
How the skipper saw the crowded and rudderless wreck of the steam-
ship, and Death chasing it up and down the storm,
How he knuckled tight and gave not back an inch, and was faithful
of days and faithful of nights,
825 And chalk'd in large letters ln a board, *Be of good cheer, we will not
desert you*;
How he follow'd with them and tack'd with them three days and
would not give it up,
How he saved the drifting company at last,
How the lank loose-gown'd women look'd when boated from the
side of their prepared graves,
How the silent old-faced infants and the lifted sick, and the sharp-
lipp'd unshaven men;

830 All this I swallow, it tastes good, I like it well, it becomes mine,
I am the man, I suffer'd, I was there.

The disdain and calmness of martyrs,
The mother of old, condemn'd for a witch, burnt with dry wood, her
children gazing on,
The hounded slave that flags in the race, leans by the fence, blowing,
cover'd with sweat,
835 The twinges that sting like needles his legs and neck, the murderous
buckshot and the bullets,
All these I feel or am.

I am the hounded slave, I wince at the bite of the dogs,
Hell and despair are upon me, crack and again crack the marksmen,
I clutch the rails of the fence, my gore dribs, thinn'd with the ooze
of my skin,
840 I fall on the weeds and stones,
The riders spur their unwilling horses, haul close,
Taunt my dizzy ears and beat me violently over the head with whip-
stocks.

Agonies are one of my changes of garments,
I do not ask the wounded person how he feels, I myself become the
wounded person,
845 My hurts turn livid upon me as I lean on a cane and observe.

I am the mash'd fireman with breast-bone broken,
Tumbling walls buried me in their debris,
Heat and smoke I inspired, I heard the yelling shouts of my comrades
I heard the distant click of their picks and shovels,
850 They have clear'd the beams away, they tenderly lift me forth.

I lie in the night air in my red shirt, the pervading hush is for my
sake,
Painless after all I lie exhausted but not so unhappy,
White and beautiful are the faces around me, the heads are bared
of their fire-caps,
The kneeling crowd fades with the light of the torches.

855 Distant and dead resuscitate,
They show as the dial or move as the hands of me, I am the clock
myself.

I am an old artillerist, I tell of my fort's bombardment,
I am there again.

Again the long roll of the drummers,
860 Again the attacking cannon, mortars,
Again to my listening ears the cannon responsive.

I take part, I see and hear the whole,
The cries, curses, roar, the plaudits for well-aim'd shots,
The ambulanza slowly passing trailing its red drip,
865 Workmen searching after damages, making indispensable repairs,
The fall of grenades through the rent roof, the fan-shaped explosion,
The whizz of limbs, heads, stone, wood, iron, high in the air.

Again gurgles the mouth of my dying general, he furiously waves
with his hand,
He gasps through the clot *Mind not me—mind—the entrenchments.*

34

870 Now I tell what I knew in Texas in my early youth,
(I tell not the fall of Alamo,
Not one escaped to tell the fall of Alamo,
The hundred and fifty are dumb yet at Alamo,)
'Tis the tale of the murder in cold blood of four hundred and twelve
young men.

875 Retreating they had form'd in a hollow square with their baggage
for breastworks,
Nine hundred lives out of the surrounding enemy's, nine times their
number, was the price they took in advance,
Their colonel was wounded and their ammunition gone,
They treated for an honorable capitulation, receiv'd writing and seal,
gave up their arms and march'd back prisoners of war.

They were the glory of the race of rangers,
880 Matchless with horse, rifle, song, supper, courtship,
Large, turbulent, generous, handsome, proud, and affectionate,
Bearded, sunburnt, drest in the free costume of hunters,
Not a single one over thirty years of age.

The second First-day morning they were brought out in squads and
massacred, it was beautiful early summer,
885 The work commenced about five o'clock and was over by eight.

None obey'd the command to kneel,
Some made a mad and helpless rush, some stood stark and straight,
A few fell at once, shot in the temple or heart, the living and dead
　　lay together,
The maim'd and mangled dug in the dirt, the new-comers saw them
　　there,
890 Some half-kill'd attempted to crawl away,
These were dispatch'd with bayonets or batter'd with the blunts of
　　muskets,
A youth not seventeen years old seiz'd his assassin till two more came
　　to release him,
The three were all torn and cover'd with the boy's blood.

At eleven o'clock began the burning of the bodies;
895 That is the tale of the murder of the four hundred and twelve young
　　men.

35

Would you hear of an old-time sea-fight?
Would you learn who won by the light of the moon and stars?
List to the yarn, as my grandmother's father the sailor told it to me.

Our foe was no skulk in his ship I tell you, (said he,)
900 His was the surly English pluck, and there is no tougher or truer,
　　and never was, and never will be;
Along the lower'd eve he came horribly raking us.

We closed with him, the yards entangled, the cannon touch'd,
My captain lash'd fast with his own hands.

We had receiv'd some eighteen pound shots under the water,
905 On our lower-gun-deck two large pieces had burst at the first fire,
　　killing all around and blowing up overhead.

Fighting at sun-down, fighting at dark,
Ten o'clock at night, the full moon well up, our leaks on the gain,
　　and five feet of water reported,
The master-at-arms loosing the prisoners confined in the after-hold
　　to give them a chance for themselves.

The transit to and from the magazine is now stopt by the sentinels,
910 They see so many strange faces they do not know whom to trust.

Our frigate takes fire,
The other asks if we demand quarter?
If our colors are struck and the fighting done?

Now I laugh content, for I hear the voice of my little captain,
915 *We have not struck*, he composedly cries, *we have just begun our part of the fighting.*

Only three guns are in use,
One is directed by the captain himself against the enemy's mainmast,
Two well serv'd with grape and canister silence his musketry and clear his decks.

The tops alone second the fire of this little battery, especially the main-top,
920 They hold out bravely during the whole of the action.

Not a moment's cease,
The leaks gain fast on the pumps, the fire eats toward the powder-magazine.

One of the pumps has been shot away, it is generally thought we are sinking.

Serene stands the little captain,
925 He is not hurried, his voice is neither high nor low,
His eyes give more light to us than our battle-lanterns.

Toward twelve there in the beams of the moon they surrender to us.

36

Stretch'd and still lies the midnight,
Two great hulls motionless on the breast of the darkness,
930 Our vessel riddled and slowly sinking, preparations to pass to the one we have conquer'd,
The captain on the quarter-deck coldly giving his orders through a countenance white as a sheet,
Near by the corpse of the child that serv'd in the cabin,
The dead face of an old salt with long white hair and carefully curl'd whiskers,
The flames spite of all that can be done flickering aloft and below,
935 The husky voices of the two or three officers yet fit for duty,

Formless stacks of bodies and bodies by themselves, dabs of flesh
    upon the masts and spars,
Cut of cordage, dangle of rigging, slight shock of the soothe of waves,
Black and impassive guns, litter of powder-parcels, strong scent,
A few large stars overhead, silent and mournful shining,
940 Delicate sniffs of sea-breeze, smells of sedgy grass and fields by the
    shore, death-messages given in charge to survivors,
The hiss of the surgeon's knife, the gnawing teeth of his saw
Wheeze, cluck, swash of falling blood, short wild scream, and long,
    dull, tapering groan,
These so, these irretrievable.

37

You laggards there on guard! look to your arms!
945 In at the conquer'd doors they crowd! I am possess'd!
Embody all presences outlaw'd or suffering,
See myself in prison shaped like another man,
And feel the dull unintermitted pain.

For me the keepers of convicts shoulder their carbines and keep watch,
950 It is I let out in the morning and barr'd at night.

Not a mutineer walks handcuff'd to jail but I am handcuff'd to him
    and walk by his side,
(I am less the jolly one there, and more the silent one with sweat on
    my twitching lips.)

Not a youngster is taken for larceny but I go up too, and am tried
    and sentenced.

Not a cholera patient lies at the last gasp but I also lie at the last gasp,
955 My face is ash-color'd, my sinews gnarl, away from me people retreat.

Askers embody themselves in me and I am embodied in them,
I project my hat, sit shame-faced, and beg.

38

Enough! enough! enough!
Somehow I have been stunn'd. Stand back!
960 Give me a little time beyond my cuff'd head, slumbers, dreams,
    gaping,
I discover myself on the verge of a usual mistake.

That I could forget the mockers and insults!
That I could forget the trickling tears and the blows of the bludgeons
and hammers!
That I could look with a separate look on my own crucifixion and
bloody crowning.

965 I remember now,
I resume the overstaid fraction,
The grave of rock multiplies what has been confided to it, or to any
graves,
Corpses rise, gashes heal, fastenings roll from me.

I troop forth replenish'd with supreme power, one of an average
unending procession,
970 Inland and sea-coast we go, and pass all boundary lines,
Our swift ordinances on their way over the whole earth,
The blossoms we wear in our hats the growth of thousands of years.

Eleves, I salute you! come forward!
Continue your annotations, continue your questionings.

39

975 The friendly and flowing savage, who is he?
Is he waiting for civilization, or past it and mastering it?

Is he some Southwesterner rais'd out-doors? is he Kanadian?
Is he from the Mississippi country? Iowa, Oregon, California?
The mountains? prairie-life, bush-life? or sailor from the sea?

980 Wherever he goes men and women accept and desire him,
They desire he should like them, touch them, speak to them, stay
with them.

Behavior lawless as snow-flakes, words simple as grass, uncomb'd
head, laughter, and naiveté,
Slow-stepping feet, common features, common modes and emanations,
They descend in new forms from the tips of his fingers,
985 They are wafted with the odor of his body or breath, they fly out of
the glance of his eyes.

40

Flaunt of the sunshine I need not your bask—lie over!
You light surfaces only, I force surfaces and depths also.

Earth! you seem to look for something at my hands,
Say, old top-knot, what do you want?

990 Man or woman, I might tell how I like you, but cannot,
And might tell what it is in me and what it is in you, but cannot,
And might tell that pining I have, that pulse of my nights and days.

Behold, I do not give lectures or a little charity,
When I give I give myself.

995 You there, impotent, loose in the knees,
Open your scarf'd chops till I blow grit within you,
Spread your palms and lift the flaps of your pockets,
I am not to be denied, I compel, I have stores plenty and to spare,
And any thing I have I bestow.

1000 I do not ask who you are, that is not important to me,   -
You can do nothing and be nothing but what I will infold you.

To cotton-field drudge or cleaner of privies I lean,
On his right cheek I put the family kiss,
And in my soul I swear I never will deny him.

1005 On women fit for conception I start bigger and nimbler babes,
(This day I am jetting the stuff of far more arrogant republics.)

To any one dying, thither I speed and twist the knob of the door,
Turn the bed-clothes toward the foot of the bed,
Let the physician and the priest go home.

1010 I seize the descending man and raise him with resistless will,
O despairer, here is my neck,
By God, you shall not go down! hang your whole weight upon me.

I dilate you with tremendous breath, I buoy you up,
Every room of the house do I fill with an arm'd force,
1015 Lovers of me, bafflers of graves.

Sleep—I and they keep guard all night,
Not doubt, not decease shall dare to lay finger upon you,
I have embraced you, and henceforth possess you to myself,
And when you rise in the morning you will find what I tell you is so.

41

1020 I am he bringing help for the sick as they pant on their backs.
And for strong upright men I bring yet more needed help.

I heard what was said of the universe,
Heard it and heard it of several thousand years;
It is middling well as far as it goes—but is that all?

1025 Magnifying and applying come I,
Outbidding at the start the old cautious hucksters,
Taking myself the exact dimensions of Jehovah,
Lithographing Kronos, Zeus his son, and Hercules his grandson,
Buying drafts of Osiris, Isis, Belus, Brahma, Buddha,
1030 In my portfolio placing Manito loose, Allah on a leaf, the crucifix
engraved,
With Odin and the hideous-faced Mexitli and every idol and image,
Taking them all for what they are worth and not a cent more,
Admitting they were alive and did the work of their days,
(They bore mites as for unfledg'd birds who have now to rise and fly
and sing for themselves,)
1035 Accepting the rough deific sketches to fill out better in myself,
bestowing them freely on each man and woman I see,
Discovering as much or more in a framer framing a house,
Putting higher claims for him there with his roll'd-up sleeves driving
the mallet and chisel,
Not objecting to special revelations, considering a curl of smoke or a
hair on the back of my hand just as curious as any revelation;
Lads ahold of fire-engines and hook-and-ladder ropes no less to me
than the gods of the antique wars,
1040 Minding their voices peal through the crash of destruction,
Their brawny limbs passing safe over charr'd laths, their white fore-
heads whole and unhurt out of the flames;
By the mechanic's wife with her babe at her nipple interceding for
every person born,
Three scythes at harvest whizzing in a row from three lusty angels
with shirts bagg'd out at their waists,

The snag-tooth'd hostler with red hair redeeming sins past and to come,

1045 Selling all he possesses, traveling on foot to fee lawyers for his brother and sit by him while he is tried for forgery;

What was strewn in the amplest strewing the square rod about me, and not filling the square rod then,

The bull and the bug never worshipp'd half enough,

Dung and dirt more admirable than was dream'd,

The supernatural of no account, myself waiting my time to be one of the supremes,

1050 The day getting ready for me when I shall do as much good as the best, and be as prodigious;

By my life-lumps! becoming already a creator,

Putting myself here and now to the ambush'd womb of the shadows.

42

A call in the midst of the crowd,

My own voice, orotund sweeping and final.

1055 Come my children,

Come my boys and girls, my women, household and intimates,

Now the performer launches his nerve, he has pass'd his prelude on the reeds within.

Easily written loose-finger'd chords—I feel the thrum of your climax and close.

My head slues round on my neck,

1060 Music rolls, but not from the organ,

Folks are around me, but they are no household of mine.

Ever the hard unsunk ground,

Ever the eaters and drinkers, ever the upward and downward sun, ever the air and the ceaseless tides,

Ever myself and my neighbors, refreshing, wicked, real,

1065 Ever the old inexplicable query, ever that thorn'd thumb, that breath of itches and thirsts,

Ever the vexer's *hoot! hoot!* till we find where the sly one hides and bring him forth,

Ever love, ever the sobbing liquid of life,

Ever the bandage under the chin, ever the trestles of death.

Here and there with dimes on the eyes walking,
1070 To feed the greed of the belly the brains liberally spooning,
Tickets buying, taking, selling, but in to the feast never once going,
Many sweating, ploughing, thrashing, and then the chaff for payment receiving,
A few idly owning, and they the wheat continually claiming.

This is the city and I am one of the citizens,
1075 Whatever interests the rest interests me, politics, wars, markets, newspapers, schools,
The mayor and councils, banks, tariffs, steamships, factories, stocks, stores, real estate and personal estate.

The little plentiful manikins skipping around in collars and tail'd coats,
I am aware who they are, (they are positively not worms or fleas,)
I acknowledge the duplicates of myself, the weakest and shallowest is deathless with me,
1080 What I do and say the same waits for them,
Every thought that flounders in me the same flounders in them.

I know perfectly well my own egotism,
Know my omnivorous lines and must not write any less,
And would fetch you whoever you are flush with myself.

1085 Not words of routine this song of mine,
But abruptly to question, to leap beyond yet nearer bring;
This printed and bound book—but the printer and the printing-office boy?
The well-taken photographs—but your wife or friend close and solid in your arms?
The black ship mail'd with iron, her mighty guns in her turrets— but the pluck of the captain and engineers?
1090 In the houses the dishes and fare and furniture—but the host and hostess, and the look out of their eyes?
The sky up there—yet here or next door, or across the way?
The saints and sages in history—but you yourself?
Sermons, creeds, theology—but the fathomless human brain,
And what is reason? and what is love? and what is life?

43

1095 I do not despise you priests, all time, the world over,
My faith is the greatest of faiths and the least of faiths,

Enclosing worship ancient and modern and all between ancient and
modern,
Believing I shall come again upon the earth after five thousand years,
Waiting responses from oracles, honoring the gods, saluting the sun,
1100 Making a fetish of the first rock or stump, powowing with sticks in
the circle of obis,
Helping the lama or brahmin as he trims the lamps of the idols,
Dancing yet through the streets in a phallic procession, rapt and
austere in the woods a gymnosophist,
Drinking mead from the skull-cap, to Shastas and Vedas admirant,
minding the Koran,
Walking the teokallis, spotted with gore from the stone and knife,
beating the serpent-skin drum,
1105 Accepting the Gospels, accepting him that was crucified, knowing
assuredly that he is divine,
To the mass kneeling or the puritan's prayer rising, or sitting patiently
in a pew,
Ranting and frothing in my insane crisis, or waiting dead-like till
my spirit arouses me,
Looking forth on pavement and land, or outside of pavement and
land,
Belonging to the winders of the circuit of circuits.

1110 One of that centripetal and centrifugal gang I turn and talk like a
man leaving charges before a journey.

Down-hearted doubters dull and excluded,
Frivolous, sullen, moping, angry, affected, dishearten'd, atheistical,
I know every one of you, I know the sea of torment, doubt, despair
and unbelief.

How the flukes splash!
1115 How they contort rapid as lightning, with spasms and spouts of
blood!

Be at peace bloody flukes of doubters and sullen mopers,
I take my place among you as much as among any,
The past is the push of you, me, all, precisely the same,
And what is yet untried and afterward is for you, me, all, precisely
the same.

1120 I do not know what is untried and afterward,
But I know it will in its turn prove sufficient, and cannot fail.

Each who passes is consider'd, each who stops is consider'd, not a single one can it fail.

It cannot fail the young man who died and was buried,
Nor the young woman who died and was put by his side,
1125 Nor the little child that peep'd in at the door, and then drew back and was never seen again,
Nor the old man who has lived without purpose, and feels it with bitterness worse than gall,
Nor him in the poor house tubercled by rum and the bad disorder.
Nor the numberless slaughter'd and wreck'd, nor the brutish koboo call'd the ordure of humanity,
Nor the sacs merely floating with open mouths for food to slip in,
1130 Nor any thing in the earth, or down in the oldest graves of the earth,
Nor any thing in the myriads of spheres, nor the myriads of myriads that inhabit them,
Nor the present, nor the least wisp that is known.

44

It is time to explain myself—let us stand up.

What is known I strip away,
1135 I launch all men and women forward with me into the Unknown.

The clock indicates the moment—but what does eternity indicate?

We have thus far exhausted trillions of winters and summers,
There are trillions ahead, and trillions ahead of them.

Births have brought us richness and variety,
1140 And other births will bring us richness and variety.

I do not call one greater and one smaller,
That which fills its period and place is equal to any.

Were mankind murderous or jealous upon you, my brother, my sister?
I am sorry for you, they are not murderous or jealous upon me,
1145 All has been gentle with me, I keep no account with lamentation,
(What have I to do with lamentation?)

I am an acme of things accomplish'd, and I an encloser of things to be.

My feet strike an apex of the apices of the stairs,
On every step bunches of ages, and larger bunches between the steps,
1150 All below duly travel'd, and still I mount and mount.

Rise after rise bow the phantoms behind me,
Afar down I see the huge first Nothing, I know I was even there,
I waited unseen and always, and slept through the lethargic mist,
And took my time, and took no hurt from the fetid carbon.

1155 Long I was hugg'd close—long and long.

Immense have been the preparations for me,
Faithful and friendly the arms that have help'd me.

Cycles ferried my cradle, rowing and rowing like cheerful boatmen,
For room to me stars kept aside in their own rings,
1160 They sent influences to look after what was to hold me.

Before I was born out of my mother generations guided me,
My embryo has never been torpid, nothing could overlay it.

For it the nebula cohered to an orb,
The long slow strata piled to rest it on,
1165 Vast vegetables gave it sustenance,
Monstrous sauroids transported it in their mouths and deposited it
    with care.

All forces have been steadily employ'd to complete and delight me,
Now on this spot I stand with my robust soul.

45

O span of youth! ever-push'd elasticity!
1170 O manhood, balanced, florid and full.

My lovers suffocate me,
Crowding my lips, thick in the pores of my skin,
Jostling me through streets and public halls, coming naked to me
    at night,
Crying by day *Ahoy!* from the rocks of the river, swinging and
    chirping over my head,
1175 Calling my name from flower-beds, vines, tangled underbrush,
Lighting on every moment of my life,

Bussing my body with soft balsamic busses,
Noiselessly passing handfuls out of their hearts and giving them to
be mine.

Old age superbly rising! O welcome, ineffable grace of dying days!

1180 Every condition promulges not only itself, it promulges what grows
after and out of itself,
And the dark hush promulges as much as any.

I open my scuttle at night and see the far-sprinkled systems,
And all I see multiplied as high as I can cipher edge but the rim of
the farther systems.

Wider and wider they spread, expanding, always expanding,
1185 Outward and outward and forever outward.

My sun has his sun and round him obediently wheels,
He joins with his partners a group of superior circuit,
And greater sets follow, making specks of the greatest inside them.

There is no stoppage and never can be stoppage,
1190 If I, you, and the worlds, and all beneath or upon their surfaces,
were this moment reduced back to a pallid float, it would not
avail in the long run,
We should surely bring up again where we now stand,
And surely go as much farther, and then farther and farther.

A few quadrillions of eras, a few octillions of cubic leagues, do not
hazard the span or make it impatient,
They are but parts, any thing is but a part.

1195 See ever so far, there is limitless space outside of that,
Count ever so much, there is limitless time around that.

My rendezvous is appointed, it is certain,
The Lord will be there and wait till I come on perfect terms,
The great Camerado, the lover true for whom I pine will be there.

46

1200 I know I have the best of time and space, and was never measured
and never will be measured.

I tramp a perpetual journey, (come listen all!)
My signs are a rain-proof coat, good shoes, and a staff cut from the
    woods,
No friend of mine takes his ease in my chair,
I have no chair, no church, no philosophy,
1205 I lead no man to a dinner-table, library, exchange,
But each man and each woman of you I lead upon a knoll,
My left hand hooking you round the waist,
My right hand pointing to landscapes of continents and the public
    road.

Not I, not any one else can travel that road for you,
1210 You must travel it for yourself.

It is not far, it is within reach,
Perhaps you have been on it since you were born and did not know,
Perhaps it is everywhere on water and on land.

Shoulder your duds dear son, and I will mine, and let us hasten forth,
1215 Wonderful cities and free nations we shall fetch as we go.

If you tire, give me both burdens, and rest the chuff of your hand on
    my hip,
And in due time you shall repay the same service to me,
For after we start we never lie by again.

This day before dawn I ascended a hill and look'd at the crowded
    heaven,
1220 And I said to my spirit *When we become the enfolders of those orbs, and the
    pleasure and knowledge of every thing in them, shall we be fill'd and
    satisfied then?*
And my spirit said *No, we but level that lift to pass and continue beyond.*

You are also asking me questions and I hear you,
I answer that I cannot answer, you must find out for yourself.

Sit a while dear son,
1225 Here are biscuits to eat and here is milk to drink,
But as soon as you sleep and renew yourself in sweet clothes, I kiss
    you with a good-by kiss and open the gate for your egress hence.

Long enough have you dream'd contemptible dreams,
Now I wash the gum from your eyes,

You must habit yourself to the dazzle of the light and of every moment
of your life.

1230 Long have you timidly waded holding a plank by the shore,
Now I will you to be a bold swimmer,
To jump off in the midst of the sea, rise again, nod to me, shout, and
laughingly dash with your hair.

47

I am the teacher of athletes,
He that by me spreads a wider breast than my own proves the width
of my own,
1235 He most honors my style who learns under it to destroy the teacher.

The boy I love, the same becomes a man not through derived power,
but in his own right,
Wicked rather than virtuous out of conformity or fear,
Fond of his sweetheart, relishing well his steak,
Unrequited love or a slight cutting him worse than sharp steel cuts,
1240 First-rate to ride, to fight, to hit the bull's eye, to sail a skiff, to sing
a song or play on the banjo,
Preferring scars and the beard and faces pitted with small-pox over
all latherers,
And those well-tann'd to those that keep out of the sun.

I teach straying from me, yet who can stray from me?
I follow you whoever you are from the present hour,
1245 My words itch at your ears till you understand them.

I do not say these things for a dollar or to fill up the time while I wait
for a boat,
(It is you talking just as much as myself, I act as the tongue of you,
Tied in your mouth, in mine it begins to be loosen'd.)

I swear I will never again mention love or death inside a house,
1250 And I swear I will never translate myself at all, only to him or her
who privately stays with me in the open air.

If you would understand me go to the heights or water-shore,
The nearest gnat is an explanation, and a drop or motion of waves a
key,
The maul, the oar, the hand-saw, second my words.

No shutter'd room or school can commune with me,
255 But roughs and little children better than they.

The young mechanic is closest to me, he knows me well,
The woodman that takes his axe and jug with him shall take me with
    him all day,
The farm-boy ploughing in the field feels good at the sound of my
    voice,
In vessels that sail my words sail, I go with fishermen and seamen
    and love them.

260 The soldier camp'd or upon the march is mine,
On the night ere the pending battle many seek me, and I do not fail
    them,
On that solemn night (it may be their last) those that know me seek
    me.

My face rubs to the hunter's face when he lies down alone in his
    blanket,
The driver thinking of me does not mind the jolt of his wagon,
265 The young mother and old mother comprehend me,
The girl and the wife rest the needle a moment and forget where they
    are,
They and all would resume what I have told them.

48

I have said that the soul is not more than the body,
And I have said that the body is not more than the soul,
270 And nothing, not God, is greater to one than one's self is,
And whoever walks a furlong without sympathy walks to his own
    funeral drest in his shroud,
And I or you pocketless of a dime may purchase the pick of the earth,
And to glance with an eye or show a bean in its pod confounds the
    learning of all times,
And there is no trade or employment but the young man following
    it may become a hero,
275 And there is no object so soft but it makes a hub for the wheel'd
    universe,
And I say to any man or woman, Let your soul stand cool and com-
    posed before a million universes.

And I say to mankind, Be not curious about God,
For I who am curious about each am not curious about God,

(No array of terms can say how much I am at peace about God and about death.)

1280 I hear and behold God in every object, yet understand God not in the least,
Nor do I understand who there can be more wonderful than myself.

Why should I wish to see God better than this day?
I see something of God each hour of the twenty-four, and each moment then,
In the faces of men and women I see God, and in my own face in the glass,
1285 I find letters from God dropt in the street. and every one is sign'd by God's name,
And I leave them where they are, for I know that wheresoe'er I go,
Others will punctually come for ever and ever.

49

And as to you Death, and you bitter hug of mortality, it is idle to try to alarm me.

To his work without flinching the accoucheur comes,
1290 I see the elder-hand pressing receiving supporting,
I recline by the sills of the exquisite flexible doors,
And mark the outlet, and mark the relief and escape.

And as to you Corpse I think you are good manure, but that does not offend me,
I smell the white roses sweet-scented and growing,
1295 I reach to the leafy lips, I reach to the polish'd breasts of melons.

And as to you Life I reckon you are the leavings of many deaths,
(No doubt I have died myself ten thousand times before.)

I hear you whispering there O stars of heaven,
O suns—O grass of graves—O perpetual transfers and promotions,
1300 If you do not say any thing how can I say any thing?

Of the turbid pool that lies in the autumn forest,
Of the moon that descends the steeps of the soughing twilight,
Toss, sparkles of day and dusk—toss on the black stems that decay in the muck,
Toss to the moaning gibberish of the dry limbs.

1305 I ascend from the moon, I ascend from the night,
    I perceive that the ghastly glimmer is noonday sunbeams reflected,
    And debouch to the steady and central from the offspring great or
        small.

50

    There is that in me—I do not know what it is—but I know it is in
        me.

    Wrench'd and sweaty—calm and cool then my body becomes,
1310 I sleep—I sleep long.

    I do not know it—it is without name—it is a word unsaid,
    It is not in any dictionary, utterance, symbol.

    Something it swings on more than the earth I swing on,
    To it the creation is the friend whose embracing awakes me.

1315 Perhaps I might tell more. Outlines! I plead for my brothers and
        sisters.

    Do you see O my brothers and sisters?
    It is not chaos or death—it is form, union, plan—it is eternal life—
        it is Happiness.

51

    The past and present wilt—I have fill'd them, emptied them,
    And proceed to fill my next fold of the future.

1320 Listener up there! what have you to confide to me?
    Look in my face while I snuff the sidle of evening,
    (Talk honestly, no one else hears you, and I stay only a minute
        longer.)

    Do I contradict myself?
    Very well then I contradict myself,
1325 (I am large, I contain multitudes.)

    I concentrate toward them that are nigh, I wait on the door-slab.

Who has done his day's work? who will soonest be through with his
    supper?
Who wishes to walk with me?

Will you speak before I am gone? will you prove already too late?

52

1330 The spotted hawk swoops by and accuses me, he complains of my
    gab and my loitering.

I too am not a bit tamed, I too am untranslatable,
I sound my barbaric yawp over the roofs of the world.

The last scud of day holds back for me,
It flings my likeness after the rest and true as any on the shadow'd
    wilds,
1335 It coaxes me to the vapor and the dusk.

I depart as air, I shake my white locks at the runaway sun,
I effuse my flesh in eddies, and drift it in lacy jags.

I bequeath myself to the dirt to grow from the grass I love,
If you want me again look for me under your boot-soles.

1340 You will hardly know who I am or what I mean,
But I shall be good health to you nevertheless,
And filter and fibre your blood.

Failing to fetch me at first keep encouraged,
Missing me one place search another,
1345 I stop somewhere waiting for you.

OUT OF THE CRADLE ENDLESSLY ROCKING

Out of the cradle endlessly rocking,
Out of the mocking-bird's throat, the musical shuttle,
Out of the Ninth-month midnight,
Over the sterile sands and the fields beyond, where the child leaving
    his bed wander'd alone, bareheaded, barefoot,
5 Down from the shower'd halo,

Up from the mystic play of shadows twining and twisting as if they
    were alive,
Out from the patches of briers and blackberries,
From the memories of the bird that chanted to me,
From your memories sad brother, from the fitful risings and fallings
    I heard,
10 From under that yellow half-moon late-risen and swollen as if with
    tears,
From those beginning notes of yearning and love there in the mist,
From the thousand responses of my heart never to cease,
From the myriad thence-arous'd words,
From the word stronger and more delicious than any,
15 From such as now they start the scene revisiting,
As a flock, twittering, rising, or overhead passing,
Borne hither, ere all eludes me, hurriedly,
A man, yet by these tears a little boy again,
Throwing myself on the sand, confronting the waves,
20 I, chanter of pains and joys, uniter of here and hereafter,
Taking all hints to use them, but swiftly leaping beyond them.
A reminiscence sing.

Once Paumanok,
When the lilac-scent was in the air and Fifth-month grass was
    growing,
25 Up this seashore in some briers,
Two feather'd guests from Alabama, two together,
And their nest, and four light-green eggs spotted with brown,
And every day the he-bird to and fro near at hand,
And every day the she-bird crouch'd on her nest, silent, with bright
    eyes,
30 And every day I, a curious boy, never too close, never disturbing them,
Cautiously peering, absorbing, translating.

Shine ! shine ! shine !
Pour down your warmth, great sun!
While we bask, we two together.

35 *Two together!*
Winds blow south, or winds blow north,
Day come white, or night come black,
Home, or rivers and mountains from home,
Singing all time, minding no time,
40 *While we two keep together.*

Till of a sudden,
May-be kill'd, unknown to her mate,
One forenoon the she-bird crouch'd not on the nest,
Nor return'd that afternoon, nor the next
45 Nor ever appear'd again.

And thenceforward all summer in the sound of the sea,
And at night under the full of the moon in calmer weather,
Over the hoarse surging of the sea,
Or flitting from brier to brier by day,
50 I saw, I heard at intervals the remaining one, the he-bird,
The solitary guest from Alabama.

Blow ! blow ! blow !
Blow up sea-winds along Paumanok's shore;
I wait and I wait till you blow my mate to me.

55 Yes, when the stars glisten'd,
All night long on the prong of a moss-scallop'd stake,
Down almost amid the slapping waves,
Sat the lone singer wonderful causing tears.

He call'd on his mate,
60 He pour'd forth the meanings which I of all men know.

Yes my brother I know,
The rest might not, but I have treasur'd every note,
For more than once dimly down to the beach gliding,
Silent, avoiding the moonbeams, blending myself with the shadows,
65 Recalling now the obscure shapes, the echoes, the sounds and sights
    after their sorts,
The white arms out in the breakers tirelessly tossing,
I, with bare feet, a child, the wind wafting my hair,
Listen'd long and long.

Listen'd to keep, to sing, now translating the notes,
70 Following you my brother.

Soothe ! soothe ! soothe !
Close on its wave soothes the wave behind,
And again another behind embracing and lapping, every one close,
But my love soothes not me, not me.

75 *Low hangs the moon, it rose late,*
It is lagging—O I think it is heavy with love, with love.

O madly the sea pushes upon the land,
With love, with love.

O night! do I not see my love fluttering out among the breakers?
80 *What is that little black thing I see there in the white?*

Loud! loud! loud!
Loud I call to you, my love!

High and clear I shoot my voice over the waves,
Surely you must know who is here, is here,
85 *You must know who I am, my love.*

Low-hanging moon!
What is that dusky spot in your brown yellow?
O it is the shape, the shape of my mate!
O moon do not keep her from me any longer.

90 *Land! land! O land!*
Whichever way I turn, O I think you could give me my mate back again if you
    only would,
For I am almost sure I see her dimly whichever way I look.

O rising stars!
Perhaps the one I want so much will rise, will rise with some of you.

95 *O throat! O trembling throat!*
Sound clearer through the atmosphere!
Pierce the woods, the earth,
Somewhere listening to catch you must be the one I want.

Shake out carols!
100 *Solitary here, the night's carols!*
Carols of lonesome love! death's carols!
Carols under that lagging, yellow, waning moon!
O under that moon where she droops almost down into the sea!
O reckless despairing carols.

105 *But soft! sink low!*
Soft! let me just murmur,

And do you wait a moment you husky-nois'd sea,
For somewhere I believe I heard my mate responding to me,
So faint, I must be still, be still to listen,
110 *But not altogether still, for then she might not come immediately to me.*

Hither my love!
Here I am! here!
With this just-sustain'd note, I announce myself to you,
This gentle call is for you my love, for you.

115 *Do not be decoy'd elsewhere,*
That is the whistle of the wind, it is not my voice,
That is the fluttering, the fluttering of the spray,
Those are the shadows of leaves.

O darkness! O in vain!
120 *O I am very sick and sorrowful.*

O brown halo in the sky near the moon, drooping upon the sea!
O troubled reflection in the sea!
O throat! O throbbing heart!
And I singing uselessly, uselessly all the night.

125 *O past! O happy life! O songs of joy!*
In the air, in the woods, over fields,
Loved! loved! loved! loved! loved!
But my mate no more, no more with me!
We two together no more.

130 The aria sinking,
All else continuing, the stars shining,
The winds blowing, the notes of the bird continuous echoing,
With angry moans the fierce old mother incessantly moaning,
On the sands of Paumanok's shore gray and rustling,
135 The yellow half-moon enlarged, sagging down, drooping, the face of
the sea almost touching,
The boy ecstatic, with his bare feet the waves, with his hair the
atmosphere dallying,
The love in the heart long pent, now loose, now at last tumultuously
bursting,
The aria's meaning, the ears, the soul, swiftly depositing,
The strange tears down the cheeks coursing,
140 The colloquy there, the trio, each uttering,

The undertone, the savage old mother incessantly crying,
To the boy's soul's questions sullenly timing, some drown'd secret
    hissing,
To the outsetting bard.

Demon or bird! (said the boy's soul,)
145 Is it indeed toward your mate you sing? or is it really to me?
For I, that was a child, my tongue's use sleeping, now I have heard
    you,
Now in a moment I know what I am for, I awake,
And already a thousand singers, a thousand songs, clearer, louder
    and more sorrowful than yours,
A thousand warbling echoes have started to life within me, never
    to die.

150 O you singer solitary, singing by yourself, projecting me,
O solitary me listening, never more shall I cease perpetuating you,
Never more shall I escape, never more the reverberations,
Never more the cries of unsatisfied love be absent from me,
Never again leave me to be the peaceful child I was before what there
    in the night,
155 By the sea under the yellow and sagging moon,
The messenger there arous'd, the fire, the sweet hell within,
The unknown want, the destiny of me.

O give me the clew! (it lurks in the night here somewhere,)
O if I am to have so much, let me have more!

160 A word then, (for I will conquer it,)
The word final, superior to all,
Subtle, sent up—what is it?—I listen;
Are you whispering it, and have been all the time, you sea-waves?
Is that it from your liquid rims and wet sands?

165 Whereto answering, the sea,
Delaying not, hurrying not,
Whisper'd me through the night, and very plainly before daybreak,
Lisp'd to me the low and delicious word death,
And again death, death, death, death,
170 Hissing melodious, neither like the bird nor like my arous'd child's
    heart,
But edging near as privately for me rustling at my feet,

Creeping thence steadily up to my ears and laving me softly all over,
Death, death, death, death, death.

Which I do not forget,
175 But fuse the song of my dusky demon and brother,
That he sang to me in the moonlight on Paumanok's gray beach,
With the thousand responsive songs at random,
My own songs awakened from that hour,
And with them the key, the word up from the waves,
180 The word of the sweetest song and all songs,
That strong and delicious word which, creeping to my feet,
(Or like some old crone rocking the cradle, swathed in sweet gar-
ments, bending aside,)
The sea whisper'd me.

From CHILDREN OF ADAM

TO THE GARDEN THE WORLD

To the garden the world anew ascending,
Potent mates, daughters, sons, preluding,
The love, the life of their bodies, meaning and being,
Curious here behold my resurrection after slumber,
5 The revolving cycles in their wide sweep having brought me again,
Amorous, mature, all beautiful to me, all wondrous,
My limbs and the quivering fire that ever plays through them, for
reasons, most wondrous,
Existing I peer and penetrate still,
Content with the present, content with the past,
10 By my side or back of me Eve following,
Or in front, and I following her just the same.

AS ADAM EARLY IN THE MORNING

As Adam early in the morning,
Walking forth from the bower refresh'd with sleep,
Behold me where I pass, hear my voice, approach,
Touch me, touch the palm of your hand to my body as I pass,
5 Be not afraid of my body.

WHITMAN

From CALAMUS

IN PATHS UNTRODDEN

In paths untrodden,
In the growth by margins of pond-waters,
Escaped from the life that exhibits itself,
From all the standards hitherto publish'd, from the pleasures, profits,
    conformities,
5 Which too long I was offering to feed my soul,
Clear to me now standards not yet publish'd, clear to me that my
    soul,
That the soul of the man I speak for rejoices in comrades,
Here by myself away from the clank of the world,
Tallying and talk'd to here by tongues aromatic,
10 No longer abash'd, (for in this secluded spot I can respond as I would
    not dare elsewhere,)
Strong upon me the life that does not exhibit itself, yet contains all
    the rest,
Resolv'd to sing no songs to-day but those of manly attachment,
Projecting them along that substantial life,
Bequeathing hence types of athletic love,
15 Afternoon this delicious Ninth-month in my forty-first year,
I proceed for all who are or have been young men,
To tell the secret of my nights and days,
To celebrate the need of comrades.

I SAW IN LOUISIANA A LIVE-OAK GROWING

I saw in Louisiana a live-oak growing,
All alone stood it and the moss hung down from the branches,
Without any companion it grew there uttering joyous leaves of dark
    green,
And its look, rude, unbending, lusty, made me think of myself,
5 But I wonder'd how it could utter joyous leaves standing alone there
    without its friend near, for I knew I could not,
And I broke off a twig with a certain number of leaves upon it, and
    twined around it a little moss,
And brought it away, and I have placed it in sight in my room,
It is not needed to remind me as of my own dear friends,
(For I believe lately I think of little else than of them,)
10 Yet it remains to me a curious token, it makes me think of manly
    love;

For all that, and though the live-oak glistens there in Louisiana
  solitary in a wide flat space,
Uttering joyous leaves all its life without a friend a lover near,
I know very well I could not.

CAVALRY CROSSING A FORD

A line in long array where they wind betwixt green islands,
They take a serpentine course, their arms flash in the sun—hark to
  the musical clank,
Behold the silvery river, in it the splashing horses loitering stop to
  drink,
Behold the brown-faced men, each group, each person, a picture,
  the negligent rest on the saddles,
5 Some emerge on the opposite bank, others are just entering the ford—
  while,
Scarlet and blue and snowy white,
The guidon flags flutter gayly in the wind.

VIGIL STRANGE I KEPT ON THE FIELD ONE NIGHT

Vigil strange I kept on the field one night;
When you my son and my comrade dropt at my side that day,
One look I but gave which your dear eyes return'd with a look I
  shall never forget,
One touch of your hand to mine O boy, reach'd up as you lay on
  the ground,
5 Then onward I sped in the battle, the even-contested battle,
Till late in the night reliev'd to the place at last again I made my
  way,
Found you in death so cold dear comrade, found your body son of
  responding kisses, (never again on earth responding,)
Bared your face in the starlight, curious the scene, cool blew the
  moderate night-wind,
Long there and then in vigil I stood, dimly around me the battle-
  field spreading,
10 Vigil wondrous and vigil sweet there in the fragrant silent night,
But not a tear fell, not even a long-drawn sigh, long, long I gazed,
Then on the earth partially reclining sat by your side leaning my
  chin in my hands,
Passing sweet hours, immortal and mystic hours with you dearest
  comrade—not a tear, not a word,

Vigil of silence, love and death, vigil for you my son and my soldier,
15 As onward silently stars aloft, eastward new ones upward stole,
Vigil final for you brave boy, (I could not save you, swift was your death,
I faithfully loved you and cared for you living, I think we shall surely meet again,)
Till at latest lingering of the night, indeed just as the dawn appear'd,
My comrade I wrapt in his blanket, envelop'd well his form,
20 Folded the blanket well, tucking it carefully over head and carefully under feet,
And there and then and bathed by the rising sun, my son in his grave, in his rude-dug grave I deposited,
Ending my vigil strange with that, vigil of night and battle-field dim,
Vigil for boy of responding kisses, (never again on earth responding,)
Vigil for comrade swiftly slain, vigil I never forget, how as day brighten'd,
25 I rose from the chill ground and folded my soldier well in his blanket,
And buried him where he fell.

SPARKLES FROM THE WHEEL

Where the city's ceaseless crowd moves on the livelong day,
Withdrawn I join a group of children watching, I pause aside with them.

By the curb toward the edge of the flagging,
A knife-grinder works at his wheel sharpening a great knife,
5 Bending over he carefully holds it to the stone, by foot and knee,
With measur'd tread he turns rapidly, as he presses with light but firm hand,
Forth issue then in copious golden jets,
Sparkles from the wheel.

The scene and all its belongings, how they seize and affect me,
10 The sad sharp-chinn'd old man with worn clothes and broad shoulder-band of leather,
Myself effusing and fluid, a phantom curiously floating, now here absorb'd and arrested,
The group, (an unminded point set in a vast surrounding,)
The attentive, quiet children, the loud, proud, restive base of the streets,
The low hoarse purr of the whirling stone, the light-press'd blade,
15 Diffusing, dropping, sideways-darting, in tiny showers of gold,
Sparkles from the wheel.

Frederick Goddard Tuckerman (1821–1873)

Tuckerman was born in Boston and educated at Harvard, where Jones Very was his tutor. He withdrew from Harvard before his courses were completed; then returned to take a law degree. He was admitted to the Bar but never practised. Instead, he devoted most of his adult life to the study of botany and the writing of poetry. He also placed a great emotional investment in his domestic life, until the death of his wife in 1857. This loss inspired the sonnet-sequences which were printed privately in 1860. They received warm praise and were reissued commercially in 1864, but thereafter Tuckerman sank into obscurity. Many of his subsequent poems were not published until the second half of this century.

From SONNETS: PART I

I

Sometimes, when winding slow by brook and bower,
Beating the idle grass,—of what avail,
I ask, are these dim fancies, cares, and fears?
What though from every bank I drew a flower,—
5 Bloodroot, king-orchis, or the pearlwort pale,—
And set it in my verse with thoughtful tears?
What would it count, though I should sing my death,
And muse and mourn with as poetic breath
As, in damp garden-walks, the autumn gale
10 Sighs o'er the fallen floriage? What avail
Is the swan's voice, if all the hearers fail,
Or his great flight, that no eye gathereth,
In the blending blue? And yet, depending so,
God were not God, whom knowledge cannot know.

II

Wherefore, with this belief, held like a blade,—
Gathering my strength and purpose, fair and slow,
I wait; resolved to carry it to the heart
Of that dark doubt in one collected blow;

5 And stand at guard with spirit undismayed,
 Nor fear the Opposer's anger, arms, or art;
 When, from a hiding near, behold him start
 With a fresh weapon of my weakness made;
 And goad me with myself, and urge the attack,
10 While I strike short, and still give back and back
 While the foe rages. Then from that disgrace
 He points to where they sit that have won the race,
 Laurel by laurel wreathing, face o'er face,
 And leave me lower still; for, ranked in place,

III

And borne with theirs, my proudest thoughts do seem
Bald at the best, and dim; a barren gleam
Among the immortal stars, and faint and brief
As north-light flitting in the dreary north.
5 "What have thy dreams,—a vague, prospective worth?
 An import imminent? or dost thou deem
 Thy life so fair, that thou wouldst set it forth
 Before the day? or art thou wise in grief,
 Has fruitful Sorrow swept thee with her wing?"
10 Today I heard a sweet voice carolling
 In the wood-land paths, with laugh and careless cry,
 Leading her happy mates. Apart I stept;
 And, while the laugh and song went lightly by,
 In the wild bushes I sat down and wept.

IV

Nor looks that backward life so bare to me,
My later youth, and ways I've wandered through;
But touched with innocent grace,—the early bee
On the maple log, the white-heaped cherry tree
5 That hummed all day in the sun, the April blue!
 Yet hardly now one ray the Forward hath
 To show where sorrow rests, and rest begins;
 Although I check my feet, nor walk to wrath
 Through days of crime and grosser shadowings
10 Of evil done in the dark; but fearfully,
 'Mid unfulfilled yet unrelinquished sins
 That hedge me in, and press about my path,
 Like purple-poison flowers of stramony,
 With their dull opiate-breath, and dragon-wings.

V

And so the day drops by; the horizon draws
The fading sun, and we stand struck in grief;
Failing to find our haven of relief,—
Wide of the way, nor sure to turn or pause;
5 And weep to view how fast the splendour wanes,
And scarcely heed, that yet some share remains
Of the red after-light, some time to mark,
Some space between the sundown and the dark.
But not for him those golden calms succeed,
10 Who, while the day is high and glory reigns,
Sees it go by,—as the dim Pampas plain,
Hoary with salt, and gray with bitter weed,
Sees the vault blacken, feels the dark wind strain,
Hears the dry thunder roll, and knows no rain.

VIII

As when, down some broad River dropping, we,
Day after day, behold the assuming shores
Sink and grow dim, as the great Water-course
Pushes his banks apart and seeks the sea;
5 Benches of pines, high shelf and balcony,
To flats of willow and low sycamores
Subsiding, till where'er the wave we see
Himself is his horizon utterly:
So fades the portion of our early world.
10 Still on the ambit hangs the purple air;
Yet, while we lean to read the secret there,
The stream that by green shore-sides plashed and purled
Expands, the mountains melt to vapors rare,
And life alone circles out flat and bare.

IX

Yet wear we on; the deep light disallowed
That lit our youth,—in years no longer young,
We wander silently, and brood among
Dead graves, and tease the sun-break and the cloud
5 For import. Were it not better yet to fly,
To follow those who go before the throng,

Reasoning from stone to star, and easily
Exampling this existence? or shall I—
Who yield slow reverence where I cannot see,
10 And gather gleams, where'er by chance or choice
My footsteps draw,—though brokenly dispensed,—
Come into light at last?—or suddenly,
Struck to the knees like Saul, one arm against
The overbearing brightness, hear a Voice?

X

An upper chamber in a darkened house,
Where, ere his footsteps reached ripe manhood's brink,
Terror and anguish were his cup to drink,—
I cannot rid the thought, nor hold it close;
5 But dimly dream upon that man alone;—
Now though the autumn clouds most softly pass;
The cricket chides beneath the doorstep stone,
And greener than the season grows the grass.
Nor can I drop my lids, nor shade my brows,
10 But there he stands beside the lifted sash;
And, with a swooning of the heart, I think
Where the black shingles slope to meet the boughs,
And—shattered on the roof like smallest snows—
The tiny petals of the mountain-ash.

XI

What profits it to me, though here allowed
Life, sunlight, leisure, if they fail to urge
Me to due motion, or myself to merge
With the onward stream, too humble, or too proud?
5 That find myself not with the popular surge
Washed off and on, or up to higher reefs
Flung with the foremost, when the rolling crowd
Hoists like a wave, nor strong to speak aloud;
But standing here, gazing on my own griefs,
10 Dark household woe, and wounds that bleed and smart;
With still lips, and an outcry in the heart!—
Or now, from day to day, I coldly creep
By summer farms and fields, by stream and steep,
Dull, and like one exhausted with deep sleep.

TUCKERMAN

XIV

Not proud of station, nor in worldly pelf
Immoderately rich, nor rudely gay;
Gentle he was, and generous in a way,
And with a wise direction ruled himself.
5 Large Nature spread his table every day;
And so he lived,—to all the blasts that woo,
Responsible, as yon long locust spray
That waves and washes in the windy blue.
Nor wanted he a power to reach and reap
10 From hardest things a consequence and use;
And yet this friend of mine, in one small hour
Fell from himself, and was content to weep
For eyes love-dark, red lips, and cheeks in hues
Not red, but rose-dim, like the jacinth-flower!

XV

And she—her beauty never made her cold—
Young-Oread-like, beside the green hill-crest,
And blissfully obeying Love's behest,
She turned to him as to a god of old!
5 Her smitten soul with its full strength and spring
Retaliating his love: unto that breast,
Ere scarce the arms dared open to infold,
She gave herself as but a little thing!
And now,—to impulse cold, to passion dead,—
10 With the wild grief of unperfected years,
He kissed her hands, her mouth, her hair, her head;
Gathered her close and closer, to drink up
The odour of her beauty; then in tears,
As for a world, gave from his lips the cup!

XVI

Yet Nature, where the thunder leaves its trace
On the high hemlock pine, or sandstone bank,
Hating all shock of hue, or contrast rank,
With some consenting colour heals the place,
5 Or o'er it draws her mosses green and dank.
So gentle Time will bring with tender craft

Another day, and other greens ingraft
On the dead soil, so fire-burned now, and blank.
What we have had, we hold; and cannot sink
10 Remembrance: patience cometh from above.
And now he breathes apart, to daily drink
In tears the bitter ashes of his love,
Yet precious-rich, and a diviner draught
Than Agria or Artemisia drank!

XVII

All men,—the preacher saith,—whate'er or whence
Their increase, walking through this world has been;
Both those that gather out, or after-glean,
Or hold in simple fee of harvests dense;
5 Or but perhaps a flowerless barren green,
Barren with spots of sorrel, knot-grass, spurge:—
See to one end their differing paths converge,
And all must render answer, here or hence.
"Lo, Death is at the doors," he crieth, "with blows!"
10 But what to him unto whose feverish sense
The stars tick audibly, and the wind's low surge
In the pine, attended, tolls, and throngs, and grows
On the dread ear,—a thunder too profound
For bearing,—a Niagara of sound!

XX

Still craves the spirit: never Nature solves
That yearning which with her first breath began;
And, in its blinder instinct, still devolves
On god or pagod, Manada or man,
5 Or, lower yet, brute-service, apes and wolves!
By Borneo's surf, the bare Barbarian
Still to the sands beneath him bows to pray:
Give Greek his god, the Bheel his devil-sway;
And what remains to me, who count no odds
10 Between such Lord and him I saw to-day,—
The farmer mounted on his market-load,
Bundles of wool, and locks of upland hay;
The son of toil, that his own works bestrode,
And him, Ophion, earliest of the gods?

XXI

O Father, God! to whom, in happier days,
My father bade me cry when troubles fall,
Again I come before thy tribunal,
Too faint for prayer, and all too blind for praise;
5 Yet owning never, through life's dim career,
The eye that would not see, the reckless ear;
Against my head no more thy tempests call!—
Refreshing that wild sorrow of the heart,
And those fierce tears: another morning raise
10 Upon this vision, now so dimmed and swoln:
Guide me, as once, unto thy feet to flee;
Claiming no price of labour, place, or part,
And only seek, before thy footstool fall'n,
Tears in mine eyes, to lift these hands of me!

XXV

By this low fire I often sit to woo
Memory to bring the days forever done;
And call the mountains, where our love begun,
And the dear happy woodlands dipped in dew;
5 And pore upon the landscape, like a book,
But cannot find her: or there rise to me
Gardens and groves in light and shadow outspread:
Or, on a headland far away, I see
Men marching slow in orderly review;
10 And bayonets flash, as, wheeling from the sun,
Rank after rank give fire: or, sad, I look
On miles of moonlit brine, with many a bed
Of wave-weed heaving,—there the wet sands shine;
And just awash, the low reef lifts its line.

XXVI

For Nature daily through her grand design
Breathes contradiction where she seems most clear:
For I have held of her the gift to hear;
And felt, indeed, endowed of sense divine,
5 When I have found, by guarded insight fine,
Cold April flowers in the green end of June;

And thought myself possessed of Nature's ear,
When by the lonely mill-brook, into mine,
Seated on slab, or trunk asunder sawn,
10 The night-hawk blew his horn at sunny noon;
And in the rainy midnight I have heard
The ground-sparrow's long twitter from the pine,
And the cat-bird's silver song,—the wakeful bird
That to the lighted window sings for dawn.

XXVII

So, to the mind long brooding but on it,—
A haunting theme for anger, joy, or tears,
With ardent eyes,—not what we think appears,
But, hunted home, behold its opposite!
5 Worn Sorrow breaking in disastrous mirth,
And wild tears wept of laughter, like the drops
Shook by the trampling thunder to the earth;
And each seems either, or but a counterfeit
Of that it would dissemble: hopes are fears,
10 And love is woe. Nor here the discord stops;
But through all human life runs the account,—
Born into pain, and ending bitterly;
Yet sweet perchance, between-time, like a fount
That rises salt, and freshens to the sea.

XXVIII

Not the round natural world, not the deep mind,
The reconcilement holds: the blue abyss
Collects it not; our arrows sink amiss;
And but in Him may we our import find.
5 The agony to know, the grief, the bliss
Of toil, is vain and vain! clots of the sod
Gathered in heat and haste, and flung behind
To blind ourselves and others,—what but this
Still grasping dust, and sowing toward the wind?
No more thy meaning seek, thine anguish plead;
10 But, leaving straining thought, and stammering word,
Across the barren azure pass to God;
Shooting the void in silence, like a bird,—
A bird that shuts his wings for better speed!

Bayard Taylor (1825–1878)

Born in Pennsylvania of Quaker parentage, Taylor saw his first poem published in a national periodical when he was only sixteen, and he was just twenty when his first book of verse appeared. The next year he began a series of trips to Europe; trips which he usually turned into popular travel-books. In 1848 he became chief of the literary department of the New York *Tribune*. Then, in 1849, he sailed to California where he spent five months with the gold-diggers. After that he travelled to the Orient, sending back letters to the *Tribune* which brought him further popularity and wealth. His subsequent life was taken up with trips abroad, letters and other contributions to the press, and innumerable lecture tours. In 1862, he was appointed secretary to the legation in Russia; and in 1878, the year of his death, he went to Germany as United States minister.

THE BISON TRACK

I

Strike the tent! the sun has risen; not a vapor streaks the dawn,
And the frosted prairie brightens to the westward, far and wan:
Prime afresh the trusty rifle,—sharpen well the hunting spear—
For the frozen sod is trembling, and a noise of hoofs I hear!

II

5 Fiercely stamp the tethered horses, as they snuff the morning's fire;
Their impatient heads are tossing, and they neigh with keen desire.
Strike the tent! the saddles wait us.—let the bridle-reins be slack,
For the prairie's distant thunder has betrayed the bison's track.

III

See! a dusky line approaches: hark, the onward-surging roar,
10 Like the din of wintry breakers on a sounding wall of shore!
Dust and sand behind them whirling, snort the foremost of the van,
And their stubborn horns are clashing through the crowded caravan.

IV

Now the storm is down upon us: let the maddened horses go!
We shall ride the living whirlwind, though a hundred leagues it blow!
15 Though the cloudy manes should thicken, and the red eyes' angry
glare
Lighten round us as we gallop through the sand and rushing air!

V

Myriad hoofs will scar the prairie, in our wild, resistless race,
And a sound, like mighty waters, thunder down the desert space:
Yet the rein may not be tightened, nor the rider's eye look back—
20 Death to him whose speed should slacken, on the maddened bison's
track!

VI

Now the trampling herds are threaded, and the chase is close and
warm
For the giant bull that gallops in the edges of the storm:
Swiftly hurl the whizzing lasso,—swing your rifles as we run:
See! the dust is red behind him,—shout, my comrades, he is won!

VII

25 Look not on him as he staggers,—'t is the last shot he will need!
More shall fall, among his fellows, ere we run the mad stampede,—
Ere we stem the brinded breakers, while the wolves, a hungry pack,
Howl around each grim-eyed carcass, on the bloody Bison Track!

ON LEAVING CALIFORNIA

O fair young land, the youngest, fairest far
Of which our world can boast,—
Whose guardian planet, Evening's silver star
Illumes thy golden coast,—

5 How art thou conquered, tamed in all the pride
Of savage beauty still!
How brought, O panther of the splendid hide,
To know thy master's will!

No more thou sittest on thy tawny hills
    In indolent repose;
Or pour'st the crystal of a thousand rills
    Down from thy house of snows.

But where the wild-oats wrapped thy knees in gold,
    The ploughman drives his share,
And where, through cañons deep, thy streams are rolled,
    The miner's arm is bare.

Yet in thy lap, thus rudely rent and torn
    A nobler seed shall be;
Mother of mighty men, thou shalt not mourn
    Thy lost virginity!

Thy human children shall restore the grace
    Gone with thy fallen pines:
The wild, barbaric beauty of thy face
    Shall round to classic lines.

And Order, Justice, Social Law shall curb
    Thy untamed energies;
And Art and Science, with their dreams superb,
    Replace thine ancient ease.

The marble, sleeping in thy mountains now,
    Shall live in sculptures rare;
Thy native oak shall crown the sage's brow,—
    Thy bay, the poet's hair.

Thy tawny hills shall bleed their purple wine,
    Thy valleys yield their oil;
And Music, with her eloquence divine,
    Persuade thy sons to toil.

Till Hesper, as he trims his silver beam,
    No happier land shall see,
And Earth shall find her old Arcadian dream
    Restored again in thee!

THE QUAKER WIDOW

I

Thee finds me in the garden, Hannah,—come in! 'T is kind of thee
To wait until the Friends were gone, who came to comfort me.
The still and quiet company a peace may give, indeed,
But blessed is the single heart that comes to us at need.

II

5 Come, sit thee down! Here is the bench where Benjamin would sit
On First-day afternoons in spring, and watch the swallows flit:
He loved to smell the sprouting box, and hear the pleasant bees
Go humming round the lilacs and through the apple-trees.

III

I think he loved the spring: not that he cared for flowers: most men
10 Think such things foolishness,—but we were first acquainted then,
One spring: the next he spoke his mind; the third I was his wife,
And in the spring (it happened so) our children entered life.

IV

He was but seventy-five: I did not think to lay him yet
In Kennett graveyard, where at Monthly Meeting first we met.
15 The Father's mercy shows in this: 't is better I should be
Picked out to bear the heavy cross—alone in age—than he.

V

We've lived together fifty years: it seems but one long day,
One quiet Sabbath of the heart, till he was called away;
And as we bring from Meeting-time a sweet contentment home,
20 So, Hannah, I have store of peace for all the days to come.

VI

I mind (for I can tell thee now) how hard it was to know
If I had heard the spirit right, that told me I should go;
For father had a deep concern upon his mind that day,
But mother spoke for Benjamin,—she knew what best to say.

VII

25 Then she was still: they sat awhile: at last she spoke again,
"The Lord incline thee to the right!" and "Thou shalt have him, Jane!"
My father said. I cried. Indeed, 't was not the least of shocks,
For Benjamin was Hicksite, and father Orthodox.

VIII

I thought of this ten years ago, when daughter Ruth we lost:
30 Her husband's of the world, and yet I could not see her crossed.
She wears, thee knows, the gayest gowns, she hears a hireling priest—
Ah, dear! the cross was ours: her life's a happy one, at least.

IX

Perhaps she'll wear a plainer dress when she's as old as I,—
Would thee believe it, Hannah? once *I* felt temptation nigh!
35 My wedding-gown was ashen silk, too simple for my taste:
I wanted lace around the neck, and a ribbon at the waist.

X

How strange it seemed to sit with him upon the women's side!
I did not dare to lift my eyes: I felt more fear than pride,
Till, " in the presence of the Lord," he said, and then there came
40 A holy strength upon my heart, and I could say the same.

XI

I used to blush when he came near, but then I showed no sign;
With all the meeting looking on, I held his hand in mine.
It seemed my bashfulness was gone, now I was his for life:
Thee knows the feeling, Hannah,—thee, too, hast been a wife.

XII

45 As home we rode, I saw no fields look half so green as ours;
The woods were coming into leaf, the meadows full of flowers;
The neighbors met us in the lane, and every face was kind,—
'T is strange how lively everything comes back upon my mind.

XIII

I see, as plain as thee sits there, the wedding-dinner spread:
50 At our own table we were guests, with father at the head,
And Dinah Passmore helped us both,—'t was she stood up with me,
And Abner Jones with Benjamin,—and now they're gone, all three!

XIV

It is not right to wish for death; the Lord disposes best.
His Spirit comes to quiet hearts, and fits them for His rest;
55 And that He halved our little flock was merciful, I see:
For Benjamin has two in heaven, and two are left with me.

XV

Eusebius never cared to farm,—'t was not his call, in truth,
And I must rent the dear old place, and go to daughter Ruth.
Thee'll say her ways are not like mine,—young people now-a-days
60 Have fallen sadly off, I think, from all the good old ways.

XVI

But Ruth is still a Friend at heart; she keeps the simple tongue,
The cheerful, kindly nature we loved when she was young;
And it was brought upon my mind, remembering her, of late,
That we on dress and outward things perhaps lay too much weight.

XVII

65 I once heard Jesse Kersey say, a spirit clothed with grace,
And pure, almost, as angels are, may have a homely face.
And dress may be of less account: the Lord will look within:
The soul it is that testifies of righteousness or sin.

XVIII

Thee mustn't be too hard on Ruth: she's anxious I should go,
70 And she will do her duty as a daughter should, I know.
'T is hard to change so late in life, but we must be resigned:
The Lord looks down contentedly upon a willing mind.

Henry Timrod (1828–1867)

Born in Charleston, South Carolina, Timrod was the son of a book-binder who had himself published a volume of poetry. The family was a poor one, and this prevented Timrod from completing the full course at the University of Georgia. Instead, he became a tutor in the family of a Carolina planter. Later, like Poe, he turned editor in an attempt to give the South its own literary magazine, but the attempt was not a success. When the Civil War came, Timrod enlisted in the Confederate Army. Ill-health forced him to resign and he became a war correspondent, first for the Charleston *Mercury* and then for the Columbia *South Carolinian*. Subsequent years were a record of misfortune. Timrod's favourite child died; his house was destroyed by Sherman's troops; his poetry was ignored; and he found himself impoverished. He died, shortly after the war, of tuber-culosis and malnutrition.

CHARLESTON

Calm as that second summer which precedes
    The first fall of the snow,
In the broad sunlight of heroic deeds,
    The City bides the foe.

5   As yet, behind their ramparts stern and proud,
        Her bolted thunders sleep—
Dark Sumter, like a battlemented cloud,
        Looms o'er the solemn deep.

No Calpe frowns from lofty cliff or scar
10   To guard the holy strand;
But Moultrie holds in leash her dogs of war
        Above the level sand.

And down the dunes a thousand guns lie couched,
        Unseen, beside the flood—
15   Like tigers in some Orient jungle crouched
        That wait and watch for blood.

Meanwhile, through streets still echoing with trade,
    Walk grave and thoughtful men,
Whose hands may one day wield the patriot's blade
20   As lightly as the pen.

And maidens, with such eyes as would grow dim
    Over a bleeding hound,
Seem each one to have caught the strength of him
    Whose sword she sadly bound.

25 Thus girt without and garrisoned at home,
    Day patient following day,
Old Charleston looks from roof, and spire, and dome,
    Across her tranquil bay.

Ships, through a hundred foes, from Saxon lands
30   And spicy Indian ports
Bring Saxon steel and iron to her hands,
    And Summer to her courts.

But still, along yon dim Atlantic line,
    The only hostile smoke
35 Creeps like a harmless mist above the brine,
    From some frail, floating oak.

Shall the Spring dawn, and she still clad in smiles,
    And with an unscathed brow,
Rest in the strong arms of her palm-crowned isles,
40   As fair and free as now?

We know not; in the temple of the Fates
    God has inscribed her doom;
And, all untroubled in her faith, she waits
    The triumph or the tomb.

THE UNKNOWN DEAD

The rain is plashing on my sill,
But all the winds of Heaven are still;
And so it falls with that dull sound
Which thrills us in the church-yard ground,

5　　　　When the first spadeful drops like lead
　　　　Upon the coffin of the dead.
　　　　Beyond my streaming window-pane,
　　　　I cannot see the neighboring vane,
　　　　Yet from its old familiar tower
10　　　The bell comes, muffled, through the shower.
　　　　What strange and unsuspected link
　　　　Of feeling touched, has made me think—
　　　　While with a vacant soul and eye
　　　　I watch that gray and stony sky—
15　　　Of nameless graves on battle-plains
　　　　Washed by a single winter's rains,
　　　　Where, some beneath Virginian hills,
　　　　And some by green Atlantic rills,
　　　　Some by the waters of the West,
20　　　A myriad unknown heroes rest.
　　　　Ah! not the chiefs, who, dying, see
　　　　Their flags in front of victory,
　　　　Or, at their life-blood's noble cost
　　　　Pay for a battle nobly lost,
25　　　Claim from their monumental beds
　　　　The bitterest tears a nation sheds.
　　　　Beneath yon lonely mound—the spot
　　　　By all save some fond few forgot—
　　　　Lie the true martyrs of the fight
30　　　Which strikes for freedom and for right.
　　　　Of them, their patriot zeal and pride,
　　　　The lofty faith that with them died,
　　　　No grateful page shall farther tell
　　　　Than that so many bravely fell;
35　　　And we can only dimly guess
　　　　What worlds of all this world's distress,
　　　　What utter woe, despair, and dearth,
　　　　Their fate has brought to many a hearth.
　　　　Just such a sky as this should weep
40　　　Above them, always, where they sleep;
　　　　Yet, haply, at this very hour,
　　　　Their graves are like a lover's bower;
　　　　And Nature's self, with eyes unwet,
　　　　Oblivious of the crimson debt
45　　　To which she owes her April grace,
　　　　Laughs gayly o'er their burial-place.

ODE

Sung on the Occasion of Decorating the Graves of the Confederate
Dead, at Magnolia Cemetery, Charleston, S.C., 1867

I

Sleep sweetly in your humble graves,
Sleep, martyrs of a fallen cause;
Though yet no marble column craves
The pilgrim here to pause.

II

5   In seeds of laurel in the earth
The blossom of your fame is blown,
And somewhere, waiting for its birth,
The shaft is in the stone!

III

Meanwhile, behalf the tardy years
10   Which keep in trust your storied tombs,
Behold! your sisters bring their tears,
And these memorial blooms.

IV

Small tributes! but your shades will smile
More proudly on these wreaths to-day,
15   Than when some cannon-moulded pile
Shall overlook this bay.

V

Stoop, angels, hither from the skies!
There is no holier spot of ground
Than where defeated valor lies,
20   By mourning beauty crowned!

Emily Dickinson (1830–1886)

Emily Dickinson spent most of her life in her birth-place, Amherst, Massachusetts. Her father Edward Dickinson, a lawyer and politician, has been described as one of the last representatives of the New England Puritan tradition. She was enrolled in South Hadley Female Seminary in 1847 but she spent less than a year there, away from home. In 1854, while away from Amherst again on a brief visit to Philadelphia, she met and apparently fell in love with the Rev. Charles Wadsworth. The love was not returned nor even expressed openly; and Wadsworth subsequently moved to San Francisco. Then, in 1862, began the period of her greatest poetic activity. During this period also, she sought the advice of Thomas Wentworth Higginson, a minor poet and littérateur who later became her first editor. In the last years of her life she seldom went beyond the confines of her house and garden and habitually dressed herself in white. Only seven of her poems were published during her lifetime.

I taste a liquor never brewed,
From tankards scooped in pearl;
Not all the vats upon the Rhine
Yield such an alcohol!

5   Inebriate of air am I,
And debauchee of dew,
Reeling, through endless summer days,
From inns of molten blue.

When landlords turn the drunken bee
10   Out of the foxglove's door,
When butterflies renounce their drams,
I shall but drink the more!

Till seraphs swing their snowy hats,
And saints to windows run,
15   To see the little tippler
Leaning against the sun!

There's a certain slant of light
On winter afternoons,
That oppresses, like the weight
Of cathedral tunes.

5   Heavenly hurt it gives us;
We can find no scar,
But internal difference
Where the meanings are.

None may teach it anything,
10   'Tis the seal, despair,—
An imperial affliction
Sent us of the air.

When it comes, the landscape listens,
Shadows hold their breath;
15   When it goes, 'tis like the distance
On the look of death.

The soul selects her own society,
Then shuts the door;
On her divine majority
Obtrude no more.

5   Unmoved, she notes the chariot's pausing
At her low gate;
Unmoved, an emperor is kneeling
Upon her mat.

I've known her from an ample nation
10   Choose one;
Then close the valves of her attention
Like stone.

Exultation is the going
Of an inland soul to sea,—
Past the houses, past the headlands,
Into deep eternity!

5   Bred as we, among the mountains,
Can the sailor understand
The divine intoxication
Of the first league out from land?

I like a look of agony,
Because I know it's true;
Men do not sham convulsion,
Nor simulate a throe.

5   The eyes glaze once, and that is death.
Impossible to feign
The beads upon the forehead
By homely anguish strung.

This is my letter to the world,
    That never wrote to me,—
The simple news that Nature told,
    With tender majesty.

5   Her message is committed
    To hands I cannot see;
For love of her, sweet countrymen,
    Judge tenderly of me!

Because I could not stop for Death,
He kindly stopped for me;
The carriage held but just ourselves
And Immortality.

5 We slowly drove, he knew no haste,
   And I had put away
   My labor, and my leisure too,
   For his civility.

   We passed the school where children played
10 Their lessons scarcely done;
   We passed the fields of gazing grain,
   We passed the setting sun.

   We paused before a house that seemed
   A swelling of the ground;
15 The roof was scarcely visible,
   The cornice but a mound.

   Since then 'tis centuries; but each
   Feels shorter than the day
   I first surmised the horses' heads
20 Were toward eternity.

   Success is counted sweetest
   By those who ne'er succeed.
   To comprehend a nectar
   Requires sorest need.

5 Not one of all the purple host
   Who took the flag to-day
   Can tell the definition,
   So clear, of victory,

   As he, defeated, dying,
10 On whose forbidden ear
   The distant strains of triumph
   Break, agonized and clear.

I never lost as much but twice,
And that was in the sod;
Twice have I stood a beggar
Before the door of God!

5 Angels, twice descending,
Reimbursed my store.
Burglar, banker, father,
I am poor once more!

Much madness is divinest sense
To a discerning eye;
Much sense the starkest madness.
'Tis the majority
5 In this, as all, prevails.
Assent, and you are sane;
Demur,—you're straightway dangerous,
And handled with a chain.

I found the phrase to every thought
I ever had, but one;
And that defies me,—as a hand
Did try to chalk the sun

5 To races nurtured in the dark;—
How would your own begin?
Can blaze be done in cochineal,
Or noon in mazarin?

One need not be a chamber to be haunted,
One need not be a house;
The brain has corridors surpassing
Material place.

5   Far safer, of a midnight meeting
External ghost,
Than an interior confronting
That whiter host.

Far safer through an Abbey gallop,
10   The stones achase,
Than, moonless, one's own self encounter
In lonesome place.

Ourself, behind ourself concealed,
Should startle most;
15   Assassin, hid in our apartment,
Be horror's least.

The prudent carries a revolver,
He bolts the door,
O'erlooking a superior spectre
20   More near.

A bird came down the walk:
He did not know I saw;
He bit an angle-worm in halves
And ate the fellow, raw.

5   And then he drank a dew
From a convenient grass,
And then hopped sidewise to the wall
To let a beetle pass.

He glanced with rapid eyes
10   That hurried all abroad,—
They looked like frightened beads, I thought
He stirred his velvet head

Like one in danger; cautious,
I offered him a crumb,
15   And he unrolled his feathers
And rowed him softer home

Then oars divide the ocean,
Too silver for a seam,
Or butterflies, off banks of noon,
20   Leap, plashless, as they swim.

Wild nights! Wild nights!
Were I with thee,
Wild nights should be
Our luxury!

5   Futile the winds
To a heart in port,—
Done with the compass,
Done with the chart.

Rowing in Eden!
10   Ah! the sea!
Might I but moor
To-night in thee!

I like to see it lap the miles,
And lick the valleys up,
And stop to feed itself at tanks;
And then, prodigious, step

5   Around a pile of mountains,
And, supercilious, peer
In shanties by the sides of roads;
And then a quarry pare

To fit its sides, and crawl between,
10   Complaining all the while
In horrid, hooting stanza;
Then chase itself down hill

And neigh like Boanerges;
Then, punctual as a star,
15 Stop—docile and omnipotent—
At its own stable door.

Farther in summer than the birds,
Pathetic from the grass,
A minor nation celebrates
Its unobtrusive mass.

5   No ordinance is seen,
So gradual the grace,
A pensive custom it becomes,
Enlarging loneliness.

Antiquest felt at noon
10 When August, burning low,
Calls forth this spectral canticle,
Repose to typify.

Remit as yet no grace,
No furrow on the glow,
15 Yet a druidic difference
Enhances nature now.

A route of evanescence
With a revolving wheel;
A resonance of emerald,
A rush of cochineal;
5   And every blossom on the bush
Adjusts its tumbled head,—
The mail from Tunis, probably,
An easy morning's ride.

I started early, took my dog,
And visited the sea;
The mermaids in the basement
Came out to look at me,

5 And frigates in the upper floor
Extended hempen hands,
Presuming me to be a mouse
Aground, upon the sands.

But no man moved me till the tide
10 Went past my simple shoe,
And past my apron and my belt,
And past my bodice too,

And made as he would eat me up
As wholly as a dew
15 Upon a dandelion's sleeve—
And then I started too.

And he—he followed close behind;
I felt his silver heel
Upon my ankle,—then my shoes
20 Would overflow with pearl.

Until we met the solid town,
No man he seemed to know;
And bowing with a mighty look
At me, the sea withdrew.

Essential oils are wrung:
The attar from the rose
Is not expressed by suns alone,
It is the gift of screws.

5 The general rose decays;
But this, in lady's drawer,
Makes summer when the lady lies
In ceaseless rosemary.

Our journey had advanced;
Our feet were almost come
To that odd fork in Being's road,
Eternity by term.

5   Our pace took sudden awe,
Our feet reluctant led.
Before were cities, but between,
The forest of the dead.

Retreat was out of hope,—
10   Behind, a sealèd route,
Eternity's white flag before,
And God at every gate.

I heard a fly buzz when I died;
    The stillness round my form
Was like the stillness in the air
    Between the heaves of storm.

5   The eyes beside had wrung them dry,
    And breaths were gathering sure
For that last onset, when the king
    Be witnessed in his power.

I willed my keepsakes, signed away
10   What portion of me I
Could make assignable,—and then
    There interposed a fly,

With blue, uncertain, stumbling buzz,
    Between the light and me;
15   And then the windows failed, and then
    I could not see to see.

A clock stopped—not the mantel's;
    Geneva's farthest skill
Can't put the puppet bowing
    That just now dangled still.

5
    An awe came on the trinket!
        The figures hunched with pain,
    Then quivered out of decimals
        Into degreeless noon.

    It will not stir for doctors,
10
        This pendulum of snow;
    The shopman importunes it,
        While cool, concernless No

    Nods from the gilded pointers,
        Nods from the seconds slim,
15
    Decades of arrogance between
        The dial life and him.

    Of bronze and blaze
        The north, to-night!
    So adequate its forms,
    So preconcerted with itself,
5
        So distant to alarms,—
    An unconcern so sovereign
        To universe, or me,
    It paints my simple spirit
        With tints of majesty,
10
    Till I take vaster attitudes,
        And strut upon my stem,
    Disdaining men and oxygen,
        For arrogance of them.
    My splendors are menagerie;
15
        But their completeless show
    Will entertain the centuries
        When I am, long ago,
    An island in dishonored grass,
        Whom none but daisies know.

What soft, cherubic creatures
    These gentlewomen are!
One would as soon assault a plush
    Or violate a star.

5   Such dimity convictions,
    A horror so refined
Of freckled human nature,
    Of Deity ashamed,—

It's such a common glory,
10   A fisherman's degree!
Redemption, brittle lady,
    Be so ashamed of thee.

What mystery pervades a well!
    The water lives so far,
Like neighbor from another world
    Residing in a jar.

5   The grass does not appear afraid;
    I often wonder he
Can stand so close and look so bold
    At what is dread to me.

Related somehow they may be,—
10   The sedge stands next the sea,
Where he is floorless, yet of fear
    No evidence gives he.

But nature is a stranger yet;
    The ones that cite her most
15   Have never passed her haunted house,
    Nor simplified her ghost.

To pity those that know her not
    Is helped by the regret
That those who know her, know her less
20   The nearer her they get.

There's been a death in the opposite house
    As lately as to-day.
I know it by the numb look
    Such houses have alway.

5   The neighbors rustle in and out,
    The doctor drives away.
A window opens like a pod,
    Abrupt, mechanically;

Somebody flings a mattress out,—
10   The children hurry by;
They wonder if It died on that,—
    I used to when a boy.

The minister goes stiffly in
    As if the house were his,
15   And he owned all the mourners now,
    And little boys besides;

And then the milliner, and the man
    Of the appalling trade,
To take the measure of the house.
20   There'll be that dark parade

Of tassels and of coaches soon;
    It's easy as a sign,—
The intuition of the news
    In just a country town.

Francis Bret Harte (1836–1902)

Born in Albany, New York, Harte lost his father in childhood. After receiving a common school education, he travelled to California where he taught school for a while. He then found work as a miner and an express-agent before becoming associated with *The Golden Era*, a San Francisco journal. In 1864 he was appointed editor of

The Californian; then, in 1868, editor of the *Overland Monthly*, the magazine in which he published the tales and poems that made him famous. With the growth of his popularity Harte decided in 1871 to move back again to the East, to become a contributing editor of the *Atlantic Monthly*. Subsequently, he was made United States consul at Crefeld, Germany, then at Glasgow. After holding these offices for a total of seven years, he finally settled in England in 1885, where he died some seventeen years later.

PLAIN LANGUAGE FROM TRUTHFUL JAMES

Table Mountain, 1870

Which I wish to remark,—
    And my language is plain,
That for ways that are dark,
    And for tricks that are vain,
5 The heathen Chinee is peculiar,—
    Which the same I would rise to explain.

Ah Sin was his name.
    And I shall not deny
In regard to the same
10   What that name might imply;
But his smile it was pensive and childlike,
    As I frequent remarked to Bill Nye.

It was August the third;
    And quite soft was the skies:
15 Which it might be inferred
    That Ah Sin was likewise;
Yet he played it that day upon William
    And me in a way I despise.

Which we had a small game,
20   And Ah Sin took a hand:
It was euchre. The same
    He did not understand;
But he smiled as he sat by the table,
    With the smile that was childlike and bland.

25   Yet the cards they were stocked
        In a way that I grieve.
And my feelings were shocked
        At the state of Nye's sleeve:
Which was stuffed full of aces and bowers,
30   And the same with intent to deceive.

But the hands that were played
        By that heathen Chinee,
And the points that he made,
        Were quite frightful to see.—
35 Till at last he put down a right bower,
        Which the same Nye had dealt unto me.

Then I looked up at Nye,
        And he gazed upon me;
And he rose with a sigh,
40   And said, " Can this be?
We are ruined by Chinese cheap labour;"
        And he went for that heathen Chinee.

In the scene that ensued
        I did not take a hand;
45 But the floor it was strewed
        Like the leaves on the strand
With the cards that Ah Sin had been hiding,
        In the game "he did not understand."

In his sleeves, which were long.
50   He had twenty-four packs,—
Which was coming it strong,
        Yet I state but the facts;
And we found on his nails, which were taper,
        What is frequent in tapers,—that's wax.

55 Which is why I remark,
        And my language is plain,
That for ways that are dark,
        And for tricks that are vain,
The heathen Chinee is peculiar,—
60   Which the same I am free to maintain.

Joaquin Miller (1841?–1913)

Born in Liberty, Indiana, and named Cincinnatus Hiner (or Heine) by his parents, Miller moved to Willamette Valley, Oregon, when he was thirteen. There and in California, Miller later claimed that he was in turn a horse-thief, a pony-express rider, and an Indian fighter. Whatever the truth behind these claims, it is clear that by 1860 he was studying law. He was admitted to the Bar, practised as a lawyer in Portland, Oregon, and edited a newspaper in the state capital of Eugene. At about this time he also wrote a defence of the Mexican bandit, Joaquin Murietta, from whom he adopted his pseudonym. A few years later he moved to San Francisco; then to London where his *Songs of the Sierras*, published privately in 1870, brought him sudden fame with the English as a 'frontier poet' and wild man from the West. He then returned to the United States, working first as a journalist in Washington before returning to California.

CROSSING THE PLAINS

What great yoked brutes with briskets low,
With wrinkled necks like buffalo,
With round, brown, liquid, pleading eyes,
That turned so slow and sad to you,
5 That shone like love's eyes soft with tears,
That seemed to plead, and make replies,
The while they bowed their necks and drew
The creaking load; and looked at you.
Their sable briskets swept the ground,
10 Their cloven feet kept solemn sound.

Two sullen bullocks led the line,
Their great eyes shining bright like wine;
Two sullen captive kings were they,
That had in time held herds at bay,
15 And even now they crushed the sod
With stolid sense of majesty,
And stately stepped and stately trod,
As if 't were something still to be
Kings even in captivity.

COLUMBUS

Behind him lay the gray Azores,
    Behind the Gates of Hercules;
Before him not the ghost of shores,
    Before him only shoreless seas.
5   The good mate said: "Now must we pray,
    For lo! the very stars are gone.
Brave Admiral, speak, what shall I say?"
    "Why, say, 'Sail on! sail on! and on!'"

"My men grow mutinous day by day;
10   My men grow ghastly wan and weak."
The stout mate thought of home; a spray
    Of salt wave washed his swarthy cheek.
"What shall I say, brave Admiral, say,
    If we sight naught but seas at dawn?"
15   "Why, you shall say at break of day,
    'Sail on! sail on! sail on! and on!'"

They sailed and sailed, as winds might blow,
    Until at last the blanched mate said:
"Why, now not even God would know
20   Should I and all my men fall dead.
These very winds forget their way,
    For God from these dread seas is gone.
Now speak, brave Admiral, speak and say"—
    He said: "Sail on! sail on! and on!"

25   They sailed. They sailed. Then spake the mate:
    "This mad sea shows his teeth to-night.
He curls his lip, he lies in wait,
    With lifted teeth, as if to bite!
Brave Admiral, say but one good word:
30   What shall we do when hope is gone?"
The words leapt like a leaping sword:
    "Sail on! sail on! sail on! and on!"

Then, pale and worn, he kept his deck,
    And peered through darkness. Ah, that night
35   Of all dark nights! And then a speck—
    A light! A light! A light! A light!

It grew, a starlit flag unfurled!
　　It grew to be Time's burst of dawn.
　He gained a world; he gave that world
　　Its grandest lesson: "On! sail on!"

40

Sidney Lanier (1842–1881)

Lanier was born in Maçon, Georgia, and attended Oglethorpe
College from which he graduated in 1860. Within a year of his
graduation he enlisted in the Confederate Army, and towards the
close of the war was taken prisoner while trying to run a blockade.
After his release, he taught in Alabama for a while; then studied and
practised law at Maçon with his father. He was an excellent musician
and in later years played first flute in the Peabody Orchestra in
Baltimore. At the same time, he was writing verse and giving a series
of lectures at Johns Hopkins University on the relationship between
music and poetry. For most of his life he suffered from a pulmonary
weakness and in 1881, when his condition grew worse, he moved to
the mountains of North Carolina. He died there a few months later.

CORN

To-day the woods are trembling through and through
With shimmering forms, that flash before my view,
Then melt in green as dawn-stars melt in blue.
　　The leaves that wave against my cheek caress
5　　Like women's hands; the embracing boughs express
　　　A subtlety of mighty tenderness;
The copse-depths into little noises start,
That sound anon like beatings of a heart,
Anon like talk 'twixt lips not far apart.
10　　The beech dreams balm, as a dreamer hums a song;
　　Through that vague wafture, expirations strong
　　　Throb from young hickories breathing deep and long
With stress and urgence bold of prisoned spring
　　　And ecstasy of burgeoning.

15 Now, since the dew-plashed road of morn is dry,
   Forth venture odors of more quality
   And heavenlier giving. Like Jove's locks awry,
    Long muscadines
Rich-wreathe the spacious foreheads of great pines,
20 And breathe ambrosial passion from their vines.
   I pray with mosses, ferns and flowers shy
   That hide like gentle nuns from human eye
   To lift adoring perfumes to the sky.
I hear faint bridal-sighs of brown and green
25 Dying to silent hints of kisses keen
As far lights fringe into a pleasant sheen.
   I start at fragmentary whispers, blown
   From undertalks of leafy souls unknown,
   Vague purports sweet, of inarticulate tone.

30 Dreaming of gods, men, nuns and brides, between
   Old companies of oaks that inward lean
To join their radiant amplitudes of green
   I slowly move, with ranging looks that pass
   Up from the matted miracles of grass
35 Into yon veined complex of space
Where sky and leafage interlace
   So close, the heaven of blue is seen
   Inwoven with a heaven of green.

I wander to the zigzag-cornered fence
40 Where sassafras, intrenched in brambles dense,
Contests with stolid vehemence
   The march of culture, setting limb and thorn
   As pikes against the army of the corn.

There, while I pause, my fieldward-faring eyes
45 Take harvests, where there the stately corn-ranks rise,
    Of inward dignities
And large benignities and insights wise,
    Graces and modest majesties.
Thus, without theft, I reap another's field;
50 Thus, without tilth, I house a wondrous yield,
And heap my heart with quintuple crops concealed.

Look, out of line one tall corn-captain stands
Advanced beyond the foremost of his bands,

And waves his blades upon the very edge
5   And hottest thicket of the battling hedge.
Thou lustrous stalk, that ne'er mayst walk nor talk,
    Still shalt thou type the poet-soul sublime
    That leads the vanward of his timid time
    And sings up cowards with commanding rhyme—
10 Soul calm, like thee, yet fain, like thee, to grow
By double increment, above, below;
    Soul homely, as thou art, yet rich in grace like thee,
    Teaching the yeomen selfless chivalry
    That moves in gentle curves of courtesy;
15 Soul filled like thy long veins with sweetness tense,
        By every godlike sense
Transmuted from the four wild elements.
        Drawn to high plans,
        Thou lift'st more stature than a mortal man's,
20 Yet ever piercest downwards in the mould
        And keepest hold
    Upon the reverend and steadfast earth
        That gave thee birth;
    Yea, standest smiling in thy future grave,
25   Serene and brave,
    With unremitting breath
    Inhaling life from death,
Thine epitaph writ fair in fruitage eloquent,
        Thyself thy monument.

30   As poets should,
Thou hast built up thy hardihood
With universal food,
    Drawn in select proportion fair
    From honest mould and vagabond air;
35 From darkness of the dreadful night,
        And joyful light;
    From antique ashes, whose departed flame
    In thee has finer life and longer fame;
From wounds and balms,
40 From storms and calms,
From potsherds and dry bones
        And ruin-stones.

Into thy vigorous substance thou hast wrought
Whate'er the hand of Circumstance hath brought;

95   Yea, into cool solacing green hast spun
       White radiance hot from out the sun.
So thou dost mutually leaven
Strength of earth with grace of heaven;
       So thou dost marry new and old
100   Into a one of higher mould;
       So thou dost reconcile the hot and cold,
          The dark and bright,
And many a heart-perplexing opposite,
          And so,
105   Akin by blood to high and low,
Fitly thou playest out thy poet's part,
Richly expending thy much-bruisèd heart
       In equal care to nourish lord in hall
          Or beast in stall:
110   Thou took'st from all that thou might'st give to all.

O steadfast dweller on the selfsame spot
Where thou wast born, that still repinest not—
Type of the home-fond heart, the happy lot!—
       Deeply thy mild content rebukes the land
115   Whose flimsy homes, built on the shifting sand
Of trade, for ever rise and fall
With alternation whimsical,
       Enduring scarce a day,
       Then swept away
120 By swift engulfments of incalculable tides
Whereon capricious Commerce rides.

Look, thou substantial spirit of content!
Across this little vale, thy continent,
       To where, beyond the mouldering mill,
125   Yon old deserted Georgian hill
Bares to the sun his piteous aged crest
          And seamy breast,
       By restless-hearted children left to lie
       Untended there beneath the heedless sky,
130   As barbarous folk expose their old to die.

Upon that generous-rounding side,
          With gullies scarified
       Where keen Neglect his lash hath plied,
Dwelt one I knew of old, who played at toil,

135 And gave to coquette Cotton soul and soil.
        Scorning the slow reward of patient grain,
        He sowed his heart with hopes of swifter gain,
        Then sat him down and waited for the rain.
    He sailed in borrowed ships of usury—
140 A foolish Jason on a treacherous sea,
    Seeking the Fleece and finding misery.
        Lulled by smooth-rippling loans, in idle trance
        He lay, content that unthrift Circumstance
        Should plough for him the stony field of Chance.
145 Yea, gathering crops whose worth no man might tell,
    He staked his life on games of Buy-and-Sell,
    And turned each field into a gambler's hell.
        Aye, as each year began,
        My farmer to the neighboring city ran;
150 Passed with a mournful anxious face
    Into the banker's inner place;
    Parleyed, excused, pleaded for longer grace;
        Railed at the drought, the worm, the rust, the grass;
        Protested ne'er again 'twould come to pass;
155   With many an *oh* and *if* and *but alas*
    Parried or swallowed searching questions rude,
    And kissed the dust to soften Dives's mood.
    At last, small loans by pledges great renewed,
        He issues smiling from the fatal door,
160   And buys with lavish hand his yearly store
        Till his small borrowings will yield no more.
    Aye, as each year declined,
    With bitter heart and ever-brooding mind
    He mourned his fate unkind.
165   In dust, in rain, with might and main,
        He nursed his cotton, cursed his grain,
        Fretted for news that made him fret again,
    Snatched at each telegram of Future Sale,
    And thrilled with Bulls' or Bears' alternate wail—
170 In hope or fear alike for ever pale.
        And thus from year to year, through hope and fear,
        With many a curse and many a secret tear,
        Striving in vain his cloud of debt to clear,
            At last
175 He woke to find his foolish dreaming past,
        And all his best-of-life the easy prey
        Of squandering scamps and quacks that lined his way

With vile array,
From rascal statesman down to petty knave;
180 Himself, at best, for all his bragging brave,
A gamester's catspaw and a banker's slave.
Then, worn and gray, and sick with deep unrest,
He fled away into the oblivious West,
Unmourned, unblest.

185 Old hill! old hill! thou gashed and hairy Lear
Whom the divine Cordelia of the year,
E'en pitying Spring, will vainly strive to cheer—
King, that no subject man nor beast may own,
Discrowned, undaughtered and alone—
190 Yet shall the great God turn thy fate,
And bring thee back into thy monarch state
And majesty immaculate.
Lo, through hot waverings of the August morn,
Thou givest from thy vasty sides forlorn
195 Visions of golden treasuries of corn—
Ripe largesse lingering for some bolder heart
That manfully shall take thy part,
And tend thee,
And defend thee,
200 With antique sinew and with modern art.

THE MARSHES OF GLYNN

Glooms of the live-oaks, beautiful-braided and woven
With intricate shades of the vines that myriad-cloven
Clamber the forks of the multiform boughs,—
Emerald twilights,—
5 Virginal shy lights,
Wrought of the leaves to allure to the whisper of vows,
When lovers pace timidly down through the green colonnades
Of the dim sweet woods, of the dear dark woods,
Of the heavenly woods and glades,
10 That run to the radiant marginal sand-beach within
The wide sea-marshes of Glynn;—

Beautiful glooms, soft dusks in the noon-day fire,—
Wildwood privacies, closets of lone desire,

Chamber from chamber parted with wavering arras of leaves,—
15 Cells for the passionate pleasure of prayer to the soul that grieves,
Pure with a sense of the passing of saints through the wood,
Cool for the dutiful weighing of ill with good;—

O braided dusks of the oak and woven shades of the vine.
While the riotous noon-day sun of the June-day long did shine,
20 Ye held me fast in your heart and I held you fast in mine;
But now when the noon is no more, and riot is rest,
And the sun is a-wait at the ponderous gate of the West,
And the slant yellow beam down the wood-aisle doth seem
Like a lane into heaven that leads from a dream,—
25 Ay, now, when my soul all day hath drunken the soul of the oak,
And my heart is at ease from men, and the wearisome sound of the
stroke
Of the scythe of time and the trowel of trade is low,
And belief overmasters doubt, and I know that I know,
And my spirit is grown to a lordly great compass within,
30 That the length and the breadth and the sweep of the marshes
of Glynn
Will work me no fear like the fear they have wrought me of
yore
When length was fatigue, and when breadth was but bitter-
ness sore,
And when terror and shrinking and dreary unnamable pain
Drew over me out of the merciless miles of the plain,—
35 Oh, now, unafraid, I am fain to face
The vast sweet visage of space.
To the edge of the wood I am drawn, I am drawn,
Where the gray beach glimmering runs, as a belt of the dawn,
For a mete and a mark
40 To the forest-dark:—
So:
Affable live-oak, leaning low,—
Thus—with your favor—soft, with a reverent hand,
(Not lightly touching your person, Lord of the land!)
45 Bending your beauty aside, with a step I stand
On the firm-packed sand,
Free
By a world of marsh that borders a world of sea.
Sinuous southward and sinuous northward the shimmering band
50 Of the sand-beach fastens the fringe of the marsh to the folds
of the land.

Inward and outward to northward and southward the beach-lines
    linger and curl
As a silver-wrought garment that clings to and follows the firm sweet
    limbs of a girl.
Vanishing, swerving, evermore curving again into sight,
Softly the sand-beach wavers away to a dim gray looping of light.
55 And what if behind me to westward the wall of the woods stands high?
The world lies east: how ample, the marsh and the sea and the sky!
    A league and a league of marsh-grass, waist-high, broad in the
        blade,
    Green, and all of a height, and unflecked with a light or a shade,
    Stretch leisurely off, in a pleasant plain,
60   To the terminal blue of the main.

    Oh, what is abroad in the marsh and the terminal sea?
        Somehow my soul seems suddenly free
    From the weighing of fate and the sad discussion of sin,
    By the length and the breadth and the sweep of the marshes of
        Glynn.
65 Ye marshes, how candid and simple and nothing-withholding and free
Ye publish yourselves to the sky and offer yourselves to the sea!
Tolerant plains, that suffer the sea and the rains and the sun,
Ye spread and span like the catholic man who hath mightily won
    God out of knowledge and good out of infinite pain
70   And sight out of blindness and purity out of a stain.

    As the marsh-hen secretly builds on the watery sod,
    Behold I will build me a nest on the greatness of God:
    I will fly in the greatness of God as the marsh-hen flies
    In the freedom that fills all the space 'twixt the marsh and the
        skies:
75   By so many roots as the marsh-grass sends in the sod
    I will heartily lay me a-hold on the greatness of God:
    Oh, like to the greatness of God is the greatness within
    The range of the marshes, the liberal marshes of Glynn.

And the sea lends large, as the marsh: lo, out of his plenty the sea
80   Pours fast: full soon the time of the flood-tide must be:
        Look how the grace of the sea doth go
    About and about through the intricate channels that flow
        Here and there,
        Everywhere,

85 Till his waters have flooded the uttermost creeks and the low-lying
lanes,
And the marsh is meshed with a million veins,
That like as with rosy and silvery essences flow
In the rose-and-silver evening glow.
Farewell, my lord Sun!
90 The creeks overflow: a thousand rivulets run
'Twixt the roots of the sod; the blades of the marsh-grass stir;
Passeth a hurrying sound of wings that westward whirr;
Passeth, and all is still; and the currents cease to run;
And the sea and the marsh are one.
95 How still the plains of the waters be!
The tide is in his ecstasy.
The tide is at his highest height:
And it is night.

And now from the Vast of the Lord will the waters of sleep
100 Roll in on the souls of men,
But who will reveal to our waking ken
The forms that swim and the shapes that creep
Under the waters of sleep?
And I would I could know what swimmeth below when the tide
comes in
105 On the length and the breadth of the marvellous marshes of
Glynn.

James Whitcomb Riley (1849–1916)

Born in Greenfield, Indiana, to parents who were determined that
their son should follow the profession of lawyer, Riley ran away from
home while still quite young and joined a patent-medicine show. He
then worked, among other things, as a house-painter and an actor
before returning to Greenfield to begin a career in journalism. He
was employed by the local newspaper and spent his spare time writing
verse for the Indianapolis magazines: an enterprise which led in
1877 to the offer of full-time employment on the *Indianapolis Journal*.
It was for this paper that he wrote a series of poems in the Mid-Western
or 'Hoosier' dialect which brought him national fame and consider-

able wealth. He was one of the most popular American poets of the second half of the century, and he consolidated his popularity by giving frequent public readings of his verse.

WHEN THE FROST IS ON THE PUNKIN

When the frost is on the punkin and the fodder's in the shock,
And you hear the kyouck and gobble of the struttin' turkey-cock,
And the clackin' of the guineys, and the cluckin' of the hens,
And the rooster's hallylooyer as he tiptoes on the fence;
5 O, it's then's the times a feller is a-feelin' at his best,
With the risin' sun to greet him from a night of peaceful rest,
As he leaves the house, bareheaded, and goes out to feed the stock,
When the frost is on the punkin and the fodder's in the shock.

They's something kindo' harty-like about the atmusfere
10 When the heat of summer's over and the coolin' fall is here—
Of course we miss the flowers, and the blossums on the trees,
And the mumble of the hummin'-birds and buzzin' of the bees;
But the air's so appetizin'; and the landscape through the haze
Of a crisp and sunny morning of the airly autumn days
15 Is a pictur' that no painter has the colorin' to mock—
When the frost is on the punkin and the fodder's in the shock.

The husky, rusty russel of the tossels of the corn,
And the raspin' of the tangled leaves, as golden as the morn;
The stubble in the furries—kindo' lonesome-like, but still
20 A-preachin' sermuns to us of the barns they growed to fill;
The strawstack in the medder, and the reaper in the shed;
The hosses in theyr stalls below—the clover overhead!—
O, it sets my hart a-clickin' like the tickin' of a clock,
When the frost is on the punkin and the fodder's in the shock!

25 Then your apples all is getherd, and the ones a feller keeps
Is poured around the celler-floor in red and yeller heaps;
And your cider-makin' 's over, and your wimmern-folks is through
With their mince and apple-butter, and theyr souse and saussage, too!...
I don't know how to tell it—but ef sich a thing could be
30 As the Angels wantin' boardin', and they'd call around on *me*—
I'd want to 'commodate 'em—all the whole-indurin' flock—
When the frost is on the punkin and the fodder's in the shock!

Edwin Markham (1852–1940)

Born in Oregon City, Oregon, Markham spent much of his youth in California, herding sheep, working as a farm hand, and going to school for only three months of the year. After attending the State Normal School at San Jose he taught in various parts of the state; but when his first volume of poetry, *The Man With the Hoe and Other Poems*, appeared in 1899 he found that he was popular and wealthy enough to concentrate on his writing. For the remainder of his life he devoted himself to the composing of verse, or to writing and lecturing on poetry and social and industrial problems. Frank Norris is said to have used him as the model for Presley, the hero of his novel *The Octopus* (1901).

THE MAN WITH THE HOE

Bowed by the weight of centuries he leans
Upon his hoe and gazes on the ground,
The emptiness of ages in his face,
And on his back the burden of the world.
5   Who made him dead to rapture and despair,
A thing that grieves not and that never hopes,
Stolid and stunned, a brother to the ox?
Who loosened and let down this brutal jaw?
Whose was the hand that slanted back this brow?
10   Whose breath blew out the light within this brain?

Is this the Thing the Lord God made and gave
To have dominion over sea and land;
To trace the stars and search the heavens for power;
To feel the passion of Eternity?
15   Is this the dream He dreamed who shaped the suns
And marked their ways upon the ancient deep?
Down all the caverns of Hell to their last gulf
There is no shape more terrible than this—
More tongued with censure of the world's blind greed—
20   More filled with signs and portents for the soul—
More packt with danger to the universe.

What gulfs between him and the seraphim!
Slave of the wheel of labor, what to him
Are Plato and the swing of Pleiades?
25   What the long reaches of the peaks of song,
The rift of dawn, the reddening of the rose?
Through this dread shape the suffering ages look;
Time's tragedy is in that aching stoop;
Through this dread shape humanity betrayed,
30   Plundered, profaned, and disinherited,
Cries protest to the Judges of the World,
A protest that is also prophecy.

O masters, lords and rulers in all lands,
Is this the handiwork you give to God,
35   This monstrous thing distorted and soul-quenched?
How will you ever straighten up this shape;
Touch it again with immortality;
Give back the upward looking and the light;
Rebuild in it the music and the dream;
40   Make right the immemorial infamies,
Perfidious wrongs, immedicable woes?

O masters, lords and rulers in all lands,
How will the Future reckon with this man?
How answer his brute question in that hour
45   When whirlwinds of rebellion shake all shores?
How will it be with kingdoms and with kings—
With those who shaped him to the thing he is—
When this dumb terror shall rise to judge the world,
After the silence of the centuries?

Paul Laurence Dunbar (1872–1906)

Born in Dayton, Ohio, to parents who had both been slaves, Dunbar
never knew the Deep South which was the setting for most of his
dialect poems. His first book of poetry was published in 1893 at his
own expense, but it was his third book, *Lyrics from Lowly Life* (1896)
with an introduction by the novelist W. D. Howells, that brought

him national fame. His dialect verse, which owed much to the work of Irwin Russell (1853–79) and James Whitcomb Riley, formed the basis for his popularity and he was continually regretting the neglect of his more conventional poetry. He died, where he had lived msot of his life, in Dayton.

WHEN DE CO'N PONE'S HOT

Dey is times in life when Nature
    Seems to slip a cog an' go,
Jes' a-rattlin' down creation,
    Lak an ocean's overflow;
5 When de worl' jes' stahts a-spinnin'
    Lak a picaninny's top,
An' yo' cup o' joy is brimmin'
    'Twell it seems about to slop,
An' you feel jes' lak a racah,
10   Dat is trainin' fu' to trot—
When yo' mammy says de blessin'
    An' de co'n pone's hot.

When you set down at de table,
    Kin' o' weary lak an' sad,
15 An' you'se jes' a little tiahed
    An' purhaps a little mad;
How yo' gloom tu'ns into gladness,
    How yo' joy drives out de doubt
When de oven do' is opened,
20   An' de smell comes po'in' out;
Why, de 'lectric light o' Heaven
    Seems to settle on de spot,
When yo' mammy says de blessin'
    An' de co'n pone's hot.

25 When de cabbage pot is steamin'
    An' de bacon good an' fat,
When de chittlins is a-sputter'n'
    So's to show you whah dey's at;
Tek away yo' sody biscuit,
30   Tek away yo' cake an' pie,
Fu' de glory time is comin',
    An' it's 'proachin' mighty nigh,

An' you want to jump an' hollah,
    Dough you know you'd bettah **not**,
35 When yo' mammy says de blessin'
    An' de co'n pone's hot.

I have hyeahd o' lots o' sermons,
    An' I've hyeahd o' lots o' prayers,
An' I've listened to some singin'
40   Dat has tuck me up de stairs
Of de Glory-Lan' an' set me
    Jes' below de Mastah's th'one,
An' have lef' my hea't a-singin'
    In a happy aftah tone;
45 But dem wu'ds so sweetly murmured
    Seem to tech de softes' spot,
When my mammy says de blessin',
    An' de co'n pone's hot.

A CORN-SONG

On the wide veranda white,
In the purple failing light,
Sits the master while the sun is lowly burning;
And his dreamy thoughts are drowned
5 In the softly flowing sound
Of the corn-songs of the field-hands slow returning.

    Oh, we hoe de co'n
    Since de ehly mo'n;
    Now de sinkin' sun
10   *Says de day is done.*

O'er the fields with heavy tread,
Light of heart and high of head,
Though the halting steps be labored, slow, and weary;
Still the spirits brave and strong
15 Find a comforter in song,
And their corn-song rises ever loud and cheery.

    Oh, we hoe de co'n
    Since de ehly mo'n;
    Now de sinkin' sun
20   *Says de day is done.*

To the master in his seat,
Comes the burden, full and sweet,
Of the mellow minor music growing clearer,
As the toilers raise the hymn,
25 Thro' the silence dusk and dim,
To the cabin's restful shelter drawing nearer.

Oh, we hoe de co'n
Since de ehly mo'n;
Now de sinkin' sun
30 *Says de day is done.*

And a tear is in the eye
Of the master sitting by,
As he listens to the echoes low-replying,
To the music's fading calls,
35 As it faints away and falls
Into silence, deep within the cabin dying.

Oh, we hoe de co'n
Since de ehly mo'n;
Now de sinkin' sun
40 *Says de day is done.*

HARRIET BEECHER STOWE

She told the story, and the whole world wept
At wrongs and cruelties it had not known
But for this fearless woman's voice alone.
She spoke to consciences that long had slept:
Her message, Freedom's clear reveille, swept
5 From heedless hovel to complacent throne.
Command and prophecy were in the tone,
And from its sheath the sword of justice leapt.
Around two peoples swelled a fiery wave,
10 But both came forth transfigured from the flame.
Blest be the hand that dared be strong to save,
And blest be she who in our weakness came—
Prophet and priestess! At one stroke she gave
A race to freedom and herself to fame.

William Vaughn Moody (1869–1910)

Moody was born in Spencer, Indiana, the son of a steam-boat pilot. He came to New York State at the age of nineteen and, with the help of a scholarship and borrowed funds, entered Harvard a year later. His academic record was a brilliant one, and by 1894 he had taken both a bachelor's and a master's degree. After teaching English and rhetoric at Harvard for a year, he was appointed assistant professor at the University of Chicago, where he stayed until 1902. The success of his *History of English Literature* (1902), written in collaboration with Robert Mors Lovett, and of his play, *The Great Divide* (1906), enabled him to devote all his attention to his creative writing; and he was at work on an ambitious trilogy of poetic dramas when he died, in Colorado, in 1910.

GLOUCESTER MOORS

A mile behind is Gloucester town
Where the fishing fleets put in,
A mile ahead the land dips down
And the woods and farms begin.
5   Here, where the moors stretch free
In the high blue afternoon,
Are the marching sun and talking sea,
And the racing winds that wheel and flee
On the flying heels of June.

10   Jill-o'er-the-ground is purple blue,
Blue is the quaker-maid,
The wild geranium holds its dew
Long in the boulder's shade.
Wax-red hangs the cup
15   From the huckleberry boughs,
In barberry bells the grey moths sup,
Or where the choke-cherry lifts high up
Sweet bowls for their carouse.

Over the shelf of the sandy cove
20 Beach-peas blossom late.
By copse and cliff the swallows rove
Each calling to his mate.
Seaward the sea-gulls go,
And the land-birds all are here;
25 That green-gold flash was a vireo,
And yonder flame where the marsh-flags grow
Was a scarlet tanager.

This earth is not the steadfast place
We landsmen build upon;
30 From deep to deep she varies pace,
And while she comes is gone.
Beneath my feet I feel
Her smooth bulk heave and dip;
With velvet plunge and soft upreel
35 She swings and steadies to her keel
Like a gallant, gallant ship.

These summer clouds she sets for sail,
The sun is her masthead light,
She tows the moon like a pinnace frail
40 Where her phosphor wake churns bright.
Now hid, now looming clear,
On the face of the dangerous blue
The star fleets tack and wheel and veer,
But on, but on does the old earth steer
45 As if her port she knew.

God, dear God! Does she know her port,
Though she goes so far about?
Or blind astray, does she make her sport
To brazen and chance it out?
50 I watched when her captains passed:
She were better captainless.
Men in the cabin, before the mast,
But some were reckless and some aghast,
And some sat gorged at mess.

55 By her battened hatch I leaned and caught
Sounds from the noisome hold,—

Cursing and sighing of souls distraught
And cries too sad to be told.
Then I strove to go down and see;
60 But they said, " Thou art not of us !"
I turned to those on the deck with me
And cried, " Give help !" But they said, " Let be:
Our ship sails faster thus."

Jill-o'er-the-ground is purple blue,
65 Blue is the quaker-maid,
The alder-clump where the brook comes through
Breeds cresses in its shade.
To be out of the moiling street
With its swelter and its sin !
70 Who has given to me this sweet,
And given my brother dust to eat?
And when will his wage come in?

Scattering wide or blown in ranks,
Yellow and white and brown,
75 Boats and boats from the fishing banks
Come home to Gloucester town.
There is cash to purse and spend,
There are wives to be embraced,
Hearts to borrow and hearts to lend,
80 And hearts to take and keep to the end,—
O little sails, make haste !

But thou, vast outbound ship of souls,
What harbor town for thee?
What shapes, when thy arriving tolls,
85 Shall crowd the banks to see?
Shall all the happy shipmates then
Stand singing brotherly?
Or shall a haggard ruthless few
Warp her over and bring her to,
90 While the many broken souls of men
Fester down in the slaver's pen,
And nothing to say or do?

ON A SOLDIER FALLEN IN THE PHILIPPINES

Streets of the roaring town,
Hush for him, hush, be still!
He comes, who was stricken down
Doing the word of our will.
5   Hush! Let him have his state,
Give him his soldier's crown.
The grists of trade can wait
Their grinding at the mill,
But he cannot wait for his honor, now the trumpet has been blown;
10 Wreathe pride now for his granite brow, lay love on his breast of stone.

Toll! Let the great bells toll
Till the clashing air is dim.
Did we wrong this parted soul?
We will make up it to him.
15   Toll! Let him never guess
What work we set him to.
Laurel, laurel, yes;
He did what we bade him do.
Praise, and never a whispered hint but the fight he fought was good;
20 Never a word that the blood on his sword was his country's own
heart's-blood.

A flag for the soldier's bier
Who dies that his land may live;
O, banners, banners here,
That he doubt not nor misgive!
25   That he heed not from the tomb
The evil days draw near
When the nation, robed in gloom,
With its faithless past shall strive.
Let him never dream that his bullet's scream went wide of its island
mark,
30 Home to the heart of his darling land where she stumbled and sinned
in the dark.

Edwin Arlington Robinson (1869–1935)

Robinson was born in Head Tide, Maine, and raised in the neighbouring town of Gardiner, which became the setting for many of his poems. He enrolled at Harvard in 1891, but the death of his father caused his withdrawal in 1893 and initiated the first of a series of mental depressions that were to plague him for the rest of his life. For the next few years he lived in Boston and New York, writing poetry and taking other work only when necessary. Then in 1905 President Theodore Roosevelt, who had read and liked his poetry, obtained a virtual sinecure for him in the New York Customs House. After five years there Robinson left to devote all his attention to his writing, spending summers at the MacDowell artists' colony in New Hampshire. By the time of his death, in New York City, he had become a well-known and even popular poet, with several Pulitzer Prizes to his credit.

LUKE HAVERGAL

Go to the western gate, Luke Havergal,
There where the vines cling crimson on the wall,
And in the twilight wait for what will come.
The leaves will whisper there of her, and some,
5   Like flying words, will strike you as they fall;
But go, and if you listen she will call.
Go to the western gate, Luke Havergal—
Luke Havergal.

No, there is not a dawn in eastern skies
10   To rift the fiery night that's in your eyes;
But there, where western glooms are gathering,
The dark will end the dark, if anything:
God slays Himself with every leaf that flies,
And hell is more than half of paradise.
15   No, there is not a dawn in eastern skies—
In eastern skies.

Out of a grave I come to tell you this,
Out of a grave I come to quench the kiss

That flames upon your forehead with a glow
20   That blinds you to the way that you must go.
Yes, there is yet one way to where she is,
Bitter, but one that faith may never miss.
Out of a grave I come to tell you this—
To tell you this.

25   There is the western gate, Luke Havergal,
There are the crimson leaves upon the wall.
Go, for the winds are tearing them away,—
Nor think to riddle the dead words they say,
Nor any more to feel them as they fall;
30   But go, and if you trust her she will call.
There is the western gate, Luke Havergal—
Luke Havergal.

THE HOUSE ON THE HILL

They are all gone away,
    The House is shut and still,
There is nothing more to say.

Through broken walls and gray
5   The winds blow bleak and shrill:
They are all gone away.

Nor is there one to-day
    To speak them good or ill:
There is nothing more to say.

10   Why is it then we stray
    Around the sunken sill?
They are all gone away,

And our poor fancy-play
    For them is wasted skill:
15   There is nothing more to say.

There is ruin and decay
    In the House on the Hill:
They are all gone away,
There is nothing more to say.

RICHARD CORY

Whenever Richard Cory went down town,
We people on the pavement looked at him:
He was a gentleman from sole to crown,
Clean favored, and imperially slim.

5   And he was always quietly arrayed,
And he was always human when he talked;
But still he fluttered pulses when he said,
" Good-morning," and he glittered when he walked.

And he was rich—yes, richer than a king—
10   And admirably schooled in every grace:
In fine, we thought that he was everything
To make us wish that we were in his place.

So on we worked, and waited for the light,
And went without the meat, and cursed the bread;
15   And Richard Cory, one calm summer night,
Went home and put a bullet through his head.

AARON STARK

Withal a meagre man was Aaron Stark,
Cursed and unkempt, shrewd, shrivelled, and morose.
A miser was he, with a miser's nose,
And eyes like little dollars in the dark.
5   His thin, pinched mouth was nothing but a mark;
And when he spoke there came like sullen blows
Through scattered fangs a few snarled words and close,
As if a cur were chary of its bark.

Glad for the murmur of his hard renown,
10   Year after year he shambled through the town,
A loveless exile moving with a staff;
And oftentimes there crept into his ears
A sound of alien pity, touched with tears,—
And then (and only then) did Aaron laugh.

Stephen Crane (1871–1900)

The fourteenth and youngest child of a Methodist minister, Crane was born in Newark, New Jersey. In the first ten years of his life his family moved continually although after 1880, when his father died, they settled in Asbury Park, by the sea. Crane attended military academy and was briefly at Lafayette and Syracuse Universities, where he won minor athletic distinction; but in 1891 he left college to become a journalist. In 1895 he achieved fame with *The Red Badge of Courage* and, impressed by a volume of Emily Dickinson's verse, began writing poetry soon afterwards. Crane subsequently worked as a reporter in the Spanish-American and Graeco-Turk wars. Then, threatened with tuberculosis, he settled in England for a while where he became a friend of Joseph Conrad, Henry James and H. G. Wells. His health continued to deteriorate and he moved to the resort town of Baden-Baden in Germany, where he died.

From THE BLACK RIDERS *and* OTHER LINES

I

Black riders came from the sea.
There was clang and clang of spear and shield,
And clash and clash of hoof and heel,
Wild shouts and the wave of hair
5   In the rush upon the wind:
Thus the ride of Sin.

III

In the desert
I saw a creature, naked, bestial,
Who, squatting upon the ground
Held his heart in his hands,
5   And ate of it.
I said: " Is it good, friend?"
" It is bitter—bitter," he answered;
" But I like it
Because it is bitter,
10   And because it is my heart."

XII

"And the sins of the fathers shall be visited upon the heads of the children, even unto the third and fourth generation of them that hate me."

Well, then, I hate Thee, unrighteous picture;
Wicked image, I hate Thee;
So, strike with Thy vengeance
The heads of those little men
5   Who come blindly.
It will be a brave thing.

XIX

A god in wrath
Was beating a man;
He cuffed him loudly
With thunderous blows
5   That rang and rolled over the earth.
All people came running.
The man screamed and struggled,
And bit madly at the feet of the god.
The people cried:
10   " Ah, what a wicked man!"
And—
" Ah, what a redoubtable god!"

XXXV

A man saw a ball of gold in the sky;
He climbed for it,
And eventually he achieved it—
It was clay.

5   Now this is the strange part:
When the man went to the earth
And looked again,
Lo, there was the ball of gold.
Now this is the strange part:
10   It was a ball of gold.
Aye, by the heavens, it was a ball of gold.

CRANE

From WAR IS KIND

XIV

A slant of sun on dull brown walls
A forgotten sky of bashful blue.
Toward God a mighty hymn
A song of collisions and cries
5 Rumbling wheels, hoof-beats, bells,
Welcomes, farewells, love-calls, final moans,
Voices of joy, idiocy, warning, despair,
The unknown appeals of brutes,
The chanting of flowers
10 The screams of cut trees,
The senseless babble of hens and wise men—
A cluttered incoherency that says at the stars:
" Oh, God, save us."

XXI

A man said to the universe:
" Sir, I exist!"
" However," replied the universe,
" The fact has not created in me
5 A sense of obligation."

A man adrift on a slim spar
A horizon smaller than the rim of a bottle
Tented waves rearing lashy dark points
The near whine of froth in circles.
5   God is cold.

The incessant raise and swing of the sea
And growl after growl of crest
The sinkings, green, seething, endless
The upheaval half-completed.
10   God is cold.

The seas are in the hollow of The Hand;
Oceans may be turned to a spray
Raining down through the stars
Because of a gesture of pity toward a babe.
15 Oceans may become grey ashes,
Die with a long moan and a roar
Amid the tumult of the fishes
And the cries of the ships,
Because The Hand beckons the mice.

20 A horizon smaller than a doomed assassin's cap,
Inky, surging tumults
A reeling, drunken sky and no sky
A pale hand sliding from a polished spar.
     God is cold.

25 The puff of a coat imprisoning air:
A face kissing the water-death
A weary slow sway of a lost hand
And the sea, the moving sea, the sea.
     God is cold.

Tell me not in joyous numbers
We can make our lives sublime
By—well, at least, not by
Dabbling much in rhyme.

Notes

The text used follows the text of the standard edition in each case, unless otherwise stated.

PHILIP FRENEAU

Standard Edition: Pattee, F. L. (ed.). *The Poems of Philip Freneau* (Princeton, N.J., 1902–1907).

The Rising Glory of America

A poem of this title was given originally as the graduating address of Freneau and H. H. Brackenridge at Princeton, and then published in 1772. Freneau reprinted his own part of the work in 1786, with drastic alterations and additions; and it is from this version that the passages included in this anthology have been selected.

ll. 11–13. *Citheron's . . . Olympus' . . . Haemus':* mountains in Greece. The first two were supposed to be the abodes of, respectively, the Muses and the gods.

ll. 14–18. *Sweet Orpheus' harp:* Orpheus was a figure famed in Greek mythology as a poet and singer. For further details see Ovid, *Metamorphoses*, X and XI.

ll. 19–20. *Alpheus' . . . Arethusa's:* Alpheus was the largest river of Peloponnesus, the waters of which were said to pass unmixed through the sea and to rise in the fountain of Arethusa at Syracuse.

l. 26. *Franklin:* Benjamin Franklin (1706–1790).

ll. 50–51. *Isaiah's . . . Jeremy . . . Amos:* prophets in the Old Testament.

l. 61. *Scipios, Solons, Catos:* Scipio Africanus Major (263–184 B.C.), Roman soldier, statesman and mystic; Solon (c. 640–c. 560 B.C.), Athenian statesman and poet; Cato Major (234–149 B.C.), Roman lawyer, soldier, statesman and writer.

l. 88. *Canaan:* originally the lowlands of Palestine, but eventually a term applied to the entire land inhabited by the Jews.

l. 90. *Pisgah:* the mountain Moses ascended to view the Promised Land (Deut. 3:27; 34:1–4).

l. 92. *lion . . . lamb:* I Sam. 17:34.

l. 97. *Siloah's:* a pool in Jerusalem.

Literary Importation

l. 8. *Sam Chandler:* 'who laboured for the establishment of an American Episcopacy, previous to the revolutionary war' (Freneau's note).

l. 13. *Sammy:* 'Bishop Samuel Seabury, of Connecticut' (Freneau's note).

ll. 22–23. *Can we . . . place:* These two lines were later slightly altered by Freneau, 'horrible' being substituted for 'damnable'. I have in this one instance deviated from the text supplied by the definitive edition of Freneau's work and retained 'damnable', since it is in this original form that the lines have become famous.

l. 30. *Magraw:* 'a noted practitioner in physic, formerly of New York' (Freneau's note).

To An Author

ll. 24–26. *Milbourne . . . Dennis:* a non-juring minister and a critic satirized respectively in Dryden's *Epistle to John Dryden* (l. 87) and Pope's *Essay on Criticism* (Bk. III, ll. 585–588).

WILLIAM CULLEN BRYANT

Standard Edition: Godwin, Parke (ed.). *The Poetical Works of William Cullen Bryant* (New York, 1883).

Thanatopsis: The title, derived from the Greek, signifies that the poem is a meditation on death.

l. 51. *Barcan:* name of a North African desert, here used to indicate deserts in general.

Inscription for the Entrance to a Wood

l. 11. *The primal curse:* Gen. 3:17.

l. 30. *causey:* causeway.

The Prairies

l. 3. *The speech . . . name:* the word 'prairie' is derived from the French.

l. 21. *Sonora:* a state in Mexico.

l. 42. *mighty mounds:* burial mounds, supposed in Bryant's time to have been built by ancestors of the American Indian, the 'mound-builders' mentioned in line 60.

l. 48. *Pentelicus:* abbreviation for marble from the quarries of Pente-likon.
l. 72. *brown vultures:* wolves.

RALPH WALDO EMERSON

Standard Edition: Emerson, E. W. (ed.). *The Complete Works of Ralph Waldo Emerson* (Boston, 1904).

Uriel

Uriel is the Archangel of the sun in *Paradise Lost*. The poem is in part an allegorical account of the New England Establishment's reaction to Emerson's *Divinity School Address*, an early statement of his Trans-cendentalist beliefs.
l. 8. *Seyd:* Saadi (1184–1291), a Persian poet and Emerson's type of the ideal poet.

Hamatreya

The title is based on two Greek words which, taken together, signify 'Earth-Mother'.
l. 1. *Bulkeley . . . Flint:* some of the first settlers of Concord.
l. 8. *flags:* wild irises.

The Snow-Storm

l. 18. *Parian:* the marble from the Greek island of Paros was renowned for its whiteness.
l. 21. *maugre:* despite.

Merlin

Merlin represents here the inspired bard, or ideal poet.
l. 49. *Sybarite:* inhabitant of the ancient Greek colony of Sybaris, noted for its luxury—by extension, any luxurious and effeminate person.
l. 126. *Sisters:* the Fates.

Concord Hymn

The poem commemorates the Battle of Concord, 1775, one of the more significant battles of the Revolution.

HENRY WADSWORTH LONGFELLOW

Standard Edition: Scudder, H. E. (ed.). *The Complete Poetical Works of Henry Wadsworth Longfellow* (Boston, 1893).

A Psalm of Life

The 'psalmist' mentioned in the sub-title may be either David (Psalms 53 and 54) or the writer of Ecclesiastes (see 3:20). The poem is in effect an answer to the psalmist's theme of 'dust to dust'.

Hymn to the Night

l. 21. *Orestes-like:* Orestes was pursued by the Furies for killing his mother to avenge his father's murder. He discovers peace in *Eumenides*, the last play in Aeschylus' trilogy, the *Oresteia*.

Mezzo Cammin

The title of the poem comes from a line in Dante's *Divine Comedy*: 'Nel mezzo del cammin di nostra vita', meaning 'Midway upon the journey of our life'.

My Lost Youth

'A memory of Portland—my native town, the city by the sea' (Longfellow).

l. 6. The source of the refrain is apparently John Scheffer's *History of Lapland* (Oxford, 1674).

l. 13. *Hesperides:* the 'blessed isles' of Greek mythology, where the golden apples grew which Ge (the earth) gave to Hera, the queen of the gods, on her marriage to Zeus.

l. 37. *the sea-fight:* 'This was the engagement between the *Enterprise* and *Boxer* [a British ship] . . . in which both captains were slain' (Longfellow's note).

Ultima Thule

The dedication is to G. W. Greene, a friend of Longfellow's youth.

l. 2. *Hesperides:* see notes on *My Lost Youth*.

l. 8. *Atlantis:* a legendary city which was supposed to have sunk into the sea.

l. 10. *Orcades:* islands off the coast of Scotland which the Greeks believed to be haunted by tempests.

The Cross of Snow

l. 2. *a gentle face:* Longfellow's second wife who was burnt to death.

JOHN GREENLEAF WHITTIER

Standard Edition: Scudder, H. E. (ed.). *The Complete Poetical Works of John Greenleaf Whittier* (Boston, 1894).

First Day Thoughts

'First day' is the Quaker term for Sunday.
l. 10. *Israel's leader:* Moses. See Exod. 31 : 18.

Snow-Bound

'The inmates of the family at the Whittier homestead, who are referred to in the poem, were my father, mother, my brother and two sisters, and my uncle and aunt both unmarried. In addition, there was the district schoolmaster who boarded with us' (Whittier's note).

l. 90. *Ammon:* an Egyptian divinity in the form of a ram.

l. 136. *trammels:* pothooks attached to the crane, a long metal arm, from which the cooking pot was suspended.

l. 215. *Gambia:* Gambia River in West Africa.

ll. 220–223. From *The African Chief*, an Abolitionist poem by Sarah Morton.

l. 225. *Memphremagog:* a lake in Quebec, Canada.

l. 226. *moose and samp:* Indian corn-meal mush.

l. 229. *St François:* a lake in Quebec, Canada.

l. 237. *Salisbury's:* a town east of Haverhill, where the Whittier family lived. To the north, on the New Hampshire coast, are the promontory of Little Boar's Head and the Isle of Shoals.

l. 274. *Piscataqua:* a river in New Hampshire.

l. 286. *tome:* William Samuel's *History of the Quakers*.

l. 410. *Ellwood's:* Thomas Ellwood (1639–1713), who wrote *Davideis* (1712).

l. 411. *heathen nine:* the Muses.

ll. 420–425. These lines refer to Andrew Jackson's war with the Creek Indians, Gregor McGregor's attempt to establish by force an American colony in Costa Rica, and the revolt of the Greeks against the Turks led by General Ypsilanti, all of which occurred in 1819–20.

l. 434. *vendue:* auction.

l. 455. *amaranth:* an imaginary unfading flower.

l. 466. *aloe:* a plant supposed to flower once in every century.

l. 474. *Flemish pictures:* Flemish and Dutch painters were famous for their portraits of domestic scenes.

EDGAR ALLAN POE

Standard Edition: Harrison, J. A. (ed.). *The Complete Works of Edgar Allan Poe* (New York, 1902).

Sonnet—To Science

l. 9. *Diana:* a Roman goddess whose 'car' was said to be the moon.
l. 10. *Hamadryad:* a wood-nymph.
l. 12. *Naiad:* a river-nymph.
l. 14. *tamarind tree:* a tree idealized in Eastern poetry.

To Helen

l. 2. *Nicean:* possibly derived from the 'Nyseian isle' mentioned in *Paradise Lost*; more probably chosen for its mystery and musicality.
l. 7. *hyacinth:* in *Ligeia* Poe associates the word 'hyacinthine' with 'raven-black . . . and naturally curling tresses'.
l. 8. *Naiad:* see notes on *Sonnet—To Science*.

Israfel

The epigraph is partly from George Sada's translation of the *Koran* (1734), and partly from the French poem, *Le Refus*, by Jean de Béranger (1786–1857).
l. 12. *levin:* lightning.
l. 13. *Pleiads:* a cluster of seven stars.
l. 26. *Houri:* a woman in the Mohammedan paradise.

Eldorado

'El Dorado'—'The Golden (Gilded)'. The place of legendary wealth long sought in vain in S. America; by extension, any ideal realm.
l. 1. *bedight:* adorned.

Annabel Lee

This poem probably refers to Poe's wife, who died in 1847.

OLIVER WENDELL HOLMES

Standard Edition: Scudder, H. E. (ed.). *The Complete Poetical Works of Oliver Wendell Holmes* (Boston, 1895).

The Last Leaf

'This poem was suggested by the appearance in one of our streets of a venerable relic of the Revolution . . .' (Holmes's note). The 'relic' was Major Thomas Melville, Herman Melville's grandfather.

The Chambered Nautilus

The title refers to a cephalopod inhabiting the Pacific and Indian oceans.
l. 26. *Triton:* A sea demigod in Greek mythology who played upon a conch shell.

At the 'Atlantic Dinner'

This poem was written for a dinner held for the *Atlantic Monthly*, a literary periodical founded in 1857 which Holmes named and to which he was a leading contributor.
l. 21. *catamount:* a common American name for the cougar ('felis concolor') or puma, also called the Mountain Lion.

JONES VERY

Standard Edition: There is no complete collection of Very's poetry. A useful selection is to be found in *Jones Very: Selected Poems*, ed. N. Lyons (New Brunswick, 1966).

Thy Brother's Blood
l. 7. *Abel's red blood:* Gen. 4: 1–16.

HENRY DAVID THOREAU

Standard Edition: Bode, C. (ed.). *Collected Poems of Henry Thoreau* (Baltimore, Maryland, 1964).
The text used follows the text of *Poems of Nature* (London, 1895).

Sic Vita
l. 8. *sorrel:* kind of acid-leaved herb.

Winter Memories
l. 16. *johnswort:* Saint John's wort genus of plants.
l. 26. *fieldfare:* American robin.

My Prayer

l. 1. *pelf:* riches.

JAMES RUSSELL LOWELL

Standard Edition: Scudder, H. E. (ed.). *The Complete Poetical Works of James Russell Lowell* (Boston, 1897).

A Fable for Critics

The passages included here from Lowell's poem of this title are all spoken by a critic who is supposed to be explaining the state of American literature to Phoebus Apollo.

l. 27. *Plotinus-Montaigne:* Plotinus (205–270) was a Roman Neo-Platonic philosopher, Montaigne (1533–1592) a French essayist renowned for his scepticism. *Egyptian's* refers to the fact that Plotinus, though a Roman citizen, was born in Egypt.

l. 51. *Griswold:* Rufus Griswold (1815–1857), an editor and critic.

l. 53. *Parnassus:* a mountain in Greece sacred to Apollo, the god of poetry.

l. 70. *what's-his-name:* Taillefer, a minstrel who sang the *Song of Roland* as he led the charge of the Norman cavalry during the Battle of Hastings.

ll. 76–77. *Anne haec ... tui:* 'Is this thy son's coat or not?' (Gen. 37:32). George Fox (1624–1691), founder of the Society of Friends, was famous for his leather breeches.

ll. 80–81. *Goliah ... Castaly's:* I. Sam. 17:49.

l. 102. *Powers ... Page:* Hiram Powers (1805–1873), sculptor of American statesmen, and William Page (1811–1885), painter of American landscapes.

l. 115. *Mathews:* Cornelius Mathews (1817–1889), like Poe, attacked Longfellow's verse vigorously.

The Biglow Papers (Second Series): The Courtin':

The Biglow Papers consist of two sets of verses published during the period 1846–1867 in various periodicals. Written in the Yankee dialect, they purported to be the work of one Hosea Biglow. The first series was begun as a means of expressing opposition to the Mexican War, which Lowell, like many Northerners, felt had been fomented by the slaveholders; and throughout their lengthy career the *Papers* continued to be vigorously Abolitionist and Unionist in their sympathies. The poem included here, however, is not concerned with politics, being simply an attempt on Lowell's part to write something 'like a pastoral'.

l. 17. *crook-necks:* gourds.

l. 19. *queen's arm:* Revolutionary musket.

l. 43. *Ole Hunderd:* a tune used with Psalm 100.

l. 95. *they was cried:* the wedding banns were read.

HERMAN MELVILLE

Standard Edition: Vincent, H. P. (ed.). *Collected Poems of Herman Melville* (Chicago, 1947).
The text used follows the text of the original editions: *Battle-Pieces and Aspects of the War* (1866); *John Marr and Other Sailors* (1888); *Timoleon* (1891).

The Portent

This and the following five poems are from *Battle-Pieces*, a volume describing various events that took place before and during the American Civil War and Melville's reactions to those events. The dates under the separate titles refer to the year in which the event described took place. John Brown was hanged on 2nd December 1859, for leading an abortive raid on Harper's Ferry, Virginia.

Shiloh

The Battle of Shiloh was fought mostly around the Shiloh Baptist Church, Tennessee. More than 23,000 men were killed in two days.

Malvern Hill

The 'Seven Days' Battle' before Richmond ended at Malvern Hill in a Pyrrhic victory for the Union army led by McClellan.

The House-Top

This poem was prompted by the 'Draft Riots' which grew out of opposition to a Federal Conscription Act. The Act included a clause permitting anyone to buy his freedom from the draft by a payment of three hundred dollars.

l. 9. *Sirius:* the dog star in Canis Major and reputedly the brightest star.

l. 19. *Draco:* the riot was quelled by militiamen. Draco drew up a harsh code of laws for Athens in the seventh century B.C.

l. 21. *Calvin's creed:* Calvin divided mankind into the predestined elect and damned. According to Melville, the draft law (by offering exemption to the rich) supplied a more cynical version of the same division.

l. 27. *never to be scourged:* Roman citizens could not legally be subjected to the degrading punishment of scourging.

Pebbles

l. 3. *pintado:* a species of petrel.

l. 8. *Orm:* presumably a reference to the author of *Ormulum,* a collection of homilies written in the thirteenth century A.D.

l. 31. *Angels Four:* Rev. 7:1–3.

l. 33. *rosmarine:* 'ros marinus' or 'sea-dew'. The herb rosemary was supposed to have healing properties.

After the Pleasure Party

'. . . a dramatic monologue, in which the speaker is a woman . . . who has devoted her years of youth to . . . intellectual pursuits, denying the sensual pleasures, only to find . . . that the scorn of love has brought its own revenge in unfulfillment ' (Vincent).

l. 29. *Vesta . . . Sappho's smart:* Vesta was a Roman goddess; the fire in her temple was tended by six Vestal Virgins, sworn to chastity. Sappho was a Greek poetess, who was supposed to have leapt into the sea when thwarted in love.

l. 51. *Cassiopea:* the mythical wife of an Ethiopian king who was carried at death to the constellation named after her, which resembles a chair.

l. 73. *Decameron folk:* the narrators of the stories in Boccaccio's *Decameron* (1353) fled to the country to escape the plague.

l. 89. *Pan's mystery:* Pan was, among other things, the god of fertility.

l. 93. *Co-relatives:* a myth recounted in Plato's *Symposium* suggests that man and woman were once parts of an androgynous whole.

l. 111. *Urania:* the narrator calls herself Urania, the patroness of astronomy.

l. 121. *Albania's porch:* the porch of a villa in Rome.

l. 124. *Thomas à Kempis:* monk and theologian (1380–1471).

l. 138. *armed Virgin:* Athena, Greek goddess of learning and armed protectress of Athens.

The Bench of Boors

l. 1. *Tenier's:* the painter David Teniers the younper (1610–1690). The painting referred to here is probably his 'Hour of Repose', which Melville saw in Amsterdam.

In a Bye Canal

l. 6. *Jael:* Judg. 4:11–22.

WALT WHITMAN

Standard Edition: Allen, G. W. and Bradley, S. (eds). *The Collected Writings of Walt Whitman* (New York, 1961).
The text used follows the text of the so-called 'death-bed edition' of 1891–1892, the last edition that Whitman saw to press.

Song of Myself

l. 49. *entretied:* carpenter's term for 'cross-braced'.
l. 109. *Kanuck, Tuckahoe . . . Cuff:* respectively, a French Canadian, a Virginian of the Tidewater district, and a Negro.
l. 272. *First-day:* Sunday.
l. 275. *jour printer:* journeyman printer.
l. 289. *Wolverine:* native of Michigan.
l. 321. *Chattahooche . . . Altamahaw:* rivers in Georgia.
l. 338. *Hoosier, Badger, Buckeye:* natives, respectively, of Indiana, Wisconsin and Ohio.
l. 366. *embouchures:* mouthpieces of musical instruments.
l. 408. *carlacue:* presumably 'curlicue'.
l. 604. *Uranus:* the Greek personification of Heaven.
l. 608. *fakes:* coiled cables.
l. 613. *quahaug:* an Atlantic-coast clam.
l. 664. *pismire:* an ant.
l. 871. *Alamo:* Battle of the Alamo, 1836. This section describes the massacre of Colonel Fannin and his troops at Goliad, Texas, in the same year.
l. 896. *sea-fight:* the victory of John Paul Jones over a British frigate in 1779.
ll. 1028–1031. *lithographing:* reproducing the best aspects of the various religions and mythologies, Hebraic (Jehovah), Greek (Kronos, Zeus, Hercules), Egyptian (Osiris, Isis), Babylonian (Belus), Hindu (Brahma), Buddhist (Buddha), American Indian (Manito), Islamic (Allah), Norse (Odin), and Aztec (Mexitli).

l. 1100. *obis:* presumably 'obeah', used in African witchcraft.
l. 1102. *gymnosophist:* member of an Indian religious sect.
l. 1103. *Shastas . . . Vedas . . . Koran:* sacred books of the Hindu and Muslim religions.
l. 1104. *teokallis:* Aztec temple.
l. 1128. *koboo:* A native of Palembang, east coast of Sumatra.
l. 1166. *sauroids:* mammoth prehistoric reptiles.
l. 1289. *accoucheur:* obstetrician, midwife.
l. 1321. *sidle:* from 'side-light', or porthole window, of a ship.

Out Of The Cradle Endlessly Rocking
l. 23. *Paumanok:* Long Island.

Children of Adam and Calamus
The poems in these two sequences celebrate relationships between, respectively, men and women and men and men.

FREDERICK GODDARD TUCKERMAN

Standard Edition: Momaday, N. S. (ed.). *The Complete Poems of Frederick Goddard Tuckerman* (New York, 1965).

The text used follows the text of the original edition; *Poems* (1860).

Sonnet I
l. 5. *orchis:* orchid.

Sonnet IV
l. 13. *stramony:* thorn apple.

Sonnet VIII
l. 10. *ambit:* circumference, border.

Sonnet IX
l. 13. *Saul:* St Paul. See Matt. 25:40, 45.

Sonnet XIV
l. 1. *pelf:* riches.
l. 14. *jacinth:* hyacinth.

Sonnet XV
l. 2. *Oread-like:* oreads were nymphs of the mountains.

Sonnet XVI

l. 14. *Agria . . . Artemisia:* 'Agria' is presumably Egeria, an ancient Italian goddess of springs. Artemisia was a goddess in Greek mythology, a bringer of fertility.

Sonnet XX

l. 4. *pagod:* a person superstitiously revered, an idol. *Manada:* Spanish word meaning 'crowd' or 'mob', used in the American West as a substitute for 'herd' or 'drove'.
l. 8. *Bheel:* name of a race inhabiting the hills and forests of certain regions of India.
l. 14. *Ophion:* an Orphic god and legendary ruler of the universe before Kronos.

BAYARD TAYLOR

Standard Edition: Taylor, M. H. (ed.). *The Poetical Works of Bayard Taylor* (Boston, 1892).

On Leaving California

l. 37. *Hesper:* the evening star.

The Quaker Widow

l. 6. *First day:* Quaker term for Sunday.
l. 14. *Kennett:* Taylor was born, of Quaker parents, in Kennett Square, forty miles from Philadelphia.
l. 28. *Hicksite:* a member of a seceding body of American Quakers founded by one Elias Hicks.
l. 30. *of the world:* not of the Quaker faith.

HENRY TIMROD

Standard Edition: Hayne, P. H. (ed.). *The Poems of Henry Timrod* (New York, 1873).

Charleston

l. 7. *Sumter:* the bombardment of Fort Sumter, in Charleston harbour, by Confederate artillery was the immediate occasion of the Civil War.

l. 9. *Calpe:* Rock of Gibraltar.

l. 11. *Moultrie:* a fort at the entrance to Charleston harbour.

EMILY DICKINSON

Standard Edition: Johnson, T. H. (ed.). *The Poems of Emily Dickinson* (Cambridge, Mass., 1955).

The text used follows the text of the original editions published in 1890, 1891 and 1896. In these editions Emily Dickinson's unusual method of punctuation was altered to conform to accepted usage and occasionally the grammar was corrected, rhymes regularized, or words changed so as to make the poems more accessible to the common reader. Those who wish to study the original text, without these alterations, are advised to consult the standard edition.

'The soul selects her own society'

l. 3. *majority:* i.e. power.

'I found the phrase to every thought'

l. 8. *mazarin:* stuff, or garment of a rich blue in colour.

'I like to see it lap the miles'

l. 1. *it:* a train.

l. 13. *Boanerges:* a surname meaning 'sons of thunder': see Mark 3:17.

'Farther in summer than the birds'

l. 3. *minor Nation:* insects, probably crickets.

l. 15. *druidic:* i.e. prophetic.

'A route of evanescence'

Emily Dickinson once wanted to call this poem *A Humming-Bird*.

l. 4. *cochineal:* i.e. scarlet.

'I started early, took my dog'

l. 10. *simple:* plain.

'Essential oils are wrung'
l. 2. *attar:* a fragrant oil obtained from the petals of the rose.
l. 8. *ceaseless rosemary:* an evergreen frequently planted in graveyards as an emblem of immortality.

'Of bronze and blaze'
l. 14. *menagerie:* various and discordant.

'What soft, cherubic creatures'
l. 5. *Dimity:* a thin cotton fabric.

'What mystery pervades a well!'
l. 16. *simplify:* to render intelligible and, by extension, to understand.

FRANCIS BRET HARTE

Standard Edition: *The Complete Works of Bret Harte* (London, 1880–1912).

Plain Language from Truthful James
l. 29. *bowers:* the highest cards in the game of euchre.

JOAQUIN MILLER

Standard Edition: *The Complete Poetical Works of Joaquin Miller* (San Francisco, 1897).

Crossing the Plains
l. 9. *briskets:* breasts.

Columbus
l. 2. *Gates of Hercules:* enclosing the Straits of Gibraltar.

SIDNEY LANIER

Standard Edition: Anderson, C. R. (general ed.). *The Centennial Edition of Sidney Lanier* (Baltimore, Maryland, 1945).
The text used follows the text of the original editions: *Poems* (1877); *Poems of Sidney Lanier* (1884).

Corn

l. 157. *Dives:* name commonly given to the rich man in the parable of Lazarus, Luke 16: 19–31.
l. 169. *Bulls' or Bears':* stock market terms for, respectively, rising and falling prices.

The Marshes of Glynn

The marshes described here are in Georgia.

JAMES WHITCOMB RILEY

Standard Edition: *The Complete Works of James Whitcomb Riley* (Indianapolis, 1913).

When the Frost is on the Punkin

This poem is written in the 'Hoosier' or Mid-Western dialect. 'Hoosier' was a term applied to the residents of Indiana.

EDWIN MARKHAM

Standard Edition: There is no collected edition of Markham's work. His most interesting verse is to be found in *The Man With the Hoe and Other Poems* (New York, 1899).

The Man with the Hoe

l. 24. *Pleiades:* The Pleiades are a small cluster of stars.

PAUL LAURENCE DUNBAR

Standard Edition: Wiggins, L. K. (ed.). *The Complete Poems of Paul Laurence Dunbar* (New York, 1913).

When De Co'n Pone's Hot

Compare this poem with Riley's *When the Frost is on the Punkin*. 'Co'n-pone' is bread made of corn meal, which was once part of the staple diet of black Americans.

l. 27. *chittlins:* chitlings, a dish made out of the intestines of a pig.

Harriet Beecher Stowe

A poem addressed to the author of *Uncle Tom's Cabin* (1852).

WILLIAM VAUGHN MOODY

Standard Edition: Manly, J. M. (ed.). *The Poems and Plays of William Vaughn Moody* (Boston, 1912).

Gloucester Moors

Gloucester Moors are near Cape Ann, Massachusetts, where Moody spent a summer vacation in 1900.

On a Soldier Fallen in the Philippines

Written as a protest against the use of American troops to suppress the Filipino independence movement.

EDWIN ARLINGTON ROBINSON

Standard Edition: *Collected Poems of Edwin Arlington Robinson* (New York, 1937).

STEPHEN CRANE

Standard Edition: Katz, J. (ed.). *The Poems of Stephen Crane* (New York, 1966).

XII

The epigraph is from Exod. 20:5.

Index

PS607
G7

Gray, Richard J   comp.
        American verse of the nineteenth century, edited wit
introduction by Richard Gray.   London, Dent; Tot
N. J., Rowman and Littlefield, 1973.

    xxxviii, 234 p.   20 cm.   £2.50 ($7.00U.S.)   GB 73–

    Bibliography : p. xxxv–xxxviii.
    Includes index.

    1. American poetry—19th century.   I. Title.

    PS607.G7   811′.3′08   74–15
    ISBN 0–87471–404–4 (Rowman and Littlefield)   M

    Library of Congress   74 [4]